KU-165-996

TONY CURTIS
Nobody's Perfect

TONY CURTIS
Nobodys Perfect

MICHAEL MUNN

LIBRARIES NI
WITHDRAWN FROM STOCK

JR
BOOKS

LIBRARIES NI

C700678318

RONDO	13/06/2011
791.43028092	£ 18.99
CLL	

Page 5: AF archive/Alamy
Page 6 top: courtesy of the author
Page 6 bottom: courtesy of the author
Page 7 top: Universal/The Kobal collection
Page 7 bottom: Hulton archive/Getty Images
Page 8: courtesy of the author
Page 9: courtesy of the author
Page 10 top: courtesy of the author
Page 10 bottom: courtesy of the author
Page 11: courtesy of the author
Page 12: courtesy of the author
Page 13 top: courtesy of the author
Page 13 bottom: Wireimage
Page 14 top: Photos 12/Alamy
Page 14 bottom: Getty Images
Page 15 top: Photos 12/Alamy
Page 15 bottom: WENN/Alamy
Page 16: Lebrecht Music and Arts Photo/Alamy

First published in Great Britain in 2011 by
JR Books, 10 Greenland Street, London NW1 0ND
www.jrbooks.com

Copyright © 2011 Michael Munn

Michael Munn has asserted his moral right to be identified as the Author of this Work in accordance with the Copyright Designs and Patents Act 1988.

All rights reserved. No part of this book may be reproduced or utilised in any form or by any means, electronic or mechanical, including photocopying, recording or by any information storage and retrieval system, without permission in writing from JR Books.

A catalogue record for this book is available from the British Library.

ISBN 978-1-907532-30-6

1 3 5 7 9 10 8 6 4 2

Printed by the MPG Books Group

This is especially for Tony . . . my son.

Contents

Author's Note

When asked who of all the movie stars I have met has impressed me the most or have just liked the most, I reply, 'Tony Curtis'. Maybe it was because he gave me my first real professional interview when I began as a journalist in 1975 and, knowing I was a fan, he allowed me two hours of his time at the house he owned in London. Or maybe it's because four years earlier he had personally escorted me onto a sound stage to watch *The Persuaders* being filmed. Or maybe it's just because I always found him to be a very nice, extremely charming and very funny man, which made being around him nice. Not everyone would agree. He could be fractious and difficult to work with. His flaws are all part of his story, as well as his better points. As he was fond of saying, nobody's perfect.

He was the subject of my first biography, hastily written through rose-tinted glasses in 1979 and hastily published somewhat incomplete in 1984 and thankfully forgotten very quickly. I had drawn on only the 1975 interview, but I interviewed him another four as well as just being around him when the opportunity was there. Each interview represented a phase in his life that was reflected in his demeanour and vocabulary. In 1975 he thought he was on the threshold of a major comeback, and so he talked about his past career with nostalgic joy, laughing at how he was given away as a prize for a weekend, or the time he gave tourists private tours of Universal studios in his car.

When I interviewed him in 1980, when he was making *The Mirror Crack'd*, he was suffering the breakdown of his second marriage and was prone to depression, although he seemed to be fighting back. In 1983, when he was filming *Where is Parisfal?* he was heavily using cocaine and alcohol – though not in my presence – and now I know why at that time he was much more flamboyant, erratic and indiscreet than usual, speaking more freely than he realised about Marilyn Monroe's obsession with marrying him and what he perceived to be the trap she set for him. He would not recall much about that interview, and was shocked he had been so carelessly candid.

In 1985, just a year after he came out of rehab, he was abjectly penitent about his drug and alcohol use and abuse, and was almost evangelical about his rehabilitation. More astonishingly he was frank about what he believed was an illness of the mind he had inherited from his mother – 'schizophrenia. He tried very hard to explain what his psychotic moments were like. But a day after the interview he called and asked me not to write about his schizophrenia because he was afraid it would harm his career, and I was happy to oblige. I publish it here, for the first time, with his career now safely enshrined in Hollywood history, because his schizophrenia provides a solid clue to his often erratic and occasional bad behaviour, and the kind of demons that sometimes possessed him. He often referred to his 'madnesses,' and questioned his sanity – 'Maybe I'm nuts!' – even if jokingly. He was given to moments of extreme jealousy, paranoia and anger, and I believe his illness was key to all that, especially when fuelled by drug abuse.

My final interview with him was in 1994 when he was promoting his first autobiography. He seemed almost to be on the threshold of lasting happiness at the age of 69, and he was very relaxed and looked amazingly well – although clearly he wasn't as he shortly after suffered a heart attack – and he still had one more divorce not far ahead of him. But he had a lifetime – *almost* a lifetime – of stories to tell and entertain with, and told them over and over on television shows both sides of the Atlantic, becoming, perhaps, better loved by the public than he ever was before.

He was yet to meet the woman who would prove to be his perfect wife, Jill VandenBerg, and who would give him better reasons for living than seeking the elusive one last really great movie role he chased. He said to me in 1994, 'Henry Fonda had his *On Golden Pond* and Spencer Tracy had his *Guess Who's Coming to Dinner?* when they were old guys and then died, and I want my *Guess Who's Coming to Dinner on Golden Pond?*' Sadly, he didn't get it.

He wrote a second autobiography in 2008 and while both versions of his life are essential sources for this biography despite the occasional contradictions between them, I have relied heavily on source material outside of his memoirs, particularly my five interviews with him, and an interview I did with Janet Leigh in 1984 when she was promoting her autobiography. Her accounts often differ from his – which proves that people recall the same events differently, and sometimes for reasons other than memory. She recalled their life together as a romantic and happy time, whereas Tony largely recalled all the pain, jealousy and misery of a failed first marriage.

Another important source comes from an assortment of American fan magazines of the 1950s which I discovered when I worked at the London office of *Photoplay*. I photocopied all the interviews with Tony Curtis, as well as with Janet Leigh, cut them up and pasted them in chronological order into a scrapbook to give a vague account of Tony's life, which I still have. They are an essential source because they are the earliest interviews which are sometimes at odds with accounts Tony and Janet gave in later interviews and in their respective books, and which supply material not given in the autobiographies. Tony Curtis always gave frank interviews and his earliest ones in those magazines are no exception. Universal Pictures executives and publicists often pulled out their hair when yet again Tony openly talked about being a Jew in Hollywood and a victim of anti-Semitism. That kind of thing just was not done. Investigating the contradictions between the differing versions of the same events often reveals as much about the personalities behind them as it does about how different Hollywood used to be.

I am grateful that I've been able to interview and know many who shared their memories of Tony Curtis over the years – some have passed on to what Tony called 'the great cutting room in the sky' while some, thankfully, are still with us. They are Janet Leigh, Kirk Douglas, Burt Lancaster, Natalie Wood, Robert Wagner, Peter Lawford, Sammy Davis Jr, Frank Sinatra, Roger Moore, Sidney Poitier, Richard Fleischer, Ken Annakin, J. Lee Thompson, Roy Ward Baker, Catherine Schell, Joan Collins, Lionel Blair, Claude Hitchcock, Susan Hampshire, Jack Lemmon, Suzanne Pleshette, Orson Welles, Eric Sykes, Terry-Thomas, Kim Novak, Rock Hudson, Walter Matthau, Robert Mitchum, Richard Chamberlain, Charles Bronson, Ernest Borgnine, Henry Fonda, Zsa Zsa Gabor, Blake Edwards, Peter Falk, Laurence Olivier, Lauren Bacall, Gregory Peck, Norman Jewison, Aaron Rosenberg and Shelley Winters. All the quotes in the book are from my personal conversations/interviews with the above and with Tony Curtis, except where otherwise acknowledged.

I am indebted to Tony Curtis. He gave me so much joy with so many of his screen adventures that I've imagined myself being the first to defiantly proclaim, 'I'm Spartacus!' or ride into battle at the head of an army of 16th-century Cossacks alongside Yul Brynner. And after seeing the first episode of *The Persuaders* on a Friday evening in 1971, I wanted to be Danny Wilde. Well, I was only 17 at the time.

I am indebted to him also because he gave me his time and attention, regardless of whether I was interviewing him or not. The first time I met him at Pinewood Studios in 1971, on an unrelated publicity errand (for *Suppose They Gave a War and Nobody Came*), he took away my cigarettes and asked, 'How old are you?' 'Seventeen!' 'You wanna die young?' 'No!' 'Never smoke again!' My colleague was impatient to get on with the work at hand. Tony told him, 'This young man's life is more important than any fuckin' motion picture.' You can't help but feel good when Tony Curtis says you are more important than one of his pictures.

In 1980 there was a very special moment in my life when I found myself standing between him and Rock Hudson in his dressing room at Twickenham Studios as we all admired his latest painting, having just appraised Hudson's latest embroidery in *his* dressing room. There I was, with these two legends from 1950s Hollywood, and we were talking about arts and crafts. I savour that moment still.

I liked Tony Curtis so much that I named my first son Tony. When I told Curtis that, he said, 'I'm very happy you didn't name him Bernard. Or Josephine.'

Michael Munn, 25 February 2011

CHAPTER ONE

A Retarded Kid

A single donkey hauled the cart that took Manó Schwartz and his father Victor on the long road from their home town of Matészalka in Hungary to Budapest during the weeks before the Great War broke out. But the road Manó was setting out on was to prove longer than he could ever have imagined, leading to New York in the United States, and then Hollywood where the son he would name Bernard Herschel became movie star Tony Curtis. It took three days for Manó and Victor Schwartz to travel the 150 miles to Budapest, but many more years to get as far as Hollywood.

Arriving in Budapest, they found the electrical store where Victor hoped his son could serve an apprenticeship closed. Victor had to return home that day and there were insufficient funds for Manó to remain in Budapest on his own. Returning in a week was not an option either because the donkey was not up to making the long journey again, so Victor took Manó into the nearest tailor's store and secured a job for him there. Thus Manó Schwartz became a tailor.

In 1917, Manó chose to remain in Hungary while Victor immigrated to America with eldest son Arthur, leaving his wife and three daughters to await the summons to join him. After Victor wrote news to his wife that he had opened a second-hand clothes shop in New York and that Arthur had joined the merchant marine, he didn't write again. After months of fruitless waiting, Mrs Schwartz packed a few belongings and her three daughters onto a boat in steerage bound for New York and arrived at his shop unannounced. She found a cheap tenement flat for her family, and Victor sheepishly moved in too.

In 1921, Manó arrived in New York. When Tony Curtis was a rising movie star, fan magazines wrote that his father, whom they called Mono Schwartz, came to America because he dreamed of being an actor on Broadway. Tony Curtis told me, 'My father tried acting when he was in Hungary. When he came to America he gave it up in a hurry. He married quite early and started raising a family. He became a tailor.' Tony later wrote that his father wanted to be some kind of entertainer.

Maybe being an actor or some kind of entertainer had been Manó's dream when he came to America, where his name was Americanised to Emanuel and evolved to Manny, but the first thing he did was get his own tailor's shop on the East Side of New York. He was barely making a living when he met Helen Klein, also from Hungary. They married on 22 May 1924. Neither had learned to speak English well and they conversed only in Hungarian, so Tony Curtis was raised in a home where Hungarian was the only spoken language.

'I remember when I was just past seven,' he said in an early interview. 'I was a real retarded kid. I spoke no English because I never heard any at home or even in our neighbourhood. For four blocks in every direction where we lived there were nothing but Hungarians, most of them as freshly over from Europe as we were, and most of them as hungry and poor.'

Bernard Herschel Schwartz was born in New York's Flower Hospital, in Manhattan, on 3 June 1925. He weighed seven pounds and had a small fuzz of black hair. According to the fan magazines, Manny told Helen – as if it was some prediction that had proven to come true by the time it was in print – 'He will be a great actor, and he will conquer this country, as I could not.'

Perhaps Manny did say something to that effect, but what is certain is he didn't give up his dream to be an entertainer, and when he saw an ad in a Hungarian–American newspaper calling for dancers, he duly applied. Asked if he could tango, he said he could. Could he do the bolero? He said he could. He was sent into a back room where there was a big vat of grapes and told to take off his shoes and socks, roll up his trousers, and start treading grapes while a Hungarian group played *czardas* music. He earned more money treading grapes into wine for a dollar an hour than he did as a tailor, and liked to boast, 'I dance for a living.'

Most of his dancing, however, was done at the First Hungarian Independent Lodge dinner and dance. Two-year-old Bernie Schwartz sat on the floor, and whenever his parents got up to dance, he grabbed hold of his mother's leg and didn't let go, hanging on for dear life, scared to death of being left on his own. He was, from his earliest recollections, intensely insecure. 'I was a baby till I was nearly five. I was scared to death when I was four and they told me I had to have my tonsils out, but they promised me all the ice cream I wanted after the operation. I ate a whole quart, right there and then, which was worth giving up my tonsils for.'

A vivid and traumatic memory from his earliest years was of his maternal grandfather coming into his father's shop in a fearful temper and picking up the hot iron to strike Manny. Bernie looked on terrified as his father just stood there, calmly staring up at this older and bigger man who was, said Curtis, 'a monster'. Bernie's grandmother walked in and stepped between them, and that was the end of that. There was no great happiness in the lives of Bernie's maternal grandparents, who both died not long after this incident.

Helen's father had been a brutal man. As a punishment for his wife for some offence, he locked her out of the house. She cried throughout the night. When Helen was five, she and her six-year-old sister Olga were hired out to work as servants and cleaners – virtual slavery. Helen grew up angry at her father and at all men, and inherited her father's violent streak, beating Bernie out of babyhood into boyhood and beyond.

'That poor woman's life was wasted,' said Tony Curtis. 'All those years of hatred and anger, and she heaped it upon another person. I don't care how smart I am, [but] getting slapped in the face and getting hit with objects certainly didn't help me say [to myself], "Take it easy, kid, she's hitting you because she's hitting someone else."'

The family often moved, intensifying little Bernie's insecurity. They moved from Manhattan to Queens, then back to Manhattan. When Bernie's first brother Julius (Julie) was born in July 1929, they lived in the Bronx, and shortly after they moved back to Manhattan where Manny had a new shop, Manuel's Valet Service, on Lexington Avenue. Helen badgered him to do better and always pointed out how well his sisters' husbands had done for themselves.

Helen resented the fact that to supplement the family's income she had to work part time. There was little affection for Bernie and Julie at home, and none between Helen and Manny. Despite the arguments and misery Manny and Helen endured, through either her fault as an embittered woman, or his as a man who just never tried hard enough to succeed, they remained married to the end.

Manny still dreamed of being an actor, and managed to appear in at least one play. Tony told me, 'I remember seeing my father in the theatre in New Brunswick, [New] Jersey. He worked with a Hungarian acting company, and I remember seeing him in one play. I have visions of it now, sitting in the balcony, looking down and seeing my father on stage. He had an axe in his hand. The play was something about someone chasing somebody else with an axe.

'That impressed me about my father, seeing him in front of all those people. I think the vision of seeing him in the theatre really sparked me. I was more sparked when I started going to the movies. I liked the idea of acting. It didn't really make sense to me until I saw the movies. Movies really turned me on.'

Manny never broke out of his trade as a tailor, and struggled to raise his family. He was a good tailor but a lousy businessman, and because times were hard, he let customers run up credit that often went unpaid. When he couldn't pay his own rent, the family was dumped in the streets. There was no welfare. Homeless families simply had to seek new premises of any kind, so Manny usually moved his family into condemned buildings until he could find another shop with a flat over it.

Tony said, in an early fan magazine interview:

> One day we moved. One day? We were *always* moving, and every time we moved into a new place it was the same old story; I had to take a beating from the kids on the block. I was too small to defend myself. I was a new kid and Jewish. So I was always in for it. Only this time I was determined to be brave. I knew I'd be knocked around, and maybe crawl home, half-conscious. Only this time I knew I was going to be fearless and stand up to it as long as I could.
>
> So I started down the tenement steps and there was just one big kid waiting for me. He was just staring me down and he was twice as tall, twice as heavy as I was. He was completely relaxed, except for his tightened fists. For all of one second I looked him fearlessly in the eye. He looked me right back, just waiting. I looked again, and then I fled, straight back up the stairs, straight to my mother. I was a coward, and I knew it.

He recalled then when he was nine, he and two Czech friends were playing on the roof of a condemned house when a big Irish boy appeared and asked one of the Czech boys his name. The Czech boy replied, 'Flanagan.'

The Irish boy turned to Bernie. 'And what's yours?'

Bernie replied, 'O'Flaherty.'

The Irish boy punched Bernie, and down he went. As he struggled to rise, the Irish boy hit him again. 'The first one was for being a Jew,' said the boy. 'The second was for not being Irish. And this one is for being a liar,' and he hit him again.

There were beatings at home too. Each morning Helen told Bernie to be quiet while his father got ready in the one-bedroomed flat they lived in. Any sound from Bernie resulted in a slapped face.

He had noticed something strange about his mother from an early age. 'She'd be looking at me, and just sometimes her face would become twisted as though she were in fear, like something was in the room trying to get her,' he told me in 1985. 'She'd talk really fast, just babbling, and her eyes would dart about the room, and then she'd bury her face in her hands and leave the room. I'd be standing there wondering what the hell *that* was all about. Nobody knew then she was schizophrenic. It was many years later, when she was in Hollywood with me, that she was diagnosed. Those times I just told you [about] – those were times when she had to be hearing the voices. Who knows what they were telling her?'

He noticed that other kids' mothers seemed kinder and warmer. An Italian friend, Frank, had a mother who always made Bernie welcome with generous portions of Italian bread. He never took friends home because his mother always treated them with suspicion. 'She didn't trust anybody,' he said, 'a feeling that must have rubbed off on me.'

Among his happiest memories of childhood were the Sundays when he walked through Central Park with his father. It was a favourite time of the week when he had no fear from bullies, or his mother. It was a 'magical time' he recalled, just being with his father.

He remembered a Sunday when he saw clusters of shacks in the park, and he asked his father what they were.

'Hooverville.'

'What's Hooverville?'

'A kind of community for people who have nowhere to live and are unemployed because of the Depression.'

Tony Curtis told me, 'I never knew that anyone was poorer than us. Then Julie and me were put in an orphanage and I *knew* nobody could be poorer than us.' Manny and Helen took the boys to Sycamore House, a government-sponsored orphanage. 'I was eleven, Julie seven or eight. It was on Sixty-second Street where my father's tailor shop was. They ran out of money and put us in an orphanage. They said they would be back soon, and we were there for ten days or two weeks while my parents relocated, but I didn't know if they were coming back.'

The brothers were separated with Julie taken to be put with the younger boys. Bernie was distressed until a woman worker talked kindly to him and led him by the hand to see Julie so he could know his little brother was all right. He was then taken to the room where he and around a dozen or so other boys were to sleep. He wet the bed every night, and so did Julie, and so both were refused the hot-chocolate drink the other boys had each night. None of the boys were allowed outside and Bernie's anxiety increased. He had no appetite and so rarely ate and became sick. 'I was so relieved when my parents came and got us, and we went and lived in the back of another tailor shop.'

Nothing had changed. They still lived in poverty, and Manny and Helen were still fighting.

Bernie went to a school – P.S. (Public School) 82 – which was four blocks away. The school was just one big room divided by mobile walls into four classrooms. 'There seemed no point in learning,' he told me. 'You had no sense of there being a future to worry about so what was the point of preparing for it? It was just somewhere to go, and as far as my parents were concerned, it was just somewhere where they didn't have to think about us, or worry about us. We were out of the way, my brother and I.'

He played truant and ventured increasingly further away from his deprived neighbourhood of the East River and the 'Seventies', going up to the elegance of the 'Sixties' and the business area of the 'Fifties'. 'With all of the madnesses, I always found a little breath of fresh air by going up to Fifth Avenue to see the people floating by.'

He had a sad and vivid memory of his father. 'I remember my father used to walk down the street with his head down, always looking in the streets as he walked. I remember when he was earning twenty dollars a week as a tailor, and he must have had a hole in his pocket because when he got home it was gone. He turned and rushed out of the house, and I went running after him. I followed him all the way back to where the shop was, which was twenty-five blocks away, and he walked the same route he had come, looking for those twenty dollars.

'And from that time on I remember my father never lifted his eyes from the streets, hoping that one day he'd maybe find those twenty bucks. That had a very profound effect on me then. I always kept my eye out for a break.'

He found a break outside of Bloomingdale's near Third Avenue and 59th Street, where wealthy women came out laden with boxes and packages, and boys offered to carry them and hail a taxi. That was 'the carriage trade'. It was also the perfect spot for a kid to shine shoes, so Manny made Bernie a little shoeshine box and stand. With his bootblack box hung over his shoulder and wearing his shabbiest clothes and usually only one black stocking that had a hole in it, he wandered to Bloomingdale's and set up his shoeshine stand outside. 'I was already learning to act,' he told me. 'I had to *look* the part, and I had a perfect smile.' He knew he had a smile that melted hearts with his full lips and clear blue eyes.

Seeing a lady leave the store with her arms laden with packages, he sidled up to her, gave his best angelic smile, and offered to carry them. If she wanted a taxi he hailed one. If she needed to cross the street he offered to help her across. He was rewarded with a dime or a quarter, and sometimes a whole dollar. 'It was the art, or craft if you will, of the carriage trade,' he said.

He laid out his shoeshine equipment on the ground. He charged a nickel a shine, and then he gave his customer's coat or suit a quick brush down and earned an extra nickel.

He would never forget one particular customer who was obviously very rich and wore English custom-made shoes. Bernie gave those shoes a gleaming shine. When he picked up his clothes brush, the man suddenly yelled, 'Get the hell out of here with that filthy brush,' and kicked over the shoeshine box. Bernie scrambled to catch the brushes and bootblack, and he looked up to see the customer throw a nickel in his face, turn and stride away.

Curtis recalled, 'This guy kicked my shoeshine box down the street, and I swore that I would never forget that man's face because I felt I might have to kill him some day. That was one of the madnesses of my life. There was always with me this feeling of sudden violence I couldn't control, just under the surface, even when I became an adult.' He had inherited his mother's sense of rage, which was so intense that she beat him to the point where he came to hate her. When recalling the beatings she dealt out, he became angry and said, 'I could see in her face an *animal* of some kind.'

During his early years in Hollywood, when interviewed for a fan magazine, he talked openly about some of the violence he endured from other kids, and of the rage that burned inside:

> There was this kid who didn't like me. In fact, we had a mutual dislike which blew up one day while we were playing on a roof top. He knocked me down and kicked me in the groin. The pain was terrific. He kept on kicking me. I tried rolling back and forth to get out of the way, and then, finding a piece of broken glass lying on the ground, I hid it in my hand. When he jumped on me, I slashed at his face with the glass. Blood gushed all over. Yelling in pain, he grabbed his face and ran down the stairs, yelling all the time at the top of his lungs.
>
> After a while I dragged myself down the stairs and over into an alley until the pain subsided. My body ached so I couldn't straighten up. Then I sneaked home, went to my room and changed clothes so my mother wouldn't find out. I never forgot this. Even years later I get riled up when I think of that kid.
>
> For a long time afterwards, this same kid kept hounding me. One day in class at school he got me so mad that I couldn't control myself. In anger, I jumped on his back, started to pull at his hair, and twisted his ears, hard, until he yelled. The teacher sent me to the office of the principal, a Mr Reskob. [In his autobiography he called the principal Mr Reskol.] He said to me, 'Bernie, we all have a cross to bear. You'll have this for the rest of your life, whether it's related to your family or something that bothers you in business. I don't tell you to take things lightly, but the kind of viciousness you displayed today by jumping on the boy's back and screaming is not the answer. You must find another way to get off this kick.'

He could hardly avoid getting into fights and his lifelong friend Victor Mikus recalled for the BBC TV series *The Hollywood Greats*, 'Every time I walked into the tailor's shop, his mother would say, "Bernie, don't fight." This was a thing with her.'

In another fan magazine interview, Curtis recalled a time when he asked a couple of his pals if they wanted to play volleyball in the gym at the end of a school day. They said that volleyball was 'a sissy's game'. A new kid was standing in the hallway, and he pointed at Bernie and said, 'You! You over there. Is it true you're a Jew boy?' Bernie didn't answer. 'What's the matter? Are you yellow? Maybe the little Jew boy's afraid to fight.'

'I'm an American,' Bernie replied. 'I was born here. In this city. So pick a fight somewhere else.'

'Don't tell me what to do,' the big kid yelled, and hit him in the jaw. He hit him again. The other kids yelled, 'Come on, Bernie. Don't let him get away with it. Fight him.'

But Bernie was no match for the other kid and quickly lost the fight. He returned home, his face bleeding and his stomach hurting. That night he told his parents, 'He called me a Jew. He said I was a sissy Jew.'

His mother, washing his face with a damp towel, told him, 'Don't let someone like that scare you. He's so stupid he's not worth fighting with.'

'But I *had* to fight him. He said all those terrible things. He had it in for me. And the other guys rooted for me. They wanted me to win. But I lost.'

His father said, 'You are a Jew and you have nothing to be ashamed of. Your heritage has deep roots. We are good God-fearing people. Our ancestors have given the world our Bible. We believe in the Word of God. Why should we throw away something that has given us a way of life rich in beauty and love for our fellow man? Look at Moses and David and Solomon. Aren't you proud of them? Their blood has come down into you.'

'What is a Jew?' asked Bernie.

His father replied, 'A Jew is like any man. He is a human being with a heart, someone with feelings, someone who wants to love and be loved. Just like anyone else. A Jew's no different than a Greek, or an Italian, or the Polish man who runs the butcher's shop across the street. And yet each man is different for what he is. Wouldn't it be a dull world if everybody was the same?'

Those words made his mother cry, and it was to be one of the few times Bernie felt some kind of family love and unity. He hugged his father and said, 'Dad, I love you,' and then ran to his bedroom because he was embarrassed to display emotion. He was proud of his father who, 'even if he were only a tailor, seemed to know so much'.

He said, 'I discovered that merely being brave isn't enough. It can be stupid. So I started trying to acquire some muscle and brawn, because that way I was going to get free and be able to do exactly what I liked, and nobody would be able to push me around ever. I did all sorts of things [to get stronger] like delivering ice, so that my arms developed and my shoulders broadened, meaning that when I went into a street scrap I could sometimes come out the winner.'

Although he developed muscles, he didn't gain height. He was smaller than all the other kids, and small too when he was an adult, standing just 5 feet 9 inches with fallen arches.

By the age of twelve he was part of a gang of kids, all from poor families and living in tenement blocks, who invented a game designed purely for the streets which they called 'victim'. The boys took it in turns to dodge through the traffic and, with deft timing and acute stupidity, fall to the ground as if hit by one of the trucks which raced from one traffic light to the next, intent on making it before the green changed to red. The truck driver invariably leaped out, leaned over the victim and pressed money into his hand, then got in his truck and sped away.

In his pre-pubescent years, he began to notice girls. 'When I was going to P.S. 82 in New York – I was going on twelve – I fell in love with a cute little blonde who wouldn't have a thing to do with me. I used to pass notes to her which she would tear up and throw away. She treated me with such terrible disdain, and once when I tried to put my arm around her, she slapped me. I felt miserable.

'Then I got acquainted with Ann. She had her troubles, too. There was a big scar on her face as a result of an accident she had been in. None of the guys would go out with her. Somebody told me that she gave kissing lessons in the back of the school, so I asked her. She said, "Sure! Ten cents a kiss." I told her I didn't have a dime, but she said that didn't matter. We went walking and when it was about dark she sat down with me on a bench under the elevated steps, and she told me to kiss her. So I did. She said, "You're terrible, you don't even know how to pucker up." Looking back on it, I guess we were both terrible, but we were a couple of lonesome kids, and we became friends.'

He was already very handsome by the age of twelve – and he knew it. 'I saw the way some women looked at me, and some guys looked at me. I felt I was paying a price for my looks. I always had to be careful when I delivered clothes for my father – I was always in danger of having the clothes torn out of my hands or get thrown up against a wall and have my pockets searched. That was the madness I felt about how I had to pay the price for my looks. I could feel the anger of guys around me. Nobody wanted to seek me out as a friend, and I was trying to be cute. The girls were easier it seemed, but these guys weren't and I wanted them to accept me, I wanted to be part of an environment.'

Victor Mikus recalled, 'He was a good-looking guy, gagging around, always full of fun.'

From an early age he had a great sense of fun, was very amiable, and could make people laugh. 'As a kid I always wanted to please everybody,' he said. 'I always wanted to show off. I wanted the adulation and friendship of people patting me and saying, "You're such a sweet little boy." Maybe I didn't get enough of it. Maybe that's a part of all my madnesses.'

All he wanted was to be liked, have fun and have friends, and escape the horrors of his home life. Out in the streets, he felt he had no responsibility – except for Julie. 'I always felt responsible for Julie,' he said in an early interview. 'I was quick. I had a sense of coordination that he lacked, but there was a sort of calm wisdom in Julie that I didn't have. I remember that one day when he was tagging after me to school, I looked around and he was gone. I went looking and found him sitting on the steps of a church, just sort of dreaming. I bawled him out. He looked up at me in his gentle way and said, "Don't hit me, Bernie. I just don't feel like going to school today." So I didn't make him go.'

Like all the deprived kids, Bernie stole. One day he went home chewing liquorice he had stolen and was caught by his father who took him back to the store to confess and pay a nickel for the candy. 'He made me feel ashamed,' Tony Curtis told me. 'He said that he didn't want the family name ruined by me or my brother. He said, "Julie looks up to you and copies you." When we got to the steps leading up to our apartment, my father said, "We may be poor, but we're honest. Next time I won't be so easy on you. We all make mistakes, but once is enough." I loved that man. He wasn't perfect. Nobody's perfect. But I always remember that everyone deserves a second chance. He never told my mother.'

Four months after the Schwartz brothers were placed temporarily in the orphanage, Bernie was with a group of friends watching an American Legion parade. Julie wanted to be with them, but Bernie told him to go away. Tony Curtis recalled, 'We'd tagged along that parade all afternoon, and we'd had a ball. Somebody said something or did something that was so funny we cried we laughed so hard, and I'm absolutely sure it was at that moment that my brother was hit by that truck.'

In an early account, he said, 'Some little kids came running over to me, shouting that a boy was knocked down by a truck, and they said, "It looked like your brother." The next minute I saw the traffic cop coming toward me. He said, "I want you to identify this kid." That was the worst moment ever.

'Julie had always been more sensible than I. I had planned how to help him over the rough spots so he wouldn't have it so tough as I had. And then the worst happened. I wanted to run for my folks. I wanted to scream for my mother. Then I knew I couldn't do it. I had to act grown up. I think maybe I did grow up right then. I certainly was never really young again after I looked down and saw it was Julie.'

Julie was taken to hospital where he died two days later.

In his two autobiographies, Tony Curtis told a slightly different story; he went home unaware of what had happened to Julie until two cops came to their home and said that a boy who might be Julie had been knocked down. They wanted someone to come to the hospital to identify him, and his parents made Bernie go. When he got to the hospital, Julie's face was so badly injured he was virtually unrecognisable except for a broken tooth he had.

Reflecting on that horrific day to Dr Pamela Connolly (a.k.a. former actress Pamela Stephenson) in 2008 on her TV programme *Shrink Wrap*, he said he whispered into Julie's ear, 'Julie, it's me. I'm here with you. Not to worry. I'm sorry I didn't want you to play with me and my friends. But when you get better we'll hang out a lot.'

The differences in the early and later accounts about when and how he identified Julie are puzzling. It was probably a simple case of Tony Curtis, as a young movie star, speaking very frankly to the fan magazines but altering the facts to protect his parents. And I don't think it was out of loyalty to them that he did so, because, as he told Dr Connolly – about being sent by his parents to identify his brother – 'I was offended by it.' He did it to protect his own image because during the 1950s a movie star was defined by *everything* about him, and that included the parents. He never revealed in those fan magazines his mother's brutal personality or her schizophrenia, and he also kept the part about them making him go and identify Julie a secret for many years, and in doing so it must have intensified the bitterness and resentment that he felt towards his parents.

The day Julie died was the day that changed Bernie Schwartz forever.

Julie's death, and the day he identified his brother, was the most traumatic event in his life which he never got over, and to his dying day he felt responsible for his little brother's death. 'Had I not chased him away from me, perhaps he would have lived. He only followed the American Legion band because I didn't want him to hang out with me. You can't have more than enough reason [for feeling responsible] than that, can you?' he asked Dr Connolly.

In an early interview, he said that he had to face up to the fact that Julie had seen him playing 'victim', and so blamed himself for Julie's death. He knew his parents blamed him. 'I was supposed to be the one who always took care of him because they never did, so maybe that's why they made me go to the hospital,' he told me in 1994. 'Maybe they were punishing me. I *never* understood why they made me do that.'

Nobody else blamed him. Victor Mikus said, 'Things happen. What are you going to do? It's unfortunate. It wasn't his fault. It's just something that occurred.'

CHAPTER TWO

Swashbuckling in Manhattan

In the depths of despair, Bernie went down to the East River and threw a stone in as a mark of remembrance for his dead brother. He prayed to God to let him see Julie. 'I think of that day a lot,' he wrote in 2008. 'I remember what the stone felt like.'

For a week after Julie's death, Manny and Helen sat shivah in the tailor's shop, and Bernie sat with them, on a box, wearing a yarmulke, as friends and family came by to express their condolences.

The funeral took place on Lexington Avenue. Julie lay in an open coffin. 'It was hard for me to look, but I did,' Tony recalled. 'Somebody lifted his head and removed the pillow from under his head, and the pillow was pink from the blood, and rearranged it. I thought, "*Why shouldn't I do that*?" I was his brother. Some strange hands lifting his head - that offended me.'

He continued, 'I heard these people mumbling and praying and wailing to what they thought God was. What good was it?' Clearly, whatever little faith Bernie had was gone.

The trucking company offered Manny and Helen a $2,000 settlement. The lawyer acting for the company told them, 'Too bad the boy didn't live. That way you would have had a steady income for life. Not big, but continuing.' When Bernie heard him say that, he was suddenly filled with a murderous rage, adding this man to his hit list. 'I guess I had a lot of people on my hit list,' he told me. 'But I was never gonna bump anyone off. I just *felt* like it, ya know?

That's how I felt as a kid sometimes, like I oughta kill someone.'

After Julie's death Helen Schwartz seemed to be more ready than usual to beat Bernie, while Manny began to slip into a depressed world of his own. Two months after Julie died, the store was broken into and every dime Manny had was stolen.

They moved to the Bronx to be closer to their relatives, and shortly after that came Bernie's Bar Mitzvah. Recalling the event for a fan magazine, he remembered his father telling him, 'See how beautiful this is? This is what makes me happy. This is all I ask from life. To see us together. The day will come when you have a family of your own. Tonight we will say our prayers together. Tonight you are a rich man.'

As required, Bernie told everyone how much he loved his parents, and how he was going to devote himself to his religion, and that he looked forward to an accomplished life. 'I didn't believe a word of it,' he later said.

He began high school, at P.S. 80, and during an English class his teacher berated him for spelling his own name wrong when he left the *tz* out of Schwartz. Tony would blame his lack of education on his family moving so many times. 'My father moved from one section of the city to another. In one school term, which was about a year, we once moved four times. So I got very little education in those early years. But I grabbed enough to learn how to read and write, and some semblance of arithmetic, which I thought was a foreign language.'

The classes at P.S. 80 were often unruly, and when there was enough turmoil and chaos to divert the teacher's attention, Bernie slipped out of school and rode the Third Avenue El (elevated railway) without a ticket. He told a fan magazine, 'Education at school took too much discipline and I only wanted to be free, and to be free I had to be an anti-discipline man and not submit to teachers and lessons. I had to stay untamed. I saw no other way for myself. So I looked out for some kind of break.'

Untamed, wanting to be free, looking for a break, he discovered 'how to maintain myself by not going to school. I'd go to museums, I'd go down streets, get on the subway, it doesn't seem like that was doing much but I was doing a lot. I was getting a different kind of education laced with wanting to be in the movies.'

When he skipped school with friends, they sometimes sneaked into burlesque shows to see the naked dancers. But Bernie's favourite place to go was the cinema, and his closest friends became very aware of his fascination with Hollywood. Victor Mikus recalled him 'talking about Hollywood – and Errol Flynn he mentioned many times'.

Another lifelong friend, Joe Franklin, figured he and Tony had seen around two thousand movies, going to the cinema every afternoon. 'On Sundays we'd always go down to Forty-second Street because there was always an Errol Flynn double bill.'

'Movies were wonderful,' Tony Curtis told me. 'To be able to end up doing that I thought would be great, and I have the feeling that I kinda geared myself up in that direction right from the beginning without really knowing it.'

He began emulating his favourite stars. When he saw Errol Flynn eating a raw onion in *They Died with Their Boots On* and still managing to talk without shedding a tear or flinching, Bernie ate onions for a week. His eyes and nose constantly streamed, and people refused to go near him, so he gave up eating raw onions.

He fantasised that he was Errol Flynn rescuing Olivia de Havilland or horse riding with Norma Shearer. He swung on balconies and fire escapes to emulate Douglas Fairbanks Jr, and he learned how he might light Greta Garbo's cigarette for her.

Then one day he actually saw Greta Garbo. Joe Franklin recalled going with him to a theatre on 57th Street for a Greta Garbo festival. 'Who's sitting a couple of seats away? Greta Garbo! She was actually staring and gazing at Bernie Schwartz.' Joe Franklin said that every time he looked over, he saw Greta Garbo peaking at Bernie. 'I said to myself, *This guy has got to go somewhere soon; he's got to be the new Rudolph Valentino*. The great Garbo was attracted to Bernie!'

Bernie swashbuckled his way around Manhattan and the Bronx as though he were Flynn and Fairbanks, climbing the trestles of the El up to the platform, all the time practising how to perform movie stunts in preparation of becoming a swashbuckling movie hero. 'It was like a bug inside of me,' he told me. 'I felt I had to try and work that bug out of me by doing dangerous things.'

He began to play games even more dangerous than 'victim'.

'I had taken a kid's dare. I had to show how tough I was. I jumped from the roof of a six-storey building across the alley to the roof of a four-storey apartment house. This was a big thing for me, a sort of symbol of success. It was as if I was saying to myself, "Maybe I'll fail in a career, but even if I do nobody else can ever say they did anything like jumping off that roof."'

He made the jump, hit a chimney and was ambulanced to hospital. He was just cut and bruised and hit the streets again to perform more dangerous feats like hanging on to the backs of moving taxis. But all the kids liked to do that, so he did something none of them dared to do. He sat on the window ledge of a high tenement block, and jumped onto a mattress below.

This was the kind of reckless and often life-threatening behaviour he exhibited after Julie's death, and he was never able to fully explain why he did them. He said to Dr Pamela Connolly it was 'to escape from the miserable environment I was in', and added, 'The death of Julie – the way they buried him.' The funeral, a stranger's hands lifting Julie's head to move the blood-stained pillow – they were visions that haunted him all his life. Perhaps being physical in the extreme was the only way Bernie could come to terms with all of that. 'I'm a very excitable person. Have been all my life. After the death of Julie I did the most bizarre things as a boy – physical things.'

He simply had no other way of dealing with his issues. 'There was no place I could go to for counselling. Today we have "counselling". Today we have "closure". There's no such thing as forgetting. Time does not heal all wounds. We imagine it does. Perhaps the initial pain and anger and frustration slowly disappear but the image is still there.'

He denied he had a death wish, or was in any way defying death. 'I had very little education, I used to deliver clothes for my father, my mother used to slap me around, and the only way I was able to achieve what I wanted was physically. When I did a stunt – if I was able to do it and not hurt myself – it was affirmation that I was doing OK. These were the madnesses that were running through my brain.'

But he was never really the tough and wild child he liked everyone else to think he was. It was all an act. He told me, 'In spite of the tough act I put on, most of the time I was shy and withdrawn, and other kids used me as a patsy just for laughs. Once I took a dare that later cost me a big dentist's bill. All of the kids at school used to be sent to the Guggenheim Clinic on Seventy-second Street. If you had a white card, it meant your teeth were to be cleaned. A blue card meant you needed a filling. A pink card meant pull it out.

'One day a kid said to me, "Bernie, you want to make a quarter?" I said, "Sure." He said, "All you gotta do is take my card to the dentist, and when you come back I'll give you two bits." So I did, and the dentist pulled out one of my rear molars. It wasn't until years later when I went to Hollywood that I could afford to have that tooth replaced. And I never collected the quarter.'

Behind the tough exterior, and hiding the inner turmoil which he was trying to understand and deal with, was a sensitive and very creative and artful personality that belied the image of the street-wise kid. He enjoyed drawing, and discovered he was good at it. It became an outlet for something nobody recognised in him, which was a need to express himself creatively. 'I could do it on my own, and it had nothing to do with anybody else,' he told me. 'Drawing is an expression of feelings, and what I draw depends on how and what I feel at the time.'

He had no idea that this simple method of expression would one day make him famous as an artist. Perhaps it was the discovery of this less physical side to him that allowed him to appreciate movie stars other than Flynn or Fairbanks, and quickly moving up his chart of favourite actors came the elegant and sophisticated Cary Grant. 'I went to see every Cary Grant movie,' he told me. 'I learned so much just from watching him on the screen. How he lit a woman's cigarette, and how he wore double-breasted jackets, and high shirt collars. It was as though he were saying to me, personally, "Bernie, when you take a girl on a date, you give the driver a five-dollar bill for a two-dollar ride, then get out of the cab and open the door for the lady." That's how I learned some of the mores and social graces of life.'

Other favourite stars were James Cagney – 'I learned from him how to be a tough guy and take care of myself' – and Tyrone Power – 'Here was a man almost as good-looking as I!'

Joan Crawford was one of his favourite leading ladies. 'She was maybe my first wet dream,' he told me. 'One day I was outside my father's shop when I saw this car driving slowly because the street was so narrow and crowded, and when I recognised Joan Crawford inside I flipped and ran up to the car, pounded on the window, and demanded an autograph. She signed her name for me, and I adored her more than ever.'

Movies became Bernie's inspiration, and his ambition in life was to be in the movies and be a star of the silver screen. 'That's all I wanted to be,' he told me. 'There was never a second or third option. It had to be the movies.'

Shortly after the family moved to the Bronx, Manny went to work with Shapiro & Sons, a major clothier in Manhattan. He supervised twenty tailors, earning good money, and suddenly his demeanour at home changed and he became more confident, even dominating Helen for the first time.

He began an affair with a buxom redhead. Helen confronted him and the other woman coming out of a cinema. The redhead walked away and Manny never saw her again. After that incident, the tension at home was worse than ever.

Manny's workers took advantage of his kindness, and productivity dropped dramatically. He was fired and went back to working for himself, but with the Depression over, he was now able to earn decent money, up to forty dollars a week. But Helen remained unhappy and went through life, as Tony Curtis put it, 'sour about everyone and everything. She was the unhappiest soul I ever knew.'

As a young teenager, Bernie was shorter than most kids of his age, but he stood out from the crowd because of his exceptionally good looks. He said, 'I knew I was a good-looking kid because of the way people responded to me. Nobody told me. *I* told me.' He corrected himself. 'There *was* someone who told me. He was a doctor. I'd come off a cart I'd made from an orange box and roller skates, and I'd injured my hand, and my finger became infected. So my mother took me to the hospital in the Bronx, and a doctor looked at it and said, "You got a serious infection." Then he said, "You're a good-looking kid. Take advantage of it. Don't neglect yourself like you've neglected your finger."

'And that was the first time anyone said I was good-looking and that I should make something of my life. My mother never told me to make something of myself. My father never did. Nobody. But what that doctor said to me stayed with me.'

Bernie slicked his thick dark hair down on the sides and left the top curly. 'I found people looked at me, and I took an interest in my appearance. Not in the clothes I wore then because most of my clothes were just street clothes, but I loved my hair, and I knew I could make it look good – make *me* look good. I was very vain even then.'

When he was 15 a female neighbour asked him to help her carry something into her apartment, and as soon as he got inside the door, she kissed him so hard that his mouth bled. She rubbed herself against him, and within a minute or two had finished with him. He left, he said, 'feeling violated'. He went home and washed his face. The experience hadn't excited him. It had repelled him. 'I have never denied that I love sex,' he told me. 'I was easily aroused, as boys are at that age, but with me it was worse. I could barely keep my erection down at any time, and I always came too soon. But that woman made me feel defiled. I decided I would never treat a woman that way. I have always tried to make it nice for the girl, and for me. Whether it was a romance or just a one-time-only thing, I was always a gentleman.'

Guys who resented him for his looks called him a homosexual because he was almost beautiful, but nothing could have been further from the truth. He was obsessed with shapely girls. 'I loved their breasts, their legs – that was what appealed to me the most. It always has.' It always did.

When he was 15 he either did or didn't have his first real sexual experience, depending on which of his autobiographies you believe. In his first, he said he never had sex with a woman until he was in the navy. But in his second, he wrote about a girl called Alicia Allen who was older than he and had her own apartment. She encouraged him in his ambition to be an actor and took him to a party held in a mansion where she introduced him to Ethel Merman who, he claimed, said to him, 'Hi, kid. Oh, what a nice-looking guy you are.'

Alicia took him to her apartment and they made love. It only happened the once, but, he said, 'that one time was truly unforgettable'. He had, however, forgotten it when he wrote his first autobiography.

In 1940, Helen gave birth to another son, Robert. 'What were they thinking?' Curtis said years later. 'They hadn't been able to take care of me and Julie, and they want to have another child? I was just a kid but I thought they were wrong.'

They didn't know it when Bobby was a baby, but he had inherited his mother's schizophrenia. His behaviour was erratic even when he was young, but it wasn't until 1950 that he was diagnosed as schizophrenic, and was later institutionalised. He was to become the second brother that Tony Curtis lost.

CHAPTER THREE

Angel With A Dirty Face

Bernie teetered on the edge of juvenile delinquency. He said, 'There were two or three street gangs. We thought we were the Dead End Kids – you know, *Angels with Dirty Faces*.' They didn't go in for big-time robberies, but he thought that given time, all of them, or some, or just him, might have headed that way. 'There were candy stores, and in back they used to have their supply places and there used to be cases of Coke, boxes of chewing gum and sometimes cigarettes.'

What he remembered most about breaking into those places wasn't how much they managed to get away with but how the merchandise had a certain nostalgic aroma which stayed with him for many years. 'I remember the smell of these places . . . mmmmm! A mixture of chewing gum, spearmint, bubble gum and candy bars and a little tinge of tobacco. Just took your breath away. We sat there more smelling it than stealing it. We'd get away with some of it. We'd keep it in a certain place, just a handful of us, and sometimes we'd get caught. We ran if we could, or if we couldn't we talked our way out of it, like, "Honestly, officer, we just found this stuff, we didn't put it there," and they knew we stole it but couldn't do anything.'

He considered himself lucky not to have moved into more serious crime. 'We never went out with guns. We were a little young then for guns. I don't know if we woulda stepped up to that. When we were kids in New York, we only used to really steal from each other. Once the big hauls were made, the gangs would try and knock off each other. So it was more of a macho game as opposed to really being in it for the material.'

Nevertheless, there was the inspiration to go on to bigger and perhaps more heinous activities. Local gangsters were a common sight, and Bernie was easily impressed by them. 'There was a guy called Herbie that I admired a lot. He was about eighteen years old, wore double-breasted suits, and every now and then he'd come around the neighbourhood in a car, a convertible. With the top down! That used to blow everybody's head! Particularly if it was wintertime. He'd have a topcoat, his hat pulled down, but still he'd come in the convertible with the top down! Those images are very clear in my head.

'I admired him, and he was always nice with the guys, the kids around the neighbourhood. I had an occasion two or three times to be in a house where he was in. He was quite a well-known character in the neighbourhood. He always seemed to me like a gentleman. Never rough or crude. But there were all kinds of stories about him.'

Bernie was at a crossroads in his life. He knew he could have gone on to do virtually anything to break out. He wasn't caught up in a poverty trap any longer because the Depression was over, and his father was earning decent money, but Bernie wanted to earn lots of money like Herbie. And he wanted to break free from the tension at home, the guilt over Julie, and the beatings from his mother, although the beatings were no longer such a problem, 'because they never hurt me coz I was able to evade them'.

He said, 'I don't know what I would have done if I hadn't ended up in the movies. I really don't know how it would have evolved. Probably would have stayed in New York, got into a profession, married some wealthy girl with a family and maybe tried to find a way out of it that way. I knew I had to find some success, to build myself some kind of estate, get some money, which is the big equaliser. Extra money can make life a shade easier. And I had enough experience with my family, where it was really lowball dough all the time, that I just wanted to improve my life, and I didn't care how I did it.'

For a while it looked as though Bernie was heading for real trouble. A friend from those days, Sam Negrin, said in an interview with a fan magazine, 'The gang was getting too old to act out a simple game of cops and robbers. That temptation to make it more real was creeping up on them. They hadn't yet done anything seriously wrong, but they were getting close. Bernie was ready to try anything to win from the gang the approval he could not give himself. I think he was close to doing something desperate.'

He was saved by a man called Paul Schwartz, not a relation but a programme director at the Henry Street Settlement House, which organised activities for local boys, including summer camp and amateur dramatics.

Curiously, Tony mentioned Paul Schwartz only once in his first autobiography, to point out that he was not a truant officer as had been reported, and said only that he 'helped set me straight, at least in some ways'. Paul Schwartz is not mentioned at all in the second auto-biography, and neither is the Henry Street Settlement House. But when I interviewed him in 1975, Tony spoke enthusiastically about Paul Schwartz, and of the programmes that gave Bernie his first real taste of acting.

'I met him when I was fifteen or sixteen. He was running a camp. He had one leg shorter than the other. Kinda buck teeth. Came from the South. He was a wonderful man who instilled a lot of confidence in me. He liked me, maybe because we had the same name, I dunno. We had a very nice relationship. He gave me a desire and a drive. He intensified my feeling about wanting to be an actor. He allowed me the privilege of putting on shows.'

Tony must have been in deep trouble with the law when he got involved in the Henry Street Settlement House, because when, in 1980, I made mention that Paul Schwartz's summer camp was a blessing for him, he said, 'It was either that or prison'. There was no other reason for the wild Bernie Schwartz to suddenly begin attending Paul Schwartz's social programmes, particularly summer camp, other than to undergo a rehabilitation programme. It might well have been Bernie Schwartz's last chance.

At camp, Paul Schwartz captured the interest of the boys with the fable of King Arthur and the Knights of the Round Table, and prompted them to create a play about the legend. They painted sets and threw together crude costumes, and all their energies went into putting on the unscripted play.

Tony told me, 'We separated into two factions, and we turned that camp into that period of time, and we became one group of men like King Arthur, and the others were the other characters of that period. It was wonderful. It was like on a movie set. There was some guy standing with a sword or a lance or a shield.'

Tony Curtis recalled none of that in his first autobiography but did write about the camp on the other side of the lake for the kids from

German immigrant families who flew the swastika alongside the American flag, and who rowed across the lake in canoes and yelled, 'You know what a Jew is? A Jew is a nigger turned inside out.' At night the German kids raided Bernie's camp with stink bombs and progressed to Molotov cocktails. Those bitter memories must have superseded all the happy memories when he came to write his life story.

In 1975 he was happy to remember that he volunteered to play Guinevere. 'Somebody had to,' he said. 'Either that or there was no play.' He wore a gold wig and a dress. He took his role very seriously, and it deepened his interest in acting. And if any of the other boys laughed at him, he laid into them with his fists, feet and teeth.

He was so enthusiastic about the settlement-house programmes that he applied for a job at the camp the following summer. So did a lot of other East Side kids, eager for a working holiday away from the slums. He met Sam Negrin while waiting for his interview with Paul Schwartz, and they both landed jobs. 'The official designation was "kitchen boy and counsellor-in-training",' recalled Sam Negrin. 'In terms of work it actually meant that we went up to Henry Street's camp at Mahopac Falls to wash dishes for one hundred and twenty-five people, scrub floors and ride herd on the smaller kids. The important thing to us was that we got a summer in the country, but we didn't lose sight of the fact that we also were paid twenty dollars for those ten weeks.'

Bernie and Sam's first task was to go up to the lake as an 'advance crew' of around half a dozen kids, and open the camp to get it ready. They slept the first night in the dining hall with their cots in close formation for security. Unused to the pitch dark without neon signs and street lights glaring in their windows, they were unable to sleep. Kids who ignored the roar of the Third Avenue El train jumped at the chirp of a cricket. And boys who prowled vicious streets without fear were too afraid to go outside the hall.

When Bernie asked if anyone else wanted to take a leak in the washing shack 50 yards down an unlit path, no one volunteered to go with him. So he set out alone.

'I set up a gag,' said Negrin. 'We agreed that when Bernie returned, we'd give him a real scare.' They heard Bernie whistling as he returned. They jumped into their cots and pretended to be asleep. As Bernie gingerly searched for his cot in the dark, the boys jumped up and yelled, 'Boo!'

'I was no more than 6 inches from his ear and no one was further than a few feet away,' said Sam Negrin. 'We thought it hilarious when we yelled, but in a minute, we knew it wasn't funny. Bernie fell back on his bed, his heart pounding so hard we could see it. For a half-hour, he couldn't get his breath. We thought he was going to die. That's when I gave up practical jokes.'

When it came to the hard work, Bernie didn't shirk. Said Negrin, 'He did more than his share of the scrubbing and never complained about blistered hands or sore muscles.'

Bernie excelled in the athletic programme. 'He was our best tumbler, a sort of Douglas Fairbanks,' said Negrin. 'He was so limber you wondered if he had a bone in his body. We spread our mattresses out on the grass so he could teach his tricks to other kids.'

Bernie was now mentoring other boys, and teaching handicapped children how to do gymnastics – when he was married to Janet Leigh, they both supported boys' and girls' clubs, and he continued to help disabled children to do physical activities as a sort of payback for what the settlement house had done for the teenage Bernie Schwartz.

Bernie and Sam worked with Paul Schwartz to put on plays at the settlement house during winter. They were largely improvised plays. Bernie invented stories on the spot. One kid was to be the cop, another the robber, another the stool pigeon, another the store keeper, and suddenly they had a play.

Sam Negrin recalled, 'Bernie carried his own weight and worked well with the group. I would have raised hell if I hadn't gotten lead roles, but not him. He'd be backstage pulling the curtain or going on in a half-dozen bit parts in each show.'

Bernie Schwartz was changing and improving himself, and even away from the settlement house he displayed a gift for improvisation and comedy, as observed by another friend from school, Sidney Schulman, who said, 'Bernie was always acting. We'd be riding the El home, and he'd get his coat up over his head, pull his arms half out of his sleeves, waggle them and announce, "Look at me, I'm a rabbit." He'd do anything for a laugh.'

Bernie wanted desperately to do some real acting, and was introduced by his sometime girlfriend, Alicia Allen, to the 92nd Street YMHA Playhouse where he auditioned for the part of the lighthouse keeper's son in *Thunder Rock* and got it. He was just fifteen. After Tony Curtis became a fledgling star at Universal, the studio put out the story that he had landed his first role in *Thunder Rock* at the YMCA rather than the YMHA, which was a Jewish organisation.

A fan magazine article claimed that Tony shaved his head for the part. I asked him if that was true, and he said it was. He loved his hair and it seems almost inconceivable that he would shave it all off, but he was prepared to do anything to fulfil his ambition to become a movie actor.

The first Manny and Helen knew about him shaving his hair was when they went to see the play. It was a decision he had made on opening night, and he had kept it a secret from everyone, including the cast and crew. Helen was mortified to see her son shaved of all his glorious locks, and when the play was over Manny tried hard to calm her down. 'What does it matter?' he asked her. 'Hair grows again. Just think! Our son was up there on stage. Did you hear him speak?' He only spoke two lines. 'Wasn't our boy handsome?'

'Handsome?' she replied incredulously. 'Bald?'

'Yes, handsome. And a boy to be proud of.'

Whether or not he shaved his head, Tony Curtis never got over his mother's apathy about his first real play. 'She couldn't see that this is what I wanted to do,' he said. 'She couldn't even be happy for me.'

He went to lengths to get the more technical aspects of acting right. 'I got a chance to play in Clifford Odets' show *Waiting for Lefty*. I had to smoke in that, and I'd never smoked in my life before. So I nearly smoked myself sick for weeks before, learning how to handle a cigarette naturally.'

When he was sixteen, the family moved back to Manhattan, which Bernie preferred to the Bronx. Manny opened a new tailor's shop where he worked in the back room sewing while Helen took care of customers. He had become too stressed to deal with the public, and Helen resented the fact that she had to work at all. The anxieties that drove Manny into the back of the shop grew into a nervous breakdown, and one day Bernie discovered his father gripping a knife in his hand, a blank look in his eyes, unable to respond to Helen's pleadings. As Manny slowly came around, he was surprised to find the knife in his own hand. Even with a nervous breakdown, he couldn't afford not to work, and the drudgery of life continued for them all.

In the part of New York called Germantown, American Nazis donned uniforms to march in parades. Bernie and his friends dropped condoms filled with urine and dog food onto the parade from a tenement rooftop. As Nazis ran into the building and up the stairs, the boys escaped over roof tops and down fire escapes into Second Avenue.

This became a regular private war for Bernie and his friends. One time Bernie found himself cornered by three Nazis with baseball bats. They would probably have beaten him to death had he not been able to outrun them. When America entered World War Two, the Nazi parades were banned.

Bernie began having nightmares in which the Nazis overran America. 'I think that was the first time I began to realise how important it was for America to be in the war,' he said. 'At first the war seemed too far away to be of concern, but then we began hearing that the Nazis were doing terrible things to the Jews. That had to make you think, if you were a Jew. It shoulda made *anyone* think.'

The whole idea of anything German became anathema to Bernie, and he even began to hate his surname, which was a German–Jewish name. He tried to find an alternative name such as David Street, David Sparrow and even David Sorrow. 'It was my way of trying to find a new identity for myself,' he told me, 'not just as a young guy but as a movie star which I hoped to be. I was already determined to change my name when I got into movies.'

He was still officially Bernard Schwartz when his parents enrolled him at Seward Park High School. But he never arrived for the first day, or the second, or any day after that. Instead he enlisted in the US Navy. He had chosen to fight the Nazis and, wrote in his autobiography, that he had originally thought of joining the marines before realising he had a better chance of surviving the war in the navy. Being underage and needing his parents' consent, he went outside the recruitment building and forged his mother's signature on the enlistment forms.

His parents were unhappy when he told them he was in the navy but didn't try to stop him, and the next day he was sent to Sampson in upper New York State to begin a six-week training period. As a school truant he had wanted to fight discipline, but all that changed. 'It wasn't until I was in the navy that I wanted to unlearn that no-discipline bit. The orders I *had* to take or get my block knocked off I took, of course.

'But the day I saw a different perspective was when an officer came round and asked which of us gobs would like to be officers. My hand shot up so fast I nearly pulled my arm out of its socket. The idea of wearing gold braid, of being constantly saluted, really reached me. So they let me be an officer candidate – for all of one class.'

He was given a test and asked to solve a simple mathematical problem. Seven plus four. He wasn't quick enough, and his paper was taken from him before he could write down the answer. 'The character who was examining my IQ said to me, "How can a bright kid like you be so dumb? Why, you can't even add seven and four." That wasn't true. I *could* add seven and four – but not easily. So I went right back to being a gob again.'

Because he wasn't eighteen, he couldn't be sent overseas, so he was sent to signalman school on the Champaign-Urbana campus of the University of Illinois where he learned to communicate with flags and Morse code. The music department at the college put on a show for the navy and a casting call went out for sailors. Bernie auditioned and was one of eight chosen. He played a romantic scene from a musical, and loved the whole experience of being on show and performing, especially as it involved nuzzling a girl.

He met one of his best friends for life in the navy, Larry Storch, who would become a nightclub comedian and actor. He recalled, 'Tony desperately wanted to become an actor, and we kind of gravitated towards each other.' Storch told him that with his good looks he should become a model. Tony told him, 'No, no, I'm gonna be an actor.'

Having thought he had left anti-Semitism behind in civilian life, Bernie was horrified to find it rearing its ugly head in the navy. 'I got that Jewish thing thrown in my face again. There we were, all fighting Hitler's Jewish persecution, but just the same, the anti-Semitic influence would appear on deck every now and then. I thought it was my duty as a Jew to go into one of the most dangerous branches of service.' He volunteered to serve in a submarine, known to be more dangerous than serving aboard any other kind of warship.

In later years he would say that he chose to serve in a submarine because he had seen Cary Grant in *Destination Tokyo* and was impressed by the sight of Grant at the periscope, his hands hanging on the handles while he pressed his eyes to the scope. There was another reason too. He said, 'I liked that fifty per cent more pay you got for sub duty.'

Studio publicity would state that he served on a submarine, USS *Dragonet*, for three years. He was in the navy for three years, but little of it was spent in a submarine. As a third-class signalman, he was sent to the submarine base in New London, Connecticut, where he trained on a submarine. Then he was sent to San Diego for more training. 'At that point I still hadn't made love with a woman,' he wrote in his first autobiography, and added that one of his first 'real times with a woman' was at a whorehouse in Panama City (in contradiction to his encounter with Alicia Allen related in his second memoir).

On a weekend pass, he and some buddies went to Los Angeles to the Hollywood Canteen restaurant and nightclub where movie stars entertained the troops. There he saw actress Gloria DeHaven, and was convinced that their eyes locked for a brief moment.

Back home, Manny was diagnosed with lung cancer. Tony recalled, 'I was given emergency leave to go home and he was already in a hospital and they took out a lung. That's at forty-two years old.' Later, his father's illness would have a profound effect on Tony and cause him to quit smoking.

From San Diego, third-class signalman Schwartz was transferred to Pearl Harbor, Hawaii, for more training, and then sent to Guam to serve on the submarine tender *Proteus*, which supplied and maintained the submarine fleet. But did he ever serve on a submarine? He told me, in 1975, that he was on the USS *Dragonet* where there was little to do but watch *Gunga Din* over and over. 'We used to run that picture without sound, and we did all the different voices ourselves. I was Cary Grant.'

Curiously, he didn't make any mention of the *Dragonet* in his second autobiography, but he did write about it in a single sentence in his first, to say that he was part of a relief crew on the submarine for a short time, which meant he cleaned the boat and got it ready for sea.

Neither did he write in his second autobiography about an injury he sustained (which he wrote about in his first memoir) when he was hit in the back by scaffolding that came away from the side of the *Proteus*, which put him in the infirmary for four days. But that account contradicts a much earlier version in a fan magazine in which he said he was hit in the back by a loading chain on the *Dragonet* and his legs paralysed. Lying in bed at a base hospital, he became despondent. 'It was like the end of the world,' he said. He was convinced he would never walk again, let alone act or do tumbles, and nothing any of the doctors and nurses said to him could convince him otherwise.

Gradually, slowly, through therapy and encouragement, he began to get the feeling back in his legs, and with hard work and a growing sense of determination, he began to put one foot in front of the other. 'I *knew* I would never walk again, and then I *knew* I would walk again, and out of that hospital, and I did after spending seven weeks in that hospital.' When I asked him about that event, he said, 'It would have killed an ordinary man, but I got up and walked out.'

If this early account was a sexed-up version of his actual injury, engineered by the studio – giving some sense of heroism to what was an otherwise generally dull and peaceful service in the navy, perhaps? – then why is there no mention of any kind of injury in his second autobiography? What makes it even more curious is that in the early account, he was *invalided* out of the navy following his recovery, which brought an end to his service in the navy, on or off submarines. Yet in both autobiographies he wrote that he was on board the *Proteus* at the signing of the peace treaty in Tokyo Bay.

In his second autobiography he wrote that he returned to Pearl Harbor before being discharged, and went to visit injured soldiers in a hospital where he befriended a guy called Steven who had broken his back, and thereafter Bernie visited him on a number of occasions. No mention of this is made in the first book. But there seem to be some similarities between the Steven of this story and the injured Bernie Schwartz who couldn't walk in the earliest account. Maybe the studios decided Steven should be transformed into Tony Curtis. And yet according to his first autobiography, he did suffer some kind of injury to his back.

Whether he was injured or not, or hospitalised or not, or invalided out, he was sent back to New York to be discharged. He received a letter saying he had served his country honourably for three years. Bernie Schwartz was back in Manhattan.

CHAPTER FOUR

R.I.P. Bernie Schwartz

Tony Curtis remained forever grateful to the navy for what it gave him. He told me, 'It was a family, and I preferred it to my own. I loved it. It did a great deal for me. And then I went back to the real world with a bump – no, not a bump, a *crash*!'

He was welcomed home with a long hug from his mother – one of the few times in his life when his mother displayed any affection for him. His brother Bobby was five years old and displaying signs of erratic behaviour. Living off his veteran's compensation, Bernie hung around pool halls for a while until he ran into Larry Storch, who was playing in the Copacabana club doing stand-up. Bernie was thrilled when Storch took him backstage and introduced him to everyone.

Influenced by the elegance of Cary Grant, Bernie became obsessive about his appearance and always dressed smartly to go out. He had managed to save three hundred dollars in the navy, more money than he had ever possessed. 'I never even owned a whole suit before,' he said. 'So the first thing I did when I got out of the navy was buy myself a new suit which cost two hundred dollars.'

He began going to the theatre, and was enthralled by Marlon Brando in *A Streetcar Named Desire*. As he headed to Broadway in the evenings, rumours spread through the neighbourhood that he was a homosexual working in a club where men dressed as women. He told everyone that his intention was to get into show business, but his neighbours taunted him, and he became paranoid about what was being said about him.

He had glossy photos taken and sent them to the Conover Modeling

Agency, and managed to get an interview. He claimed that this led to some modelling jobs but he was never specific about what those were except that he got on the cover of a magazine which earned him a hundred dollars.

His clothes always looked as good as new because his father fixed them up for him, but he always felt there was 'something threadbare about them'. Or maybe, he reasoned, 'it wasn't the clothes that were second class; maybe it was me'.

After coming out of the navy he felt incomplete, 'which led me to behave strangely sometimes'. He was overly sensitive, even paranoid, that anything anyone said was some kind of insult at him for being a Jew. He even thought that the agent at the Conover Modeling Agency had reacted to hearing the name Schwartz. 'I was always finding myself in confrontation just walking through a neighborhood. "Here comes the fucking Jew." How did they know I was Jewish? I guess I looked Jewish or I looked Mediterranean, or whatever I looked like. These are the things that had a profound effect on me.'

In an early interview with a fan magazine, he told how he tried to deal with his feelings of hatred and despair for all the anti-Semitic abuse he'd put up with.

> Shortly after my discharge, I woke up one morning feeling particularly disturbed. For some strange reason I felt drawn back to my neighbourhood, so I got dressed, put on my new suit and tie, and took a subway train from the Bronx to the Seventies where I used to live. As I walked along Seventy-second Street near First Avenue, I remembered a German boy who lived in the neighbourhood, who used to roust me around. I went looking for him.
>
> I described him to a kid who pointed out where he lived, and said that he was working. I hung around the neighbourhood, went to the corner and got myself a chocolate egg cream, walked around some more, came back and bought a doughnut. I called my mother and told her I'd be late coming home for dinner. Then I sat down on the front stoop to his place to wait.
>
> Just at dusk a figure came down the street, and I recognised him at once. He walked up to me, stopped and said, 'Wait a minute. Don't tell me. Why, you're Bernie Schwartz!'

> With that I came up off the stoop, and I must have hit this
> boy as hard as I ever hit anybody. He flew about twelve feet. I
> looked down on him and I started to cry.

In 1983, I showed him that story and asked him why he had cried. He said, 'I don't know where that came from. Maybe it was the sheer relief of having turned the tables on him. Or maybe I felt ashamed. I never understood. I have always thought I was better than that.'

He tried to overcome his inadequacies by being attentive to what others were saying, laughing at their jokes and generally 'kissing up to people', because he wanted people to like him, and to show that he cared about other people. He said he had tried to recover from Julie's death 'by being kind and considerate to everyone I meet. I make a point of it. I find that this affection I feel from people [and] that I can reciprocate [it] has had a great calming effect on me.'

Helen nagged him to find a job. He told her, 'What can a guy do who can't even add seven and four in two seconds?'

'Then what will you do?' she demanded.

'I'm going back to school.'

He hadn't got over his failure to solve a simple mathematical sum, so aged twenty he re-enrolled in Seward Park High School. He missed a lot of classes because he was doing the rounds of talent agents, spending up to six hours a day looking for work. He called himself David Street because he was convinced that nobody would give a Jew work as an actor or as a model.

Home life was as miserable as ever. His parents still fought, and Helen listened to all the local gossip and believed her son was a homosexual. She questioned him relentlessly about where he had been, and whenever she ranted at him, he let her carry on until she ran out of steam. Manny kept out of it, and Bobby just played in a world that was becoming increasingly his own. Bernie stayed out of the house as much as possible to avoid the constant arguments with his mother, and it drove him to want to escape his family and make something of himself.

He had thought school would be the answer, but he later made confusing and contradicting statements about whether he got any qualifications. He said in a fan magazine, 'I hustled around trying to get my diploma from high school. But I soon goofed off. I told myself I was now too old to study.' In another article, he said that he wasn't at school long enough to get a diploma.

He made no mention of going back to school after the navy in his first autobiography, but in his second he said that after going back to school he emerged with a GED – a General Educational Development qualification basically equal to a high-school diploma – which made him eligible for university, paid for by the GI Bill.

He described a photograph that shows him wearing a mortarboard and gown as 'an early head shot, 1946'. Whether he had some kind of qualification or not, when he discovered that the Dramatic Workshop on the West Side of Manhattan was accepting students on the GI Bill, he applied there. According to his first autobiography he was accepted by the Workshop because all veterans had to be accepted. 'You couldn't be turned down,' he wrote.

But in the second book, he wrote that he had to 'try out and be selected in order to attend school there', and was so desperate to disguise his working-class Jewish background that he auditioned by miming his way through a scene from *Dr. Jekyll and Mr. Hyde* in which he became the monster. He was good enough to be accepted. Or perhaps, as he wrote in the first book, he couldn't be rejected.

In either event, in February 1947 he enrolled at the Dramatic Workshop, which was located in the New School of Social Research. It had its own theatre, The President, on 48th Street, and among his classmates were Walter Matthau, Harry Belafonte, Rod Steiger and Bea Arthur.

Walter Matthau recalled, 'I was in a class with Tony Curtis and Harry Belafonte, two of the most handsome men you ever saw, and there was me with this mug of mine, and I knew I was never going to be able to get the girl.

'Tony and I were competing for the part of the officer in *Twelfth Night*. He didn't have the delivery to play Shakespeare then, and God knows neither did I, but we were going for it anyway. We had to say the line, "Orsino, this is that Antonio . . . That took the Phoenix and her fraught from Candy." Tony came to me and said, "Walter, what the hell does it mean, *took the Phoenix and her fraught*?" I said, "How the hell should I know, but don't worry about it because you're going to be a movie star." It was that obvious.'

During the spring semester Bernie landed a job with the Stanley Woolf Players, a non-union stock (the US equivalent of repertory) company, performing in after-dinner abridged versions of *This Too Shall Pass* and *The Jazz Singer* in hotels in the Catskills. He got paid ten dollars a week. Then, in Chicago, he joined the Yiddish Theatre, run by Oscar Oskeroff and when spring was over he returned to the Dramatic Workshop. The students put on plays at the Cherry Lane Theatre, taking it in turns to play the leading roles. It was Bernie's turn when they produced *Golden Boy*, and somehow he became a Universal Pictures contract player. Just how is unclear.

According to early studio publicity, Bob Goldstein, a senior talent scout at Universal Studios, saw him in *Golden Boy* and immediately signed him to a contract with a starting salary of a hundred dollars a week.

According to Tony's first autobiography it was a theatrical agent, Joyce Selznick, who saw him and liked him. In the second autobiography, he wrote that he was doing the rounds of agents and went to see Joyce Selznick to ask if she could help him get into movies. She thought he would look great in movies so she took him to see her uncle, producer David O. Selznick, who rejected Bernie because he had a funny walk, which was caused by packs of cards he had put in his shoes in an attempt to look taller.

Continuing this account from the second autobiography, Joyce Selznick took him to meet Bob Goldstein at Universal Pictures' New York office. (Tony's memory was faulty in later years, writing that Goldstein's brother, Leonard, ran Universal Studios in Los Angeles, but Leonard Goldstein was just one of the studio's producers. He also wrote, in his first autobiography, that Joyce Selznick wasn't related to David O. Selznick, but, of course, she was.). A few days later he got a call asking him to come to the Universal office in New York where Bob Goldstein told him that one of his scouts had seen him in *Golden Boy* and recommended him, so he was sending him to California for a screen test.

(In his first autobiography, Tony wrote that he had a phone call from Bob Goldstein's secretary telling him he was going to California and there was a ticket all ready for him, but there was no mention of a screen test.)

He caught a TWA Super Constellation four-prop aeroplane from New York's Idlewild Airport (later to be renamed JFK Airport). He recalled that trip for a fan magazine.

For a long time I assumed a wise-guy attitude to cover up my lack of self-confidence. I remember how I flew out to the coast, when I had been signed to a contract by Universal, I sat next to a fellow with whom I struck up a conversation. He asked me what I did and I told him I was going to Hollywood to be an actor with Universal.

He said, 'Very interesting, but how does it happen that you chose that company?'

I said, 'Oh, they were all after me, but this is the studio where a young actor gets a break. Now you take a place like Warner Brothers. Nothing! Why, they even let Clark Gable go over to Metro.'

My companion laughed. Just before we landed, he introduced himself. Jack Warner!

In both his autobiographies, Tony Curtis elaborated on that story. Jack Warner told him, 'If Universal drops you, come and see me. I'll change your name to Tyrone Goldfarb.' If Warner had been that impressed, he would have offered Bernie a contract because he had not yet been screen-tested, and he hadn't yet signed a contract.

Bernie got off the plane to discover that nobody from Universal was there to meet him. But then, why should there have been? He was not yet a contract player but just a hopeful actor who had had his aeroplane ticket paid for so he could come and be screen-tested.

Tony Curtis wrote (in his second autobiography but not the first) that Jack Warner had his chauffeur drive Bernie to the Knickerbocker Hotel where he had a room booked. In earlier accounts, he said that he found his own way to Universal but couldn't get in because the guard on the gate didn't know who he was. It took him two days to trace Bob Goldstein, who straightened everything out. Bernie supposedly arrived inside Universal Studios on 3 June 1948. 'I landed on the lot on my birthday,' he said. 'It's weird how so many of the important dates in my life have coincided with my birthday.'

In an early interview, he said, 'This was my twenty-third birthday, and I was quite disappointed with myself because I'd read in the movie magazines how Tyrone Power had started when he was twenty-two. I'd missed it by a day! To my mind, this put me a year behind in the race for fame, but I actually didn't have too much doubt that I'd soon overtake Ty and every other actor, too.' Maybe this was the day he was screen-tested.

His autobiographies are unclear on the matter; in the first no screen test is mentioned. In the second he arrives at Universal, is sent straight to see Leonard Goldstein and signed to a contract – no screen test. As one of Universal's producers, Leonard Goldstein was unlikely to have signed Tony but he did have the authority to give him a screen test, and in fact fan magazine accounts reveal that he made a screen test with Ann Blyth, and also tested on his own, responding to directions to look one way, then another, establishing that he looked good whichever way he looked. (Shots from his solo screen test appeared in the TV documentary *Tony of the Movies*.)

He signed a seven-year contract with six-month options, which meant every six months the studio could decide whether to drop him, starting at a hundred dollars a week. He had more regular money than he'd ever had before, and he had a studio to take care of him. Then reality set in.

'That's when I discovered that the opulent one hundred dollars a week I was to start with turned into thirty-five dollars when all the deductions, agent's fees and the like were taken out of it.' This included twenty dollars a week deducted to pay off his dues to the Screen Actors Guild, which came to one hundred and fifty dollars. 'That's also when I discovered that while everybody on the lot was very pleasant to me, nobody was actually dying to get me into a picture.' He was actually on 'lay off' until work could be found for him, which meant that contractually the studio didn't have to pay him, but they did allow him thirty dollars a week until he could be put to work.

He needed somewhere to live. Shelley Winters, who was under contract to Universal, said he arrived at her house where she lived with her parents and sister. 'He turned up with his sea bag stuffed with all he owned in life, and said, "My mother knows your Aunt Fanny in the Bronx and she said you should take care of me till I find somewhere." So I invited him in, and he told me he was just out of the navy and was under contract to Universal. He was very sweet, and very handsome, and had the worst Bronx accent I'd ever heard.

'I managed to get him on the waiting list of The Sycamore House, which was an enormous old boarding school where other young actors lived and got fed breakfast and dinner for eight dollars a week. He lived with my family until a space was available for him.'

He attended acting classes at the studio run by Abner Biberman, who was unimpressed by Bernie Schwartz and did his best to humiliate him. Curtis told me, 'He seemed to take delight in humiliating me by standing me in front of the whole class and yelling at me, "You are a lousy actor.

Just a punk out of New York." Biberman had his work cut out. We weren't all exactly budding John Barrymores.'

Rock Hudson recalled, 'You couldn't get into Universal if you were the greatest actor in the world unless you looked good, and then they gave you a contract and hoped that you could be taught to act.' Always self-deprecating, he added, 'With me they failed.'

Eventually Biberman was fired and Bernie continued his lessons with a great deal more enthusiasm. He also attended a speech class at MGM where his female instructor tried to rid him of his New York accent. The most he could do was reduce it when required, but his distinctive accent was always a large part of the charm and chemistry that was Tony Curtis – which he wasn't yet; he was still Bernie Schwartz.

He made a number of good friends at the studio, notably Jeff Chandler, one of the studio's biggest stars, and Rock Hudson who, like Bernie, was a newcomer. During those first weeks in Hollywood, Bernie was shocked to discover that a lot of men in the movie industry were hitting on him. 'I got frightened that maybe I was a homosexual – that's what I said, *frightened* that I was a homosexual – because I was getting hit on by so many of the men, and I didn't like that. All my life I wanted to sit across a table with a girl like Cary Grant did, and have small talk and have a drink. I didn't want to do that with a guy.'

Rock Hudson was one of those who tried to hit on Tony during the early days of their friendship. 'But you know, he was so big, he didn't want to fool with a little kid like me,' said Tony. 'But they all hit on me. Henry Wilson, the agent, had a lot of gay clients, and he would love to have [had] me in his coterie of clients but I wasn't that way.'

About a week after signing with Universal, he landed a tiny part in *Criss Cross*, which starred Burt Lancaster and Yvonne De Carlo. He explained how he got the part:

I got to Universal June 3, on my birthday, and, oh, around June 10, I'm walking to the commissary and a short man comes up to me and says [*guttural accent*], 'My name is Robert Siodmak,' and I say, 'How do you do?' He said, 'What is your name?' I said, 'Bernie Schwartz.' 'What are you doing here?' 'Well, I'm under contract now.' He says, 'Well, I'm making a movie called *Criss Cross*. Can you dance?' Well, what am I gonna say? Here's my chance to get into a movie and he asks me can I dance. I mean, he shoulda asked me something hard. Can I fly? 'Sure!'

He says, 'Can you do the mambo-conja?' or whatever it was. I say, 'Are you kidding?' 'Ya got it!' And that's how I got my first part. Next thing I know, the head of the Casting Department is acting like he's the one giving me the break. 'Mr Siodmak is looking for a young man, and I thought I'd send you down and maybe you can get the part.' Bullshit, bullshit, bullshit!

Anyway, I show up and I'm rehearsing with Yvonne de Carlo in this dance. Didn't know one step of it. It was called the Mambo Rhythm or The Jungle something. Very fast music. They only photographed us from the shoulders up for the close-up, and from a distance any kind of Latin movement looked like it [was real], so I faked it.

I came in the morning and thirty-seven minutes later I was outta pictures!

His time on the set was brief, but after dancing with Yvonne de Carlo he was sharing a bed with her not long after.

The story goes that his one scene in *Criss Cross* resulted in hundreds of letters flooding into the studio asking who the guy was who danced with Yvonne de Carlo, and because of that the studio had to sit up and take notice of him. But this story is at odds with the story Tony told in one of his earliest interviews, following his appearance in his third film, *The Lady Gambles*, which starred Barbara Stanwyck. Tony had one short scene, as a bellhop who delivers a telegram to Stanwyck. He said, 'I got one fan letter from that. Just one, but I've still got it. It said, "Who was that boy who delivered the telegram? Why doesn't he star in a picture?" At the time it arrived that much faith [the letter writer] showed in me was very important [to me].'

Either there was a flood of fan letters following *Criss Cross*, or just the one letter following *The Lady Gambles*. Whatever the facts behind the fan letters, his movie career had begun. 'I did get *City Across the River* – not the lead, nor the second lead, or even the fourth. The fifth! Most of the time my back was to the camera, yet the miracle happened, and a few people noticed me and the critics were unbelievably kind. I zoomed emotionally, and deflated again as the studio continued to ignore both me and my notices.'

The studio didn't really ignore him. He was being groomed, being tested, but he was impatient. He wanted to play the kind of parts Marlon

Brando got. But all Universal cared about was that their new boy was extremely good-looking, and they were carefully testing the water as far as his talent and potential popularity were concerned.

In *City Across the River* he played a member of a New York gang. He later claimed that the studio wanted to give him the lead role because of all his fan mail but the director, Maxwell Shane, refused him the part. That couldn't have been the case, whether there was fan mail or not, because the studio called all the shots, not a contract director like Shane. I doubt Tony exaggerated the facts to elevate himself but simply came to believe in the studio publicity that was eventually generated about all the fan mail he had supposedly received. What is true is that over a relatively short period of time the studio was able to exploit his good looks in photographs which they placed in fan magazines, making him famous before he had actually starred in a movie.

Some scenes for *City Across the River* were filmed on location in New York, in a tenement building near the Bowery. The public gathered to watch, and he enjoyed being on show and signing autographs. He stayed with the rest of the cast at the Sherry-Netherland Hotel but spent some evenings, out of a sense of obligation, with his parents. Helen began visiting the set. 'She didn't care about whether I was doing well or not,' he said. 'She only wanted to be a part of show business but without actually doing anything.'

During the week spent filming there, Walter Matthau spotted him. 'He was in a chauffeur-driven car, which apparently drove all the young guys who played the gang to and from their hotel, and Tony wanted a drive on his own. I hadn't seen him in years, and his first words as he leaned out the window were, "Hey, Walter, I fucked Yvonne de Carlo." Not, "Hey, Walter, how are ya doing?"'

The film tried to maintain a realistic tone by not crediting the cast of young actors at the beginning of the film, but instead had a narrator introduce them at the very end as the camera tracked from one face to another. When it got to Bernie the narrator introduced him as Anthony Curtis.

How Bernie Schwartz came to be called Anthony Curtis, and then Tony Curtis, is a matter of some confusion. Tony once said that Bob Goldstein had told him, 'Schwartz ain't a name to get you into the big time. Not even George Bernard Schwartz.' That might just have been a funny story Tony thought up.

He once told Roderick Mann of the *Sunday Express*, 'What I really wanted to call myself was Ricardo Cortez. Unfortunately, that name was already taken. If it hadn't been, who knows how I'd have turned out?'

In his first autobiography he wrote that he tried out a whole series of names including Steven John and John Stevens. Then he hit on the name Curtis because he had an ancestor called Kertész, which he anglicised to Curtis. He tried Jimmy Curtis for size, then Johnny Curtis and finally hit on Anthony Curtis. It wasn't long before it was shortened to Tony Curtis.

In his second autobiography he said that the only book he ever read was *Anthony Adverse* by Hervey Allen – he read it in the navy – and so wanted to call himself Anthony Adverse, but there was already an actor called Anthony Adverse – (I can't find any actor by that name) – so Tony came up with Curtis because he had a relative, Janush Kertiz.

Janet Leigh said that she had asked Tony how he got his name, and he told her that he had been told 'Schwartz has to go!' because it was a German name, and so there was much discussion between Universal executives about what the new name should be. Anthony Adverse was suggested (presumably by Bernie) but there was a film and book by that name (but no actor), so they kept the Anthony and somehow out of the discussion came the name Curtis.

He told me, 'I never liked my name – Schwartz. It was German, and with what they were doing to Jews in the Holocaust, I didn't like having a name that in some way was a reflection of that horror. So I changed it to Curtis, which was a Hungarian name, and became Anthony Curtis and then Tony Curtis.'

Shelley Winters came up with her own account. 'His first night with us in our house, he had dinner with us, and I told him, "Don't take offence, Bernie, but you can't be a movie star with the name Bernie Schwartz," and then my mom said, "Why don't you use your mother's maiden name like Shelley did?" so he did, and they were going to call him Bernie Curtiz, and then it became Tony Curtis.'

Helen's maiden name was Klein. There may have been a relative called Janush Kurtis – or Kertész – and this person might have been someone on Helen's mother's side of the family. Tony later wrote of Winters, 'She tells everyone she "made" me, but I remember her as being pretty irascible and mean.' He also described her as 'a real yenta, a big-mouthed busybody'. No love lost there, although she did get him into The Sycamore House.

Somewhere in the mix of all those accounts is how Bernard Schwartz became Anthony Curtis, although everyone began calling him Tony. He had another very good reason to change his name. He said, 'I didn't want to be Bernie Schwartz any more. He was another guy. I was re-inventing myself as Tony Curtis. As far as I was concerned Bernie didn't exist any more. R.I.P. Bernie Schwartz.'

His career was slowly but steadily being built up by Universal, which may or may not have been responding to fan letters. In his third picture, *The Lady Gambles*, he was billed as Antony Curtis. He recalled being given what he said was the best piece of direction he ever received.

> Michael Gordon was directing *The Lady Gambles*. I went to Warner's and they gave me a bellhop's uniform with the little round hat, and I went back to the set and they gave me an envelope. I was supposed to knock on Barbara Stanwyck's door, and I say, 'Looks like this has followed you halfway across the country.' She'd give me a tip or whatever and then I'd leave.
>
> I practised. I tried every possible way to say it. I'm in my corner backstage and the director comes walking around. He knew it was the first time I was going to be in a movie and he knew I came from New York. And he said to me, 'All you want is a tip.'
>
> Bells went off in my head. When I was shining shoes all I wanted was a tip. When I carried clothes for my father in the tailor store, carried packages – whatever I did when I was a kid, all I wanted was the tip. So I did the scene and said the line, and I gave her one of the best smiles I ever had. I even ad-libbed a few words, 'Thank you!' That to me is what acting is. Personal.

After *The Lady Gambles*, he was a racing car driver in *Take One False Step*, working just a few days. It would seem his fleeting appearance was left on the cutting room floor. Then he had a tiny role in *Johnny Stool Pigeon*, a crime drama about a federal agent, played by Howard Duff, who makes an alliance with an Alcatraz inmate, played by Dan Duryea, in his attempts to smash a narcotics ring. Searching for a young actor to play the part of a deaf-mute killer who is murdered and shipped from Mexico to Los Angeles in a coffin full of cocaine, producer Aaron Rosenberg, a former USC All-American football player, found Anthony Curtis. (Rosenberg's brother George became Tony's agent.)

Aaron Rosenberg told me, 'I really liked Tony. He had those wonderful looks, and he really shone on the screen. I cast him in a number of movies and we became good friends. He was young and naive, and the director played a terrible gag on him. He told Tony to lie in the coffin while a nurse administered a shot to make him so relaxed he would look like he was really dead. When he saw the long hypodermic needle, he shot out of that coffin. Everyone laughed and he realised it was a practical joke.'

Tony wrote in his autobiographies that he enjoyed having jokes played on him, but in a fan magazine of the time he said:

> I hate to be the butt of a practical joke. Like the one a couple of publicity guys played on me when I first began to work in pictures. I was so anxious to make good, I fell for anything people told me. I'd played a cowering deaf-mute in one of my first pictures, and these guys kept telling me afterwards that since I had done so well the studio was going to cast me as spineless characters forever. They kept building up the idea for days until I finally burst in on the casting director and shouted, 'If you think I'm going to play those kind of parts, you're crazy!' 'What are you talking about?' he asked. 'We don't have anything planned for you right now.' I was so angry, I wouldn't talk to the publicity guys for days.

He was making a lot of friends, including Marlon Brando, whom he admired and envied for his great talent. Burt Lancaster had taken a liking to Tony. 'We both came from Manhattan in New York, and when you meet someone from Manhattan in New York you're brothers,' Burt Lancaster told me. 'Tony was like my little kid brother, fun to be around but not all the time.'

He had made friends with Howard Duff when making *Johnny Stool Pigeon*, and Duff and Lancaster were friends too, and they knew of an apartment on Sierra Bonita in Hollywood that would suit Tony better, so he moved out of The Sycamore House and into an apartment of his own.

Jerry Lewis was another new friend. Tony met him at a nightclub owned by prizefighter Benny Leonard, where Lewis and his partner Dean Martin were performing. 'Jerry was my best friend at that time,'

Tony told me. 'He was a very funny guy in a little-kid kind of way. He was always doing childish things. He'd put a piece of candy in his pocket, and he'd take it out at a party and drop it down a girl's blouse as if it was an accident and then go after it. A lot of people didn't like him coz he could be very domineering. He always thought Dean Martin worked for him.'

Tony was still shy of girls. When he took a girlfriend, actress Betty Thatcher, to Benny Leonard's nightclub and introduced her to Jerry Lewis, it quickly became obvious that Betty and Jerry were attracted to each other. Too intimidated and shy to object, Tony slipped quietly away.

Meanwhile, Tony was falling in love with a beautiful starlet called Marilyn Monroe.

CHAPTER FIVE

WIN TONY CURTIS

He met Marilyn Monroe in the autumn of 1948.

'I'll never forget the moment I first saw her,' he told me. 'She wore a see-through blouse through which I could see her bra, and I could see she was very voluptuous which I liked. She had red hair then, tied in a ponytail. Not much make-up. She took my breath away. She was walking down one of the streets at Universal. Those studios were like small cities. I smiled and said, "My name is Tony." She said, "My name is Marilyn." She was like me, new to Hollywood and wanting to be a star.'

He had bought himself a used pale-green Buick convertible with Dynaflow Drive for just thirty-five dollars. It was cheap because it had a rusty hole in the floor through which he could see the surface of the road. He offered her a lift in his cheap Buick convertible and drove her to the small hotel where she was staying; it turned out she had been installed there by Twentieth Century-Fox executive Joseph Schenck, with whom she was spending weekends. She gave Tony her number, but it was a week before he had the courage to call her and ask her out. They began what he said was his first true love affair. 'I never felt like that about a girl before,' he said. 'I really liked her and she liked me. We went out for a while, sometimes to a club, sometimes to a restaurant.'

Because of her affair with Schenck, which Tony was unaware of at the time, she was only available during the week. Howard Duff had a beach house which he allowed Tony and Marilyn to use on weekdays. After their first few dates they went to bed at Duff's beach house. 'Her breasts were every teenage boy's fantasy come true,' he recalled. He realised he was falling in love with her. He told me in 1983, 'I knew I really loved this girl, and she loved me – simple as that. We taught each other what it was like to be a man and a woman with those subtleties of feelings, those subtleties of loving, those subtleties of being able to reach out to another person.'

The subject of marriage came up. 'We had our careers to worry about without having the pressure of getting married. It confused me, this whole idea of being married to anyone, let alone Marilyn. Maybe that was because I'd never seen my parents happy together. Or maybe I could sense that my career was more important. But we talked about it. I think you do when you're in love the first time. And I said, kind of half-jokingly, "We should get hitched," and she said she couldn't because she had to take care of her career, which I later learned meant taking care of Joe Schenck. She was prepared to let men use her to get to the top, but I didn't know that then, although I began to sense it a little later.'

Tony said that Marilyn refused to marry him. 'I did kinda feel like she'd rejected me, even though I wasn't serious about getting married, but it made me stop and think that maybe I wasn't good enough, or maybe she didn't love me, and it was all kinda confusing for the both of us. So we didn't see each other quite so much, and then one day she said, "You still wanna get married?" and by then I knew that would have been a mistake, so I said, "You know, one day we might get married," and she said, "You promise?" and I said without thinking it through in any way whatsoever, "Of course". And from then on she musta thought we were engaged because even though I got married and she got married, when we were making *Some Like It Hot* she said to me, "OK, now let's get married."'

He never forgot 'the way she smelled, the way she'd lie in bed. She was funny. Whenever she laughed her bosom shook.'

He recalled, 'I think we were a sweet couple. She was so vulnerable, so fragile that I wanted to take care of her, and I never married anyone like her – my wives were the opposite, none of them needed my protection; they were domineering.' (I think by that he meant they weren't compliant.) 'We were almost teenagers in love, and you don't ever get over your first love.'

Talking to Dr Pamela Connolly in 2008 about Marilyn, he said, 'I defy anybody – any guy or any girl – in their first love experiences to not find them unique and different.'

Tony, then, never quite got over Marilyn, and apparently she never got over him.

After he stopped seeing Marilyn, he got rid of the car. He told me about that car: 'I bought a car for thirty-five bucks. I polished it up with the best wax you ever saw. I jazzed that car up – it looked *beautiful*. You wouldn't believe it cost thirty-five bucks. I once went to a premiere when I first started in movies. When I got to the premiere, I gave the keys of the car to the theatre doorman and said, "Keep the car!" I thought that was a chic thing to do!'

The Universal publicity department continued to steadily build his profile. He talked to me in 1975 about 'the wonderful trips' he was sent on. 'We once went on a tour to Washington DC and the Bakers' Union was having a huge annual affair. Alben Barkley, who was then the Vice President of the United States, was an honorary guest. Jack Diamond (studio publicist) had just joined Universal and he came with me on tour for two or three weeks – that was his first job. So we went on the road, and he walked into the Bakers' Union thing, and before I knew it I was sitting next to Alben Barkley, and he and I were cutting this huge cake like we had just got engaged.

'Jack had simply walked in and took the place over. He said to the head of the union, "This is Tony Curtis, an actor with Universal," and to the Vice President he said, "We're here to help you out with the celebration of the Bakers' Union." And before you knew it I was running the whole show. It was incredible. Yes, they were really interesting days for me.'

The fan magazines became full of photos of Anthony Curtis (which is how he was still officially billed), with long, wavy, black, greased hair and a huge quiff to match (Tony always claimed that Elvis Presley copied his hairstyle), and in swimming trunks at the beach.

Through 1949 Tony went from picture to picture, most of them minor films like *Francis*, the first in a series about a talking mule. He had a few lines to speak in *I Was a Shoplifter*, a forgotten melodrama with Mona Freeman. At the end of 1949 he was given a substantial role in an unsubstantial Western, *Sierra*, starring Audie Murphy and Burl Ives.

Although he hated practical jokes, he was constantly targeted. One time they locked him in the steam room at Universal Studios. And somebody put sleeping tablets in his drinks. After Tony had got his own apartment, he came home from the studio to find the locks had been changed and he couldn't get in. He got the landlady to open up, and inside he found all his furniture and belongings were gone, and there was a man claiming to be the tenant. It was a gag played Burt Lancaster and Howard Duff. Tony didn't laugh but shook with rage.

It was probably around this time that Tony met Frank Sinatra for the first time:

> The first time I met him was at the Paramount where he was playing, but I don't remember what year it was. But what I do remember is that I was invited to his birthday celebration at his house. I was surprised coz he didn't really know me, but he invited all the young people in Hollywood who were starting out like me – he was generous that way. And there were all these other people in the business – those who were established, so the young people got to meet some of the important people, but more important we were being given a good time at a very nice party. I recall his children were there – certainly Frank Junior was; that's where I met him. And Fran had – Frank Senior that is – he had with him Gloria DeHaven. At least, I *think* it was Gloria DeHaven. That's who I thought it was at the time, and now I can't be sure, but I remember being so excited because I had seen Gloria DeHaven during the war at the Hollywood Canteen, and I was nuts about her. What always impressed me about Frank, if I may say so, was that he always insisted on having the *best*. He wouldn't stand for anything that was not the best. He demanded it, and he deserved it, and he got it, and that allowed him to have a wonderful life, the way he wanted it to be. He didn't care what anybody else thought he should have or thought how he should be. I liked that, I liked that a lot, and I think that lit something in me to want to have the best for myself, and to have nice things that *I* wanted, and to be how *I* wanted to be.

Late in 1949 Tony's family arrived in Los Angeles, presumably just for a holiday. But they were not going home again, and they were suddenly his responsibility. Tony was bewildered and angered. Landed with his family's welfare, he hoped to lighten his sudden financial burden by getting Manny a job in the wardrobe department at Universal. But Manny turned the job down. Tony then spoke to top dress designer

Orry-Kelly, who said he would be happy to meet with Manny, but Manny never went.

'My mother [was] demanding that I pay for everything, like I was going to pay her off – for what? She treated me like a dog when I was a kid,' he said.

He had dedicated his life to his work and had been free of distractions for a whole year, and, more importantly, he was free of Bernie Schwartz. Suddenly he was Bernie again, surrounded by his mother, father and brother Bobby. He found them a place to live and paid their rent.

He recalled, 'My father had a serious heart attack before they came out so he wasn't strong, my mother was just as aggressive if not more so, and my brother wasn't manageable. So I had to find someone that could help me to ease the pain of my family and ease the pain of my brother.'

Bobby looked up at things that weren't there and tried to grab at things that no one else saw. He sometimes threw himself to the floor and screamed for no apparent reason. His schizophrenia, still undiagnosed, was getting worse. Helen's illness was also still evident to Tony, who found it frightening when it erupted.

'She knew she couldn't beat me any more,' Tony said, 'but there were a few times when she suddenly got into a terrible rage that was like something from a monster movie, when her face contorted, and she raised her fists to hit me, and I grabbed her by the wrists and said, "No you don't, Mom," and she froze and looked off into the distance and said, "Bernie? You home yet? You know I told you to be home early. Now you'll be punished." And I kept calm and gently said, "Bernie's home, Mom, and he's not late. He's here. Just calm down, OK?" And she'd come back and she'd say something like, "He was calling me from the street." And I knew she thought she'd heard something.'

He later heard voices of his own. 'I'll be honest. I have always been afraid of going nuts. I mean really mad! Of getting lost in that world my brother and mother – my brother most of all – went to. I went there too, sometimes. But I always came back.'

He had to pay for doctors to diagnose Bobby's illness and treat him, costing three hundred dollars a time. Helen denied Bobby was ill and continually nagged Tony to get him parts in his films. Bernie Schwartz, and everything he had been, and all the memories and guilt, had come back to haunt Tony Curtis.

Aaron Rosenberg gave him a good supporting role in an important film, *Winchester '73*, and he appeared in one lengthy episode about a cavalry troop pinned down by marauding Indians until help arrives in the form of James Stewart and his Winchester '73 rifle. Universal renewed his contract and gave him a raise to two hundred and twenty-five dollars a week. He was back in the saddle again in *Kansas Raiders* as Kit Dalton riding with Quantrill's Raiders. Audie Murphy was top-billed as Jesse James. For the first time he was billed as 'Tony Curtis'.

Tony was insecure on a horse. 'The only horse I ever saw was in New York City pulling ice wagons. And there I am dressed like a cowboy, and they throw me on this horse, and off we go. I fall off the horse and the horse takes off. One of the guys comes running over and says, "See if Tony's all right," and the other guy says, "Tony? We got all the actors in the world we need, we only have four horses," and off they all went after the horse.'

He became the subject of some clever if tacky studio merchandising by selling his much-loved hair (much loved by the girls, and by Tony). He recalled, 'They'd have these envelopes, and I'd go [to the barbers] and they'd say, "OK, Tony, come in and sit down," and they'd cut off my hair and parcel it in these envelopes and send it to all the fans.

'I was even once a prize for a movie magazine. I forget now – I think they had to write a paragraph or a story on why they would want to have Tony Curtis as a weekend guest. Somebody in Terre Haute, Indiana won, and I went there with Piper Laurie, and I thought I'd probably spend some time with the lucky winner and pose for a few photographs. But this lady had really got me for the weekend. She was disappointed. She'd wanted to win a refrigerator, but she won me instead for the weekend, and she never let me forget that I couldn't freeze her food.'

He received some hostility from the winning lady's neighbours, who hadn't heard of Tony Curtis. 'They said, "What do you do with all that long hair?" I said, "I'm an actor." "Have you starred in a movie yet?" "I've been in films, but not as the star," I said. "Then why do you need long hair?"

'I found that humiliating. I found the whole deal humiliating, being turned into some cheap fan package. When I was won as a prize a second time, I escaped during the night, climbing out of my bedroom window. I walked five, six miles to the hotel where the studio publicity guy was staying and I made it clear to him in no uncertain terms that I wasn't going to be given away as a prize again.'

Despite such indignities, Tony admitted to having had 'a really wonderful time' in those first few years in Hollywood. He got to meet a whole host of famous movie stars, including his idol Cary Grant. He told me, 'I met him at a dinner given in honour of L.B. Mayer at the Cocoanut Grove in Los Angeles. This was about 1950, and Cary Grant was at that dinner. We met in the men's room! I just went up and said, "Hello, my name is Tony." I even have a photograph of that stuck somewhere. That was the first time I met him. It meant a lot to me. I admired that man. I still do.'

He had learned from Grant when watching his movies, and now he learned from being in his presence. 'Cary Grant was once describing how you judge a bottle of white wine. He said, "When it's chilled, it tastes like a cool glass of water." He said, "It's so artful, it's artless." And I swear, when he said that to me, bells went off in my head. That's what acting is. So artful, it's artless.'

Tony told me that in those early days he didn't really expect to become a big star and certainly didn't think he could be as big a star as Cary Grant. 'In the beginning, when I met Cary and all the other stars I met, I didn't give myself a tinker's chance of making it. But that's because I really hadn't thought it through like that. I never really laid it out in my mind that I was going to be very successful. All my energies I just concentrated in those areas I was trying to be successful in at that time.' Which was just getting work and surviving.

'When I first came to Hollywood, I was really like a nature boy. You never saw such a left-footed, clumsy-looking guy. I'd never been in a private home. I didn't know what it was to have a private bathroom or what forks to use. Once I had dinner at Cole Porter's home, and he had some beautiful champagne glasses, obviously blown by an angel, just like paper. I was holding this glass in my hand and sure enough, I broke it into fourteen pieces. The table was soaked with champagne. Ethel Merman was sitting right across from me, and she said, "Kid, don't worry about it," and she grabbed her glass and crushed it into bits. I never forgot that.'

Burdened with having to provide for his family, he moonlighted as a studio tour guide to make extra money. He told me:

I bought a limousine – an *old* limousine. I had a friend, Nicky Blair, who was an actor who later opened a restaurant in Hollywood. And Nicky had a friend who worked at the Knickerbocker Hotel. So Nicky's friend used to tell the tourists that came to the hotel that he could get them a tour of the studios and get autographed pictures of the stars. Then he'd phone me at the studio and I would take my limousine, which I polished up, and I'd go down to the hotel and pick up maybe five or six tourists. I was their tour guide!

I'd drive them to the studio, and I'd park the car and go over to the cop on the gate. And I'd say, 'I've got some relatives here from New York. Is it OK if I drive them on the lot?' He'd say, 'Sure, kid, go ahead.' I'd say, 'Thanks a lot,' and I'd get in my limousine and drive through. I'd take them out to the back lot and say, 'This is where Tom Mix shot the bad guy and this is where he shot the Indian.' I'd make it all up.

Then I'd go back to the publicity department and get all these ten-by-eight black-and-white glossy stills of Ann Blyth and Jimmy Stewart and Audie Murphy – all those that were under contract to the studio, and I'd autograph them. *I'd* autograph them in whatever way I thought those stars might sign. I even misspelled names.

I almost got caught one time. I pulled up by one of the cops at the gate, and I said, 'Got some relatives in the back. Can I take them on the lot?' And he kinda flicked his eyes in the back of the car and he kinda half-smiled and said, 'OK!' I drove them once around the lot and I pulled up to hand out the auto-graphed pictures, and then I saw who was in the back of my car for the first time. They were Chinese. And I'd been passing them off as my Uncle Irvin and Aunt Ellie from New York!

That's how ingenious my early days in movies were, y'know. It was nice and easy in those days. It was never a problem. It was only a problem after I started becoming successful. Then all of a sudden people would stop and look at me. I'd walk into the commissary and everyone would say, 'What's his number? What's he doing and to whom? Why is he being picked out and not me?' That's when I began to feel the tension. I began to feel that strong. But before that, life wasn't at all bad, ya know. Even when I was being given out as a prize.

He also enjoyed the personal perks which he dreamed up for himself. 'There were these beautiful girls put under contract every two or three weeks, and I was under contract, so everybody had to go to dancing classes, speech classes, fencing classes, horseback-riding classes, so I came up with the idea of kissing classes. So I'd go up to a beautiful young woman who was just put under contract and I'd say, "Hi, my name is Tony, and I'm your kissing instructor." I'd say, "You have to kiss differently on the screen than in your personal life." I got a few kisses that way.'

Wanting him to enhance his acting skills, Universal sent Tony to study acting at the Actors Studio in Los Angeles in 1950. He didn't care for the Method style of acting taught there even though Marlon Brando had been its most famous student. 'Marlon didn't need to learn *anything* from *anyone* about acting,' said Tony. 'That Method crap is all about having to suffer. You don't have to suffer. You just turn up knowing your lines, listen to what the director wants, find the subtleties of the part, and do it. Marlon could do that in his sleep. But he liked that Method way of acting, and that's fine because you can't deny he's one of the greatest actors of our time. I *had* to go to the Actors Studio but the only method I was interested in was the rhythm method . . . with the girls.'

Around that time he began sharing a house with Brando. They made an odd couple. Brando never cleaned up after himself or took out the garbage, so Tony did all that. Brando drank a lot. Tony didn't. Brando was a slob. Tony sought refinement. But Tony gained a lot of confidence being with Brando because Brando rarely extended the hand of friendship to actors.

'I couldn't help but compare my career to his,' Tony told me, 'and I was envious that he was making such great movies and doing great plays, and I was stuck in small roles in small budget movies at Universal, and I figured I could have been doing better if anyone gave me the chance. I was insecure as an actor, about my background, about being a Jew, and being uneducated. Marlon didn't try to boost my ego, but just showed friendship and kindness – I mean *real* kindness – to me, and that helped me to feel confident about myself, because if *he* didn't care about those things I was insecure about, then why should *I* worry about any of it?'

But, of course, Tony did worry about it. And then, in 1949, he met someone who would have a great deal to do with the shaping of the old Bernie Schwartz into the new Tony Curtis. She was twenty-two-year-old Janet Leigh.

CHAPTER SIX:

The Jew and The Christian Girl

anet was born Jeanette Helen Morrison to Helen and Fred Morrison in Merced, California, on 6 July 1927. She was an exceptionally intelligent child, graduating from high school at the age of fifteen. A lonely child, she eloped with nineteen year-old John Carlyle shortly before her sixteenth birthday. The marriage soon ended, and Jeanette returned home in disgrace. 'That left a scar with me,' she told me, 'because I realised I'd done a wrong thing, and I thought I was a bad person because I'd upset my family, and I was ashamed.'

She began studying music and psychology at the University of the Pacific and was married a second time, to the band leader Stanley Reames, in October 1945. She was spotted by Norma Shearer in 1946 at the Northern Californian ski resort where Jeannete's parents worked, Fred on the reception desk and Helen as a maid. Shearer was struck by Jeanette's stunning but fresh and wholesome beauty and personally recommended Jeanette be given a screen test at Metro-Goldwyn-Mayer. Now called Janet Leigh, she made her screen debut in 1947 opposite Van Johnson and Thomas Mitchell in *The Romance of Rosy Ridge*.

Janet and Reames divorced in September 1949 – she was married and divorced twice by the age of twenty-two. She had quickly achieved considerable success as a movie star, and by 1950 had made ten films, all in starring roles, and was MGM's most popular ingénue.

Janet Leigh and Tony Curtis had nothing in common. And yet they became one of Hollywood's most celebrated married couples during the 1950s.

'I don't remember where I met her,' Tony Curtis said in 2001. 'But I do remember meeting her.'

He gave his earliest version of their first meeting to a fan magazine.

> A friend of mine was invited to a party given by the Sazerac people. [The Sazerac Company owned a particular cocktail as well as a rye whiskey.] Why didn't I come along and we'd go to a movie later, he suggested. Well, across a crowded room I saw this girl who suddenly made the evening seem enchanted. She was wearing a black dress, there was a bun-thing on her head, and she was super-special. I couldn't take my eyes off her. When a cameraman asked if I'd mind posing with Janet Leigh, we were introduced and boom – it happened. I felt just like I'd been smacked with a steam roller! Before I left, I found out who had brought her. 'What has Arthur Lowe Jr got that I should have?' I asked. 'Janet Leigh!' they came back at me. 'I've got news for you,' I said. 'I'm working on it.'

Presumably, the Sazerac party was being held at Lucy's Restaurant, because Janet Leigh told me that's where she first saw him. 'I was making a movie at RKO, *Jet Pilot*, with John Wayne' – she had a contract to make three films with RKO, although Jet Pilot would not actually be released until 1957 – 'and at the end of a long day at the studio I was taken by Perry Lieber, who was head of publicity, to Lucy's, which was a restaurant where all the big stars would be taken for interviews and the studio executives would have lunch or dinner. And it was there that I was introduced to Tony Curtis, who was this beautiful young man with large blue eyes and all that black hair, and a really charming personality. He told me he was from New York and under contract to Universal, but we didn't talk for long because we were separated by the Universal publicity man who was with him and by Perry Lieber who wanted me to meet all the other people there.'

Tony told a fan magazine about their second meeting. 'The next time I saw Janet we were in the same class at the Actors Lab.' (This, presumably, was a new experimental class starting up, as the famous Actors Lab in Los Angeles wasn't established until 1990.) He continued:

For a month and a half I kept waiting for a chance to invite her to Schwab's around the corner for a cup of coffee. But there was always some ham hovering and I couldn't make any progress. Finally, the Mel Tormés invited me to go swimming at Donald O'Connor's house. When I heard Janet was coming, I was practically there before I learned another guy was bringing her. I ended up at the movies.

When the Tormés had their house-warming, I went, and took a date. Janet was there with her date and later asked us to stop by her house to watch television. There was a new class in acting that might be formed, and we talked about it. When Janet said she was interested, I casually suggested that if she would give me her telephone number, I'd be glad to make inquiries and relay the information.

In 1984, Janet remembered Tony's phone call. 'It sounded like Cary Grant on the phone when he said, "Hello Janet," and I couldn't figure out why Cary Grant was calling *me*. And as we talked, I remembered that I'd read in the trade papers that Tony Curtis had fooled quite a few people with his impression of Cary Grant. He asked me if I would have dinner with him next Saturday, so I said, "I'd be delighted but unfortunately I have a previous engagement with Tony Curtis." And then he knew I'd caught him out, and we arranged to have dinner, and it turned out to be something very special.'

In his fan magazine interview, Tony went on to say, 'I'm not a bit shamefaced when I say that the acting class never got started – but guess who did? For our first date, I thought it was a good idea to also invite the Mel Tormés, so Janet and I wouldn't have to pay too much attention to each other. Let us face it, I wasn't too sure of my luck either. On our fifth date I asked Janet to go out with me alone. I couldn't afford to take her to Ciro's or Mocambo, but I didn't apologise because somehow I knew it wasn't necessary.' The fact that it took five double-dates before Tony had the courage to take Janet out on his own illustrated his lack of confidence and anxiety about girls at that time.

'I remembered the Villa Nova, a crazy kind of an attractive place with very good food. I'd been there before with my friends Howard Duff and Mike Meshekoff' – (Meshekoff was Duff's agent) – 'so I knew I wouldn't have too much trouble ordering. Later on we could go to a movie. Janet listened to the plans and loved them. What a girl! We were in business!'

He lacked cash as most of it went on his family, but he couldn't admit that when giving his reason to a fan magazine for being unable to afford to take Janet somewhere special:

> In Hollywood, after you've finished a picture and until you start another, they put you on 'layoff.' Literal translation: 'No money!' When they put me on layoff after *Kansas Raiders*, it made no difference as far as Janet was concerned. We went for long hikes, we had picnics at the beach. We'd stop at a drive-in for a hamburger. Janet said, 'If we get too hungry we'll eat with my family one night and your family the next. If you still have an appetite, I'll fry you an egg.'
>
> For the Sadler's Wells ballet, Janet paid for her ticket and I paid for mine. No, I'm not kidding, and furthermore, instead of it embarrassing a fellow, with her understanding, she made it seem all right. Through her understanding, I'd like to add, I've become a much more tolerant person.
>
> Like one night when I was fussing and fuming, trying to decide where I could take her to have a real wonderful time. When I first arrived in Hollywood, I arrived with a Bronx accent. I worked hard to lose it but occasionally, when I get excited, it comes creeping back. Finally I stopped pacing the floor, turned to Janet and groaned, 'I give up. I can't think of a place. I'm *dead*!' Those wonderful eyes began to sparkle. Stealing my Bronx line, she quietly answered, "Why, Tony! It doesn't matter where we go. After all, I'm *witcha*!'

Janet said in 1984, 'Although we were two entirely different people from different backgrounds, together we were a wonderful couple. I was swept off my feet. He was so handsome and charming and funny and really very thoughtful, and we just did what we had to do to overcome the differences between us. I didn't care if he didn't earn as much as I did, although it bothered him, but as far as I was concerned, as long as we were together, that's all that mattered. It really was a very special and wonderful time in my life, and I think it was for him too.'

Tony told me, 'I felt very good that someone like Janet Leigh could find me appealing and nice to be around. That did a lot for my confidence.'

Their second daughter, Jamie Lee, would recall seeing a photograph of them during those early times, at a Hollywood party, sitting at a table, and in that photo her father was, she said, 'looking to her to see what fork to pick up'. He had not yet perfected being Tony Curtis.

The studios had considerable control over the private lives of their contract players, and Universal arranged Tony's dates to premieres and Hollywood functions. This led Tony to a surprising yet whimsical conclusion. 'There was a lot of small print in my contract and I'm convinced that somewhere in there it said that when I worked in a movie with a leading lady there was no reason why I couldn't have an affair with her. So I did.'

When the studio discovered that he was romancing Janet, they were displeased and dismayed. He told me, 'When I started going with Janet, there was opposition from the studio. They were afraid what the newspapers might say or worse, what the public would say. I was like, OK, bring it on, tell me what the problems are and I'll deal with it. The problem was, here's the Jew and the Christian girl. They wouldn't say it, but that's what it was. Was that the best they could throw at me? That was the least of my problems. I'd been called a dirty Jew all my life. And now in Hollywood it was happening again. I couldn't believe it.'

Against the studio's demands, he insisted on taking Janet to the *Harvey* premiere. Tony recalled for a fan magazine:

The studio said, 'Wear a tuxedo and take a pretty girl. The fans will expect to see you.' 'The fans will expect to see *who*?' I wanted to ask them again to make sure it wasn't a dream. Well, I didn't have a tuxedo and I couldn't afford to buy one. When I told my trouble to my good friend Jerry Lewis, he opened his clothes closet. 'I've got four of them. Grab one!'

The day of the premiere I polished my car, cleaned the white tyre walls and bought a new top on a credit plan. That night, in Jerry's tuxedo and with Janet looking like moonlight, we drove up in front of the Carthay Circle Theatre. It was my first premiere [this sounds unlikely] and I felt my knees turning into jelly. When the fans in the bleachers screamed out our names, that finished me. 'I'm going to die, Janet,' I gasped. Then I felt a small, quiet hand in mine. It squeezed encouragingly. 'No, you're not going to die,' she barely whispered. 'The fans love you and want to see you. Let's go over and talk to them.'

I felt so useless, so inadequate standing there. I wanted to shout back, 'What do you want from me? What can I do for you? Take my money, take everything!' Crazy things go through your head at exciting times like this. I kept thinking, just five years ago it would have been *me* up in the bleachers! How glad I am I had this experience in the beginning, and, because of Janet, I'll know what to do.

Janet would recall, in 1984, what she thought was their first premiere together, and although in her account it wasn't *Harvey*, it demonstrated the point she wanted to make, which was that despite the opposition both she and Tony had from the studios, the public were quick to accept them as a romantic couple.

'We went to the opening of *Ice Follies of 1950*, and it was our first time appearing in public as a couple at an event. We walked along the red carpet and photographers were everywhere and cameras flashing, and there was a huge crowd, and they were screaming, "That's Janet Leigh! There's Tony Curtis, and they're together!" and they screamed and cheered and were happy for us, and I think they really loved us together.'

Wherever they went, they were mobbed by adoring fans who loved seeing them together. 'There was one sweet moment when we went to Boston,' she said, 'and there were hundreds to greet us, and some young girl grabbed my arm and said, "Now, when are we going to have our baby?"'

Tony introduced Janet to his best friends, which included Aaron Rosenberg, his agent George Rosenberg and his wife Meta, writer Marty Ragaway, Larry Storch, Danny Arnold, Jeff Chandler, Rock Hudson, Jerry Gershwin (who was an agent at MCA), and Jerry and Patti Lewis.

In a joint interview for a fan magazine, Janet and Tony described when the time came to meet the parents. It was decided that Janet would meet his first. She said she and Helen took to one another the minute they met, and she spoke about how delicious the soup, the roast chicken and the stuffed cabbage were, and recalled how both she and Helen kept glancing at the way Manny and Tony tucked into their food. Janet told Helen, 'It seems we both like to see our men eat.' (Janet probably knew that Tony had paid for all the food but that wasn't to be revealed in those early fan magazines. And although Janet never spoke publicly, or wrote, about Helen's brutality towards Tony, I doubt that he had revealed that aspect of his mother's personality so soon.)

Janet continued, 'The important thing when you meet your fellow's folks is to be yourself, and I guess I was that night. After dinner, we stacked the dishes and Mom Schwartz tried to shoo me into the other room with the men. But they weren't calling me "General Leigh" at home for nothing. I don't believe in putting things off, and I won our mock battle. We both did the dishes.'

While some of this runs like a studio-controlled bit of cutesy publicity, Janet really did make a huge effort to integrate with the Schwartz family. She told me, 'I studied Judaism so I could get a better understanding of Tony's family. And I always did the dishes with Helen whenever we ate there.'

After the success of Janet's first meeting with the Schwartzes came the disaster of Tony's first meeting with the Morrisons. Janet lived with her parents, and was paying for the house they all lived in, so she made the decisions (hence her nickname 'General Leigh'). She told her parents, 'It's all set. Dinner, and nightclubbing this evening.'

During their joint interview, Janet recalled, 'Mother announced him. She rushed into my room grinning, "He's here. And he's so handsome!"'

Tony said, 'I seem to recall being strictly myself when I met the Morrisons,' and then they described what was called 'a minor comedy of errors' as Tony walked across the lawn and found his heels were sinking into the ground. 'Your lawn is awfully soggy,' he told Mr Morrison.

'We just had it replaced,' Fred Morrison informed him.

The evening got worse at the restaurant where there was very little conversation. The stress took its toll on Janet, and halfway through the first course, her mother looked at her and said, 'You're tired, aren't you, dear?'

'Beat,' Janet said.

'As a matter of fact,' said Fred, 'I've had a hard day too.'

'That makes three of us,' said Tony.

Mrs Morrison said, 'I count four cases of fatigue. Let's all go home.'

They returned to the Morrison home, and as Tony said goodbye to Janet on the porch, he told her, 'Your father is certainly a nice fellow. What a sweet way of saying, "Keep the heck off the grass."'

'There's just one thing,' Janet pointed out to him. 'You kept calling them Mr and Mrs Leigh.'

'Well?'

'The name's Morrison.'

And with that Tony left, believing that Fred Morrison would never take a liking to him. Janet said of her father, 'He's quite reserved and doesn't give an opinion for an eternity. He didn't say whether he liked or disliked Tony. But I can tell when he disapproves and I was fairly certain he didn't disapprove.'

But Morrison didn't think Tony was good enough for his girl, who was a major star at a major studio, MGM, while Tony Curtis was only a supporting player at an inferior studio. Although Morrison claimed not to be anti-Semitic, he thought Tony being Jewish would be a problem, especially for Janet's career.

By Christmas 1950 Tony and Janet had been seeing each other for four months. She told me, 'When I heard that the [Schwartz] family had never experienced Christmas I brought them a little tree with all the trimmings and gifts to go under it. I remember his little brother Bobby's eyes like saucers at the sight of the tree. Helen and Manny said that they usually observed Hanukkah but since they weren't strict Orthodox Jews they would have Christmas for the first time.'

She and Tony had given a slightly different account of that Christmas in a joint interview given. The article ran like a duologue, and while cutesy in a typical fan magazine way, it demonstrates the chemistry and connection the couple had in those early days. It began with her saying, 'We started going together in August.'

'And that Christmas you took me home to your folks, and I saw their tree –'

'And you'd never seen one before –'

'Oh, I'd *seen* one, but only in store windows and things. I hadn't actually ever been in someone's house at Christmas when there was a tree. I never knew any Gentiles that well, I guess.'

'But you liked it, and what you said was, "Let's get one for my folks". And your poor father didn't know *what* to make of it.'

'Yeah! Yeah, my father.' (The article mentions that Manny had died the year before this interview, meaning it was published towards the end of 1959.) 'Jan, remember how he looked at that tree? He didn't like it at first, remember? Only he was so nuts about you, he didn't want to say anything.'

'And when he saw how excited and pleased your brother Bobby was –'

'And how pretty Mom made it with all that tinsel –'

'And then we put a six-pointed star on top instead of a regular five-pointed one –'

'Yeah, a Star of David.'

'Then he said, "How can anything that gives so much pleasure be bad for the soul?" And he loved it.'

'He must have because the next year he went out and got one for the family himself.'

This, then, was Tony's first real Christmas, introduced into his life by Janet. In later years, he described that first Christmas as 'a means to get Janet's father to accept me', he told me. 'He felt once I was celebrating Christmas, I must have been a regular guy, which meant I wasn't so Jewish after all.'

In 1951, Tony landed his first starring role in the Arabian adventure *The Prince Who Was a Thief*. Suddenly he was no longer a mere supporting player, but he was still a minor actor at a minor studio compared to Janet at MGM, and Fred Morrison was still finding it hard to accept him.

The Prince Who Was a Thief, a colourful Arabian Nights – or 'sand and tits' as he called it – swashbuckler, was a dream come true as he had always wanted to emulate Errol Flynn and Douglas Fairbanks Jr. A month before filming began, he took lessons in sabre, foil and epée, and discovered he had a real love for fencing. He was able to perform most of his sword-fighting scenes himself in this and subsequent films, and in later years stage his own fencing scenes (in *The Persuaders* and *The Count of Monte Cristo*).

Rudolph Maté was the film's director, and the producer was Leonard Goldstein. The leading lady was 18-year-old starlet Piper Laurie, who had signed a contract with Universal just the year before after dating Bob Goldstein. To generate publicity for the film, Universal sent Tony and Piper on dates to Hollywood parties. 'She was kind of pretty,' he told me, 'but not an attractive person, I thought. I couldn't see what it was about her that Bob Goldstein liked so much. She was a piece of work, I'll tell ya. Unprofessional and suspicious of everyone, even the make-up artist; she'd redo all her make-up in secret, and then she looked terrible on film. Those make-up people know what they are doing, and when they found out what she'd been up to, they had to shoot her stuff again.'

Tony would recall in an early interview how overawed he was to be the star of a movie. 'The day the picture started, when I walked on the set, a chair with my name on it was standing there. Another gag, I thought. It'll probably collapse when I sit on it.

'They told me, "You're the star in this one, Tony." And they weren't kidding. I nearly died.

'That evening when I saw Janet, I told her how everyone kept trying to help me.'

Shelley Winters claimed she was on set the first day: 'Tony was nervous on his first day on the set so I went with him. The first thing he said on screen was "Yonda lies de castle of my fodder, de prince."' [This line – misquoted by Winters and everyone else – actually came from *Son of Ali Baba*, a follow-up movie the following year.] 'The director Rudy Maté said, "Cut! Tony, is dat how you alvays talk?" Maté was also Hungarian. Tony said, "Sure, and you don't talk so hot yourself." I told Rudy, "Look around at everyone laughing. Let Tony talk the way he does and you'll have a hilarious comedy." And I was right.'

Janet recalled in 1984, 'I remember visiting him on the set and seeing how wonderfully dashing he looked in his harem pants and turban. He wore a vest and no shirt. He was insecure and after each take he looked to Rudy Maté for approval, but he saw Rudy shaking his head very slightly, and Tony thought he must have been doing a lousy job, so eventually he asked Rudy what he was doing wrong, and Rudy said, "But I'm very pleased. You're doing really well." And as he said that, Tony noticed that Rudy had a minor tic which made his head shake.'

Tony told a fan magazine that when the picture was almost finished, he felt so grateful to everyone involved that he wanted to buy them all a gift each, but Janet talked him out of it. 'A few days before the picture was finished, she called me and said, "I know how you feel about the people on the set, but you can't afford to give each one a present. So may I suggest that you write personal notes instead of just saying *Thank you*". It was so thoughtful of her and it never would have occurred to me. I rushed out and ordered stationery with my name on it. If only the kids back at P.S. 82 could get a load of me now, I wished. I broke myself up just thinking about it!'

The Prince Who Was a Thief, which cost $400,000 to make, grossed over two million, and Curtis and Laurie became teenage idols. Casting director Bob Laze told Tony the studio would pay him $30,000 to marry Piper, and he was tempted by the money. At that time, he was overwhelmed by his insecurities, his anxiety about becoming a better actor, he was being hassled by Universal to stay away from Janet, he felt inferior to her, and he had the burden of maintaining his parents. He was already on the verge of a nervous breakdown. He discovered something to help calm him down.

'What a crazy business it all was,' he told me in 1985. 'Just *crazy*! I felt like I was going crazy, and I guess I was. I would sense that illness that my mother had creeping in, and it scared me. I needed something to settle me down and I tried dope for the first time. I thought that was the answer to my problems. In the long run it wasn't, but it helped calm me down enough to get me through it all. I didn't even *like* Piper Laurie, so I made the right decision not to marry her. What a disaster *that* would have been for *both* of us.'

It was Robert Mitchum who introduced him to marijuana. Mitchum had been busted for possessing marijuana in 1948, spent time in jail, and came out more popular than when he went in. He continued to use it and was smoking it in 1977 (in front of me) when he told me, 'I gave Tony Curtis his first spliff. He was strung out and so I said, "Try one of these," and he did, and he came back and said, "Got any more?" I said, "Sure!" and then I told him how to get his own.'

From time to time, when things were rough, Tony smoked cannabis, and when everything was OK he stuck to legal cigarettes.

Helen Schwartz made it known to Janet that she wanted her to marry Tony. Janet recalled that she and Tony had argued in front of his family, and she refused to talk to Tony throughout the rest of the meal. As they washed up, Helen told her, 'You shouldn't get mad at Tony. He loves you very much.'

Janet replied, 'I felt he was very wrong, but that doesn't mean I don't love him.'

'Well then, why don't you two hurry up and get married?'

'We have a lot of things to work out right now. Tony's thinking about his career and I don't want to clutter his worries by adding to them.'

'You won't clutter them,' Helen insisted.

'When it happens, it'll happen,' Janet told her.

'But you do want to marry Tony, don't you?'

Helen thought a marriage between Tony and Janet would enhance her new lifestyle in Hollywood. She seemed not to care about Tony's accomplishments. 'She never showed any kind of approval for what I did, never a word of praise. She only cared about mixing with Hollywood society,' he told me. 'One of her best friends was Gary Cooper's mother. She thought being in a club with Gary Cooper's mother would complete her life and that terrible background she came from, but it didn't. She just couldn't find pleasure in anything. And eventually she said to me, "I'm so sorry I used to slap you around." She had to try and find a way to rid herself of all that guilt and obliterate the pain and anger that she created in me, and in herself. But it didn't help her or me. I loved my mother and I mourned for the mother that I never had.'

Painting a rosier picture of that time, Janet recounted, for a fan magazine, a party she threw for friends and family. Tony climbed onto a coffee table at around eleven that evening, and said, 'Silence! I have an announcement to make.'

Janet said, 'Oh no, Tony, let me make it.'

'I'll do it,' he insisted.

'We'll both do it.'

Everyone expected to hear an engagement being announced. Janet and Tony said in unison, 'Dinner will be served,' and the disappointed crowd made their way to the dinner table.

In 1984 Janet gave a slightly different account. 'I gave a party with Mom and Dad in December 1950, and during the evening I stood on a chair and said, "Ladies and gentlemen, I have an announcement to make." I could hear a murmur going through the room, "Here it comes, they're going to announce an engagement," and I knew this, and said, "I am pleased to tell you . . . dinner is served."'

The prank shook her dad who asked her, 'Are you ever going to announce your engagement?'

'Would you mind?' she said.

He replied, 'No!' and that, Janet said, was the only hint he ever gave that he approved of Tony.

But in fact he never approved, and his attitude was coloured by his own long-term marriage problems.

'Janet's dad was not keen on me – I knew that,' Tony told me. 'But her mother liked me, and I liked her mother a great deal. She was also called Helen, like my mother, but a different kind of lady. She always laughed at the practical jokes I played. One time I jacked up the rear of her car, and I stood behind it and held it, and she came out and almost screamed. Janet came running out, and she said to Janet, "Look what Tony's doing." Then I let go and walked round from the back, and the car stayed up in the air and she realised it was jacked all the time, and she was hysterical, tears running down her cheeks.'

One time he walked in with his hand tucked into his sleeve, saying that he lost his hand in a game of poker, and that was enough to send Mrs Morrison into further hysterics. 'Best audience I ever had,' he said.

Tony and Janet became the Great Hollywood Love Affair. And yet, long after their romance was over, Tony was unable to remember being *in love* with Janet. In fact, by 1983, he was saying that he had not truly been in love with any of his wives (three by then). But the pain of three failed marriages and so much history since his days with Janet had scarred him, and he just couldn't remember being in love. Janet, however, never had any doubt how they had felt about each other. 'We were passionately in love,' she told me. 'I'm in no doubt how we both felt at the time. It's easy to forget the happy times when a marriage ends badly, but I make sure I remember.'

There weren't any meaningful discussions between Tony and Janet about getting married. 'We didn't talk about it,' he said. 'There was so much to think of and deal with. I had my own thoughts about it. I really admired Janet's sophistication and I figured some of it would rub off on me if we were married. And, you know, I really wanted her to admire me because then I would know that if she married me it would be because she really liked who and what I was. I couldn't do anything for her in her career. She had nothing to gain other than a husband, and I know she was anxious on that subject because she had been married and divorced twice already.'

But there was speculation about an impending marriage, and so Universal and MGM, by design or accident, managed to separate them. Universal sent Tony on a tour of America to promote *The Prince Who Was a Thief*, and Janet was sent by MGM to Pittsburgh to film scenes for her new movie, *Angels in the Outfield*, in April 1951.

'That was difficult,' Janet remembered. 'He was away for weeks. But it was good for him because everywhere he went huge crowds turned out to see him. Girls were tearing his clothes off. I'm sure he loved all that! Well, it shocked him at first, but he overcame it! He came to Pittsburgh for a day and a half, which was not enough time. We were so much in love.'

He found himself missing Janet so much that he called her hotel in Pittsburgh at two in the morning. She hadn't yet returned from a promotional party, so he continued to call her every ten minutes until she was back in her suite and answering his call.

He told her, 'I can't stand it. I've been so worried, I couldn't sleep. I've got to know you belong to me. Will you marry me?'

She said, 'Yes!' and the engagement was officially on. But they kept the news from the studios and even from their families.

Janet returned to California to continue filming at MGM's Culver Studios and, shortly after, Tony returned for a brief respite from the gruelling publicity tour. They agreed to marry as soon as possible in Greenwich, Connecticut. Two weeks later, Tony left to continue his tour while Janet was sent to New York by MGM to do publicity, accompanied by the studio's PR man John Springer, who had become a close friend of hers. She swore him to secrecy about the engagement and enlisted his help in setting a wedding date. They found a judge who was available on 4 June. Janet had the requisite blood test, and was promised Tony could have his done on the big day. The marriage was applied for under the names of Jeanette Morrison Reames and Bernard Schwartz.

She flew to Chicago to be with Tony on 26 May, rushing into his arms at the airport where he had been fending off reporters and had let it slip that they were engaged. Asked where and when, they said it was probably going to be in August or maybe later. They didn't want the wedding to become a publicity event.

After dinner in the Pump Room at the Ambassador East Hotel, they went to see Jerry Lewis and Dean Martin in the hotel's Chez Paree nightclub. They stood at the back of the packed club until a waiter asked them to follow him, all the way up onto the stage where they were seated at a table for two. Lewis and Martin introduced the 'betrothed couple' to the delighted audience. 'We were so embarrassed and had to sit there in full view for the entire show,' Janet recalled. After, they went to Jerry's dressing room and asked him to be best man and his wife Patti to be matron of honour.

Exactly what happened leading up to the wedding isn't totally clear as Tony and Janet later gave differing accounts. In his account, the night before the wedding he and Janet were in New York. Jerry Lewis cornered him and said, 'What are you doing? Are you nuts? Getting married will kill your career.'

Then Leonard Goldstein called and told Tony Universal thought it best if they didn't get married. He told Tony, 'You have a big career in front of you. Don't blow it.' Tony also believed Janet was getting the same kind of pressure from MGM and from her father who, said Tony, 'didn't want to lose his meal ticket'.

He became so angry and confused that he called her at her hotel – in his account they had separate hotels! – and said, 'Maybe we shouldn't get married.'

'That's fine, because I don't want to marry you either,' she said, and hung up.

He called her back, apologised, and begged her to marry him. They talked for an hour by phone and patched things up. The wedding was back on.

According to Janet, she had gone to New York while Tony, back in California, confided to Leonard Goldstein that they had set a wedding date. Goldstein warned him that Universal wouldn't be pleased, and Tony arrived in New York upset. They went to see Jerry Lewis and discovered Leonard Goldstein had somehow got there and was discussing the situation with Lewis, who made it clear to Janet and Tony that he agreed with Goldstein. Janet, in tears, ran all the way back to the Waldorf Hotel (where, in her account, they were *both* staying).

Tony was close behind, and when he burst into her room he told her that he didn't care what Goldstein or Universal or MGM or RKO thought, and he didn't want to lose her. Minutes later Jerry Lewis called by phone and told Janet that he wasn't thinking straight because of his workload and was truly sorry. 'When Tony spouted off, I knew he was right,' he told her.

Then Leonard Goldstein called and apologised, saying, 'You have my blessing.'

Tony and Janet both remembered what they did next, which was to visit Julie's grave. 'I used to go to his grave a lot,' Tony said in 1985, 'and I talked to him, and I swear he talked right back to me. A day or two before I married Janet, we went there to get some kind of peace because there was so much bullshit coming from the studios about us getting married, and so I said a little prayer over the grave like I always did, and ya know, I just felt much better. I don't know why, but I felt kind of at peace.'

Janet wrote that Tony told her it was 'almost as if Julie had sent out his voice of approval to us'. Tony didn't say if he actually heard, or thought he heard Julie's voice that particular time at his graveside, but he did tell me, 'I sometimes feel cursed with my mother's illness, and sometimes blessed coz it allowed me to hear my little brother when I needed to. Julie always seemed to know the right thing to say. Did I hear him from beyond the grave? Or was it schizophrenia? I'm too afraid to analyse it.'

The wedding went ahead in Greenwich on 4 June 1951. Tony gave a fan magazine a detailed account of his day from the start. 'I thought daylight would never come. I'd feel chilly so I'd get up and close the window. In five minutes I'd get up and open it because it got so hot and I was sweating. So what's the matter with you, I asked myself. I was afraid I might never get to marry my wonderful girl.'

When morning came he showered and shaved. His polished his shoes again. He got into his suit and was ready too early. He ordered orange juice from room service while he resisted phoning Janet. When he couldn't resist any longer, he called her and said, 'Good morning, Mrs Schwartz, it's that man again.'

Janet heard a nervous tremor in his voice, and said, 'It's just a little wedding, darling. Brace up, it's only for the rest of our lives.'

Thanks to the dedication of a journalist on hand to record the wedding for posterity in print, we know that Janet wore a pastel-blue cotton dress. 'Tiny pastel plaid pleats, inserted down the back, fanned out gracefully as she whirled and turned. There was an underskirt of the same plaid, and a matching collar. She wore a white straw cap on her soft blonde curls and white shoes and gloves.'

When a few pleats came loose, the housekeeper hurried to fetch a needle and thread for the repair. Then somebody warned her, 'It's unlucky to sew a dress while it's on,' so she stepped out of it while it was fixed.

The wedding party gathered on the green outside of the courthouse. Friends included John Springer, actor Tommy Farrell, songwriter Mack David and Joe Abeles, who was one of Tony's oldest friends from New York. But for unexplained reasons there were no parents of either the bride or the groom.

A call came through from Jerry Lewis in New York to say he and Patti were going to be late. 'It won't be legal without us, but go on with the wedding. We'll see you later.' A little later he phoned again to say they could make it after all and asked them to delay the wedding.

While anxiously waiting for the best man and matron of honour to arrive, Tony and Janet posed for photos on the terrace, the judge settled on a comfortable chaise, and a waiter served champagne to the guests. One of the female guests told Janet her slip was showing, so she rushed inside to tuck it away neatly. Tony complained that his new shoes hurt. Janet looked at her face in her small mirror and cried out, 'My nose shines. *Everything* shines!'

Everything was now a very long hour behind schedule and nerves were fraying by the time the Lewises arrived. One side of a large room had been arranged for the ceremony with a dais surrounded by flowers and palms. The other half was for the wedding breakfast with 'a long flower-laden table centred by a huge three-tiered white cake that looked like a castle'.

Janet described the ceremony as 'short, sweet, sedate and solemn'.

The bride and groom gave their vows, the judge pronounced them man and wife, and Tony kissed the bride. Jerry Lewis took Janet in his arms, bent her back and gave her a movie-hero kiss. Then he waltzed her round the floor, after which he announced that he didn't bring his wedding present because he was too weak to carry it. The gift turned out to be an enormous TV set which would be delivered to their apartment.

Midway through the afternoon, the guests left. The bride and groom, in a chauffeur-driven black limousine, headed for New York and the Waldorf Astoria where they had the suite MGM had permanently reserved. Tony wanted to go via the Bronx. He saw, sitting on a stoop, one of his aunts. (It would seem that the poor relatives from New York had not been invited.) Tony wound down the window and called to her; when she saw him in the limousine, she asked, 'Who died?' The family, it seems, had not been told.

When they got to the Waldorf, he carried his bride in his arms into the large suite. Telegrams and flowers kept arriving, thanks to MGM, who alerted the wire services at the final moment. That afternoon the newspapers announced the marriage of Tony Curtis and Janet Leigh.

They called both sets of parents. Janet told Helen Schwartz, 'Hello, Mrs Schwartz, this is Mrs Schwartz.' According to Janet, there was 'a lot of screaming and crying and long-distance hugging and kissing. A lot of love.' And yet the parents had not been invited. Could it be there was hostility between the Morrisons and the Schwartzes? Tony told me, 'Janet's dad didn't think any of my family was good enough.'

Although it was their wedding day, they both had publicity obligations to fulfil, and they went their separate ways for the next few hours. Janet returned to the suite first. There was a knock at the door. Standing there was a beautiful girl who enquired, 'Is Mr Curtis here? I have something for him.'

'No, he isn't here.'

'Then I'll wait for him,' she said, and she walked in, or 'wiggled inside', as Janet described the moment. She had no idea what business this girl had with Tony (and, curiously, didn't ask). When he arrived, the girl said, 'Mr Curtis, I am your present from the boys,' and she bent him backwards in a big smooch – a joke from Jerry Lewis. Fortunately, Janet saw the funny side.

That evening the wedding party was held in a room at Danny's Hideaway, a popular club run by their friend Danny Stradella. All the wedding guests were there, as well as executives from Universal, MGM and RKO, plus Mel Tormé, Dean Martin, Vic Damone, Cyd Charisse, Tony Martin and Phil Silvers. The DeMarco Sisters, from the Copa, performed. 'It was glorious, it was happy, it was fun, it was volatile, it was crazy – it was wonderful,' said Janet.

The honeymoon was about to begin.

CHAPTER SEVEN

Hollywood Honeymoon

'We should have had a honeymoon, but we had too much work,' Janet Leigh told me.

The honeymoon was put on hold.

The very next day after the wedding, Tony caught the train to continue the publicity tour for *The Prince Who Was a Thief*, which had been interrupted by the wedding. Seeing him off at the railway depot, Janet was dismayed to discover Piper Laurie wearing an exotic negligee in the cabin adjoining Tony's. 'Hardly a comforting sight to a new bride,' she wrote. She needn't have been jealous; the friction between Tony and Piper was increasing. He was convinced Piper was unhappy because the publicity about the wedding eclipsed the publicity about the movie.

Janet had the task of finding their first home together. It turned out to be a new modern one-bedroomed rented apartment at 10600 Wilshire Boulevard. Helen Schwartz insisted on helping her move in, and she began to discover how dominating Helen could be. Her mother-in-law was insisting where things should go until Janet finally told her, 'Look, mother, I'm sorry, but you do it your way in your house and I'll do it my way in mine.'

Upon his return, Tony arrived at the apartment, picked her up in his arms at the doorstep and carried her over the threshold. She remembered the apartment as 'our own special home'. It had a cramped kitchen and a small lounge that was dominated by the large television bought for them by Jerry and Patti Lewis.

'We were young, in love and attractive, working and surviving in a highly glamorous profession, and stimulated by diverse circles of friends,' Janet recalled. They spent a lot of time at Jerry and Patti Lewis' house on Amalfi Drive in Pacific Palisades where a large group of friends invariably gathered. They watched movies, played games and filmed home-made movies on Jerry's 16mm camera. Dick Stabile, whose orchestra travelled with Lewis and Dean Martin, and Mack David composed music for the movies, and Danny Arnold wrote the scripts. Lewis directed, and their acting friends all played parts.

They even held premieres at the house. A hundred guests were invited to see *Fairfax Avenue*, a spoof of *Sunset Boulevard*, in which Janet played the Gloria Swanson part and Tony the William Holden role. Tony remembered those home-made movies: 'They were just for fun, and we didn't take them seriously, but I think that's how Jerry Lewis taught himself how to direct and edit movies. We were all great pals in those days. Me and Janet were doing well. I guess that's how it is when you're young and only just married, but we had our problems right from the start.'

Janet paid the rent and living expenses because Tony earned less than she did, and he was still keeping his family who, to his dismay, moved so they could be closer to him. He hated being unable to pay his own way and insisted on an arrangement with Janet whereby he would reimburse his half of the expenses when he was able. And in time he did. 'It was important to him,' said Janet.

In November 1951, Tony and Janet were asked by businessman John Haskell (husband of columnist Dorothy Haskell) if they would appear in a show in London in December for the International Variety Club in aid of the National Playing Fields Association, of which the Duke of Edinburgh (the future Prince Philip) was the president. There would follow a tour of Germany and France for a series of 'one-night stands' for the servicemen and women stationed there. 'We saw the Variety Club show and the tour of Germany and France as our chance to get the honeymoon we never thought we'd get,' said Janet.

The honeymoon was on.

They were going to be among an elite group of entertainers including Frank Sinatra, Ava Gardner, Orson Welles, Noel Coward and Rhonda Fleming.

The couple flew out to New York and spent a hectic and happy week there, shopping, being photographed, doing interviews, seeing lawyers about contractual difficulties Tony's agent was having with Universal, seeing Charles Laughton on stage in *Don Juan in Hell*, seeing other plays, nightclubbing at the Copa, socialising and throwing a party in their hotel suite.

'It was a marvellous free honeymoon,' said Janet.

Tony didn't remember it quite that way. 'I felt out of my league with all those great entertainers. What could I do? I'm not going to out-sing Frank Sinatra.' But Janet remembered him having a wonderful time. Tony would find it hard to ever remember a wonderful time, and perhaps that's because he felt, from the beginning of the marriage, that he had made a terrible mistake. 'I should never have gotten married. I had my career to think of. That shoulda meant more to me. I dunno – it's hard to think back.'

They took time out to visit the Bronx. Tony often took pilgrimages to the Bronx and Manhattan. Because of his insecurity and anxiety, he needed reassurance that he really had escaped. There were still a lot of his old friends living there, still struggling to earn a living. One old friend saw him and said, 'It's been a long time, Bernie. What happened to you? Where've you been?'

'California!'

'No kidding! How is it there?'

'The climate couldn't be better.' Satisfied, he left the Bronx and Manhattan behind until the next time.

They arrived in London on 5 December, gave a press conference at a special luncheon, and were installed in their hotel suite complete with their own maid. They had more interviews to do, then saw a show and had dinner with Peter Lawford and Don Weis.

The next day they managed to take in some of the sights before attending a huge party at the Embassy Club for the stars hosted by the Duke of Edinburgh and the chief barker of the Variety Club, C.J. Latta.

The show was held at the Coliseum theatre at midnight, and was a huge success, ending with a spectacular display by the Royal Marine Band and Grenadier Guards Band, and a line-up which included Tony, Janet, Frank Sinatra, Ava Gardner, Noel Coward, Rhonda Fleming, Orson Welles, Max Wall and Tommy Trinder. After this big finale, Princess Elizabeth was brought on stage and they were all introduced to the future Queen of England.

The stars then gathered at the hotel for breakfast where Orson Welles entertained them with feats of magic. Finally, at around 6 a.m. Tony and Janet fell into bed.

Then it was on to Germany where they played Wiesbaden, Neuburg

Air Base, Munich and Frankfurt. Frank Sinatra and Ava Gardner had taken off on a belated honeymoon; they could afford one, Tony and Janet couldn't. This tour was their honeymoon. And despite Tony's gloomy and vague recollection, it was, by Janet's account, a wonderful and happy time.

Tony's contribution to the shows was more a case of just being there to say hello and thanks to the soldiers. Janet sang and looked beautiful. Tony recalled, 'I'm sure they appreciated seeing Janet more than they did me.'

On a flight to Frankfurt in an air-force plane, one of the engines caught fire. The passengers were paralysed with terror, not least of them Tony and Janet, while the pilots fought to keep the aircraft under control. Janet huddled into Tony's chest, and he held her tightly and they said their prayers. The pilots shut down the flaming engine and safely brought the plane down. Ambulances and fire engines were already on the landing strip, but fortunately no one was hurt. Tony, however, had gone into shock and went on to develop such a severe fear of flying that for many years after he refused to fly anywhere.

A highly strung young man, often insecure, sensitive to criticism and paranoid in a business which breeds paranoia, all his emotions were brought out in the extreme during their first visit to Germany. Janet recalled:

When we spent time in Germany doing shows for the troops still there, it was, for both of us, I think, a surreal kind of place. I remember Tony said he could almost hear the cries and screams of two great aunts he had who were slaughtered in Dachau. He spoke also of a cousin who died in Buchenwald. So Tony was really very suspicious – he was suspicious of strangers anyway, always wondering if they were prejudiced towards him because he was a Jew, but he felt it a lot more in Germany. I saw how it got to him – each day he hated being in Germany, and it got worse each day.

At the end of our tour there was a party, and we had caviar and really good Scotch, and the Germans were very polite. Nobody said anything out of order, but Tony was growing angry with each polite question which was asked through an interpreter. I think the more polite they were, the angrier he became. He was wondering what they were really thinking and figured that because they were Germans, they *had* to hate Jews. When somebody asked him if his name was really Curtis, he said very clearly, to the whole room, so that everyone fell quiet, 'My name is Bernard Schwartz and I am a Jew.'

There was complete silence, and before anyone spoke, Tony took my arm and we left.

Because Tony refused to fly, they caught the night train to Paris. On arrival, they discovered to their surprise and delight that they were not going to doing any shows there after all. It was, in fact, a bonus holiday for all the stars in the company – Christmas in Paris, all expenses paid. Not everyone wanted it. Orson Welles and Noel Coward begged off. But there was a price to pay; Tony and Janet conducted interviews arranged by MGM, Universal and RKO, and also took part in publicity for TWA.

On Christmas Eve the company gathered in Tony and Janet's suite for a champagne celebration and an exchange of presents. Janet bought Tony a pair of cufflinks he had spotted and admired in a shop on the Left Bank. After the last guest had left, they put in calls to their parents. Janet said they were both 'teary-eyed and homesick'.

Just before midnight they decided to take a walk. In a joint interview for a fan magazine, Janet asked Tony, 'Remember Paris that first Christmas? We went walking along the Left Bank and we found a little church that had Midnight Mass, and we decided to go in. Remember? At first you didn't quite want to. We were still feeling our way around each other's religions then – kind of afraid of offending each other. And you said, "How can I go into a church and not pray?" And I said, "Well, I'm not Catholic either, and this is a Catholic Church. But I'll say the prayer I want to say, and you say the one you want to say, and God will hear us both.'

The honeymoon was finally over, and the couple tried to make a home life for themselves. But they were both too busy for that. At the beginning of 1952, Janet made *Fearless Fagan* at MGM, while Universal rushed Tony into his second starring role, in *Flesh and Fury*, playing a deaf-mute who stumbles into the boxing game, becomes a champ and ultimately finds a cure for his handicap.

There had been times, in his childhood, when he had become so angry he vowed to kill. While filming *Flesh and Fury* he unleashed some of that pent-up anger and again felt a murderous rage come to the surface. He recalled:

There was a moment of realisation – *revelation* – when I knew I could have killed this guy who had knocked me on my ass in a scene in the ring. I still recall every sense of it. Something was building up all morning long when we were preparing to shoot the scene. I don't know what started it. I always go out of my way to try not to create any tension and bad vibe on a set because these are people you have to work with coz I know how angry *I* can get when aroused, and I can always take care of myself. So I don't know what *his* problem was.

This guy was just working me over unnecessarily, really pissing me off, getting me angrier and angrier, until finally I couldn't take it any longer and I felt this blind flash of rage and an urge to punch him to a pulp. He'd knocked me on my ass, and when I got up I coulda killed him. He was standing there, right in front of me, and I had this vision – this really strong vision – of being a gladiator with nothing on but leather thongs with little metal points on them, and all I had to do was hit him. One hit! *Boom*! And he'd be dead.

These were feelings I'd had before, in New York. There were people I wanted to kill. That's not so bad. The bad thing is if you let it take you over. Like that vision of being a gladiator – I knew that it was the kind of thing you couldn't let take you over, because one thing builds on another and before you know it you're a gladiator . . . in your own head, and I can see how some people are the way they are if they go on to kill people. I've always had some kind of mental trip switch and I can stop myself, like I stopped myself on that movie, or I coulda killed that guy.

Critics began to take notice of Tony's acting as well as his athleticism. 'There is Tony Curtis, who can box and who does a fine job of acting, both as a mute and as one who learns to talk and hear,' said the *Motion Picture Herald*. 'In fact, the picture gives a handsome Curtis for the women, and a skilful, fighting Curtis in some very convincing fight scenes for the men.' *Kinematograph Weekly* thought, 'Tony Curtis does a good job and distinguishes himself in the ring.'

Immediately after *Flesh and Fury*, Universal cast Tony and Piper Laurie in *No Room for the Groom* as a newly married couple with problems caused by the bride's family moving in with them. Tony believed Universal had planned this film when they offered him money to marry Piper. The friction between them continued to overshadow their work, and their relationship deteriorated further. 'Making this movie was just torture,' he recalled. It did well because of the popularity of Curtis and Piper, even though it was nothing special. 'The comedy is strained and tedious with only an occasional bright spot meriting a chuckle,' said *Variety*. 'Curtis and Miss Laurie are generally satisfactory although [the] former plays a big drunk sequence, what should have been his best comedy scene, very poorly.'

To Tony's horror, Universal put them back into harem pants and turbans for *Son of Ali Baba*. Again, Tony displayed his considerable athletic prowess, with many acts of derring-do, leaping from one parapet to another, climbing walls and beating off Arabian heavies with panache. He trained every day with his stand-in, stuntman Davy Sharpe, who taught him to ride a horse properly, to jump, leap and tumble.

The screenplay was hardly poetic prose, and he had a particularly awful line to speak, 'Yonder in the valley of the sun is my father's castle.' After the movie came out, Debbie Reynolds said on television, 'Did you see the new guy in the movies? They call him Tony Curtis, but that's not his real name. In his new movie he's got a hilarious line where he says [adding a heavy New York accent] "Yonda lies de castle of my *fodda*."' That line, which he never said, was to be repeated often and became, 'Yonda lies de castle of my fodda, de caliph.' It became a joke at Tony's expense, and appeared in just about every one of his obituaries by journalists who never saw the film to know he never said it.

The critics of the time noticed his charm and athleticism more than his acting ability. 'Tony Curtis displays plenty of agility,' thought *Kinematograph Weekly*, which found the film, 'Spacious, extravagant and disarmingly juvenile fun', while *Today's Cinema* noted, 'The main roles are vivaciously played by Tony Curtis and Piper Laurie,' and that the film 'makes confident entertainment with spirited action in the cloak and dagger style'.

Tony hoped one day to be allowed to do serious drama, and he continued studying at the Universal drama class, now run by Sophie Rosenstein. She allowed actors to present extracts from plays in the studio's small theatre. Janet recalled Tony being excellent in an excerpt from *All You Need Is One Good Break*.

Each film he made was followed by a gruelling publicity tour, and at each stop Tony was mobbed by girls who ripped his clothes off. He told me that some of that was rigged. 'Y'know, I'd get my clothes torn off by fans. And if they couldn't tear my clothes off, they'd make me a suit that *could* be torn off. They'd get some girls that worked at the exchange at Universal to come and pull my sleeves off, and they'd take photographs of it and put it on the wire services – *Tony Curtis raped*! They created all of it. I know the whole bag. I couldn't sing or dance. It's not like I was Frank Sinatra. I didn't have a guitar. I didn't have *anything*. I just walked out on stage. But I tell you, it created a furore.'

In June 1952, Janet went to Colorado to shoot tough location scenes in the Rocky Mountains for *The Naked Spur* and, because he finally had some free time, Tony went too. They were housed in a complex of cabins with the rest of the cast and crew. To celebrate their first anniversary, Gloria Stewart, there with husband James Stewart, the star of the film, threw a party for the Curtises.

While Janet worked, Tony took easel and paints to the streams to paint, a pastime he was finding highly therapeutic. His pastime became a passion, a great escape from his general paranoia, and his best efforts were hung on the walls of their apartment.

He remained insecure and was becoming increasingly more of an hypochondriac. His back ached a lot (not surprisingly considering the back injury he probably sustained in the navy), he suffered from stomach cramps, and also periods of fatigue. He was prescribed all kinds of medications – for pain, for his stomach, for colds and flu, and for sleeping. He told me in 1985, 'I've been taking drugs ever since I went into the movies. I'd work all day and come home so wired that the studio doctor would give me Seconal or Nembutal to sleep. In the morning I'd be so bushed he'd hand out Dexedrine to buck me up.'

He didn't drink much alcohol in those early days, although he was a heavy smoker. Cigarettes also eased his anxiety, and smoking was common among most film stars and throughout society. And from time to time he smoked cannabis.

He had long been vain, but his vanity became an obsession, and among the worst things that could happen to him was to find a spot or pimple on his face. When one appeared he was likely to stay at home and brood, unable to face the world looking anything less than dazzlingly handsome. He knew his career, in the beginning, depended wholly on his looks. 'I had little but my good looks in those days,' he told me. 'Nobody cared whether I could act or not. I'd get on the set to do a scene and I'd have trouble with the dialogue. If it took more than four takes, the director would say, "Don't worry about it, kid. We'll change it." Change it? That's the worst thing in the world you can do to a man. It was always made easier for me. I was never allowed to fight my way through anything. If a scene called for a rainstorm, they'd warm up the water. I wasn't given the simple joy of getting wet and shivering. And I wasn't that skilled an actor that I could fabricate it.'

He became a client of MCA, run by Lew Wasserman, one of the most powerful agents in Hollywood. Jerry Gershwin at MCA had persuaded him that he would get much better representation from them, including extensive studio coverage, more effective influence on decisions and greater promotion, than his current agent, George Rosenberg, ever could. Tony had felt loyalty to Rosenberg and wasn't immediately convinced, but he eventually decided to switch agents. Janet recalled that he was in a state for days before finding the courage to tell Rosenberg that he was fired.

Lew Wasserman took a special interest in Tony's career and began to personally represent him and Janet. The couple joined an elite group of people that gathered at the home of Wasserman and his wife Edie on Sundays for cocktails, a barbecue and the use of their pool.

It was a turning point in his career. 'That man did everything for me,' Tony told me. 'He was more than an agent. He was my mentor. You know, he was so powerful and by far the most intelligent man in Hollywood that MGM begged him to take over their studio, but he didn't want to let all his own clients down. They offered him the moon, and he turned it down. He was an honourable human being, and from the moment I signed with him, everything changed for me.'

Wasserman renegotiated Tony's contract with Universal, who agreed to pay him $50,000 a picture and allow him to make movies for other studios. The first film under this new agreement was *Houdini* at Paramount, about the legendary escapologist and illusionist Harry Houdini. Tony had become anxious about being typecast as Piper Laurie's screen partner, so Wasserman had a plan to dissolve the Curtis/Laurie partnership by creating a new one, that of Curtis and Leigh, and to that end Janet was cast as Houdini's wife. MGM quibbled over billing, wanting their star's name above Tony Curtis. Janet told them bluntly, 'There is no question. My husband should be billed first.' The deal was made, and Janet played Mrs Houdini.

Manny Schwartz had been working for Tony's press agent, Warren Cowen, doing very light work, just collecting and clipping press articles into scrapbooks. Tony secured his father a job at the Paramount wardrobe department, and as he ran to call his father with the news, he tripped on a cable and tore the ligaments in his right knee. There was no time to recuperate, and he began filming with a limp. And Manny stuck with his job, sticking press pieces in scrapbooks.

Tony dedicated himself to spending hours learning how to do Houdini's illusions, coached by magician George Boston and also Joe Dunninger, who had been a close associate of Harry Houdini. As a consequence of his dexterity and ability to perform the illusions, he and Janet, who assisted him in many of the tricks, were both initiated into the Magicians Society, honour bound never to reveal their secrets.

On the first day of filming, Janet and Tony were both nervous about working with each other. She suffered from stress-related colitis and was always unwell for the first few days on any film. They were both quickly put at their ease by the film's director, George Marshall, who, said Janet, 'was so funny and sanguine, immediately setting the tone of the set'. Marshall had discovered that she used to love having water fights with her parents. Their water battles started with flicking washing-up water, moved on to whole glasses of water, then buckets, and finally the hose. It was a peculiar but hysterical pastime enjoyed by the Morrisons. Even Fred had fun doing it. So from day one, George Marshall began throwing paper cups of water at Tony and Janet, who merrily retaliated.

There was a basket with a big bow waiting for Janet on the set on the first day. Inside was a poodle puppy, a present from Tony. She named her Houdina. 'I adored her and lavished all my motherly instincts upon this innocent,' wrote Janet. 'And my desire to have a child intensified daily.'

Jerry Lewis and Dean Martin were making a movie at Paramount at the same time, so they all visited each other. 'It was a lively lot,' said Janet.

For the first time, Tony was host to important visitors on a film set. One was director Billy Wilder and another was Yul Brynner, then a Broadway star in *The King and I*. 'Tony had a great dexterity,' Brynner told me. 'When he played Houdini, he learned how to do many of the actual tricks, and that impressed me about him, that he would take the time to really learn how to do them rather than rely on tricks of the camera.'

There was one trick which should have required a stunt double –

Houdini would be submerged in ice. Tony insisted on doing the stunt himself and suffered ice burns to his skin.

For the first time in his career he was called upon to play someone older than himself, ageing throughout the movie. Tony was 28 years old, and his extreme boyish good looks allowed him to pass for much younger, but turning him into the older Houdini was a challenge for the Paramount make-up department. They tinted his sideburns grey and drew lines on his face. Because he had taken to shaving his chest to keep it smooth for beefcake photos, hairs had to be painted on to his chest. It was a shock for his teenage audience to see him looking so different, although the effect wasn't totally convincing. Tony knew it was a flaw in the film, telling journalist Tony Crawley in 1975, 'I'd like to do another approach to *Houdini*. My age at the time kinda dictated the way they wrote the script.' When Crawley suggested it should have been called *Houdini Junior*, Tony said, 'Exactly! That's what they shoulda done, played it up to the time Houdini Junior became Houdini Senior. That would have been smart, instead of trying to bring him to the end like that. I was asked to age unnaturally, and you just couldn't at twenty-eight.'

The water fights came to a climax during the shooting of the final scene where Houdini was to escape after being hung handcuffed upside down in a glass cage full of water. George purposely placed Janet some distance away from everyone else, including Tony and all the camera, lighting and electrical equipment. When he called 'Action!' several buckets of water were poured over her from the rafters above, drenching her. She loved it!

Janet recalled that there was always laughter and friendship while making *Houdini*, and it was a happy time for both her and Tony.

Filming ended on an unscripted and highly dramatic note. Tony performed the glass-cage stunt himself. When he began to act as if he was running out of air and was struggling to escape, he was so convincing that the propmen smashed the fake glass with axes, and Tony came spilling out onto the floor along with gallons of water. It was captured on film and edited into the movie.

Reviews were not enthusiastic. 'In the title role, Tony Curtis is as unrevealing about Houdini the man as about Houdini the magician, hardly hinting at his dynamic personality, strength, ingenuity and resourcefulness,' said *Time*. The *Monthly Film Bulletin* concluded, 'With firmer direction, and with make-up that indicated ageing through more than powdered temples, Tony Curtis and Janet Leigh might well have been convincing.' The *Hollywood Reporter* had kinder words. 'Curtis and Miss Leigh make a winning team, playing the love scenes with moving tenderness and performing many of the magic tricks themselves.'

Tony's loyal fans, and those of Janet, ensured the film did well, and a new screen partnership had been established. They had embarked on a whole new phase of their lives and careers. To Janet it was bliss. To Tony it would become a burden. The honeymoon was over.

CHAPTER EIGHT

A Sliver of Schizophrenia

Universal finally felt they could take a chance and give Tony roles that were several stages up from his Arabian Nights pageants. Aaron Rosenberg, recalling his own glory days as a player in the USC All-American football team, cast Tony in *The All-American* as a college football star with a huge chip on his shoulder. It cost little to make, turned a decent profit and kept the fans happy, as well as a few critics. 'Curtis is thoroughly believable as a football star,' said the *Hollywood Reporter*. *Variety* found this 'rah-rah football feature with Tony Curtis as a star quarterback an entertaining offering. While no great classic, it is plenty of fun.'

He could now afford to contribute more to the living expenses which had been Janet's responsibility, and they moved to a bigger apartment, a penthouse, at 10814 Wilshire. They even employed a housekeeper to clean and cook. Life was looking good.

In 1953 he starred in *Forbidden*, set in Macao, in which he fought off racketeers and rekindled an old flame, played by established leading lady, Joanne Dru; but he felt they had no chemistry because, at 32, she was older than him. He said, 'My job was to do the pictures they put me in, and I always got them done, which was all they wanted from me.' The setting for the movie might have been Macao, but none of the cast got much further than the back lot of Universal Studio.

Tony's next picture was a tough war movie, *Beachhead*. He had hoped to star with Janet at Warner Brothers in *Prince Valiant*, but Warner had its own contracted boy, Robert Wagner, to play the knight with long hair.

Beachhead was to be filmed in Hawaii, separating the couple for the first time since they married. At the last minute she decided to travel with him to Hawaii and spend six days with him in Honolulu before she had to return to Hollywood for *Prince Valiant*. Tony still refused to fly so they went by ship, the *Lurline*.

I found three accounts of their Hawaii adventure: Tony's version in his 2008 autobiography, Janet's in her 1984 memoir; and an early version in a fan magazine. They all differ, which wouldn't matter much but for one question – did Tony know that Janet was pregnant?

According to the earliest version, she suspected she was pregnant and he insisted on her having a pregnancy test before leaving for Hawaii. The results were not to be known for several days. In the hope of avoiding publicity, she had it done under the name Jeannette Morrison.

Although anxious about the results, they tried to relax in the presence of their friends Van Johnson (from Janet's debut movie *The Romance of Rosy Ridge*) and his wife Evie – Van Johnson was on his way to Hawaii to make *The Caine Mutiny*.

According to Janet's 1984 account, she had the 'faint hope' that she was pregnant and 'had to wait a while longer to be positive before I said anything, even to Tony'. So in this version they sailed without her having taken a pregnancy test, and Tony didn't yet know she might be pregnant. She wrote that during the crossing she became certain she was going to have a baby and told Tony, who 'wanted to shout it from the highest mast', but they agreed to keep it quiet.

In the fan magazine account, the *Lurline* came under siege from reporters because the news had leaked about Janet's pregnancy test, and she told them that she knew no more than they did at that time. In the article, she described the 5am docking in Honolulu as being like 'New Year's Eve at five o'clock in the morning'. There were three hours of celebratory chaos as kayaks and catamarans and divers came to meet the ship. The press boat came alongside, and Janet and Tony were greeted with kisses and alohas and had leis heaped upon them until they could hardly see over the top of them. Her 1984 version pretty much concurs with all this.

Their suite at the Royal Hawaiian on Waikiki was spacious and airy with wicker furniture, panoramic windows and a wide veranda. They had six glorious days which were, by both accounts, happy in the extreme, with sightseeing, dinner at the Royal Hawaiian in formal dress, a luau under the stars and the chance to ride an outrigger canoe and a twin-hulled catamaran. While Tony was able to burn to a golden bronze before he began filming, Janet had to keep herself protected because she had promised Warners she would keep her skin fair for *Prince Valiant*.

According to the fan magazine account, they could wait no longer for the results of the pregnancy test and telephoned through for it. When told it was positive, they were both ecstatic.

When it came time for Janet to leave, Tony told her, 'You gotta rest as much as possible.'

'Yes, Tony.'

'You take real care of yourself. I know it'll be hard for you coz you never sit down long enough to grow bored.'

'Stop fussing.'

'But you must look after yourself because we have more to think about than just us.'

It was all very sweet and romantic.

In Janet's 1984 account, no pregnancy test was ever taken, but it must have been confirmed at some point. She didn't say when.

According to the fan magazine piece, Tony was unable to see her off on her flight back to Los Angeles because he was already on his way to the island of Kauai for the first day of filming *Beachhead*, so she was seen off by friends including the Van Johnsons.

For both of them, making their respective pictures was a lonely time. Tony's location was unpleasant and very hot and humid and lacked the luxury he had enjoyed in Honolulu. In California, Janet kept a promise made to Tony that she wouldn't attend parties because of the pregnancy, and she relaxed as much as possible between scenes. According to the earliest story, he also made a promise, to phone her every other day, and each time he did, he asked her the same anxious question, 'How are you?'

And she always replied, 'I'm fine. Just fine.'

When he called her on her birthday, 6 July, she said she didn't feel well at all. She hadn't been sleeping, and was depressed and feeling sick. She was sure it was just because of the separation (and she often suffered from colitis).

Tony was supposed to call only every other day, but he was worried about her and called their apartment the very next day. There was no answer. He called his mother, who said she had talked to Janet earlier that day and everything had seemed all right, and that she would be home that evening. Tony began to panic, and called Mrs Morrison, who gave him the bad news that she had just returned from St John's Hospital where Janet had been admitted earlier that evening and given emergency surgery. She had lost the baby.

Mrs Morrison told Tony that the doctor had assured Janet she would be fine and be able to have babies in the future. Tony immediately sat down and wrote a letter to Janet, telling her how sorry he was that she had lost the baby and that he knew how disappointed she would feel. When she read the letter, her only thought was how disappointed he was feeling. It was a time when they should have been together, but he was unable to get home.

That was the earliest version of the episode.

In 1984, Janet revealed that two weeks after she had returned from Hawaii, she had begun to bleed. Her doctor told her to stay off her feet. Production on *Prince Valiant* hadn't yet begun so she didn't need to go to work. George, a favourite uncle, was in town and came to stay with her at the apartment to keep her company and keep an eye on her. When she began to cramp and haemorrhage, he had bundled her into his car and driven her straight to the hospital. Uncle George went back to the apartment and took the call from Tony and broke the news to him.

Much of the above was contradicted by Tony, who wrote in his second autobiography that he didn't know Janet was pregnant until he learned of the miscarriage. The foremost thing on his mind was, why hadn't she told him, and he wondered if she had reasons of her own to keep it from him, suggesting that he suspected the baby's father was someone else. It was pure paranoia. And it was driven by something else.

'Schizophrenia,' wrote Tony Curtis, 'ran in the family.' He told me, 'My mother was schizophrenic, and I believe her father was too, and that was passed down through the genes to my brother Bobby. And I have it too.'

In his first autobiography, he made mention of his schizophrenia just the once. 'That sliver of schizophrenia runs in the family. I have little flares of it myself.'

His brother Bobby was severely schizophrenic. Tony's was moderate. During the darkest days of his life, in moments of despair, most especially when he was sinking into an abyss of hard drugs and alcohol, that 'sliver of schizophrenia' occasionally slipped into his life.

'I have heard voices at times in my life when I have been at my lowest. I mean, in deep, dark despair. I never noticed them when I was young. It only came when I was working hard to make something of myself, and [when] my personal life was difficult – and when I was a drug user.'

Tony often referred to his 'madnesses' in interviews. In the BBC documentary about him in *The Hollywood Greats* series, he said, 'Maybe I'm nuts.' I think he had long accepted that there was some kind of mental illness which plagued him from time to time, and which he kept hidden during the height of his success, afraid that knowledge of it would destroy his career. His schizophrenia ran through his life, probably to the very end. At times he could fight it, and at other times he was defeated by it.

When Janet miscarried, that sliver of schizophrenia must have slipped through. He was, by nature, paranoid and jealous when he had no cause to be, and those were the times he suffered schizophrenic moments. He told me in 1985, 'I used to wonder where I got these jealous rages from, believing everyone and everything was against me, and accusing people of all kinds of betrayal. It scares the shit outta me, but I know it's an illness – the kind my mother had. I can't let it beat me. It's something I gotta fight to my dying day, I swear.'

Tony could often be brutally honest about himself and his failings, and highly critical of others, usually with some justification. He was often negative, sometimes in the extreme, about his first marriage, tending to see the dark side of everything, while Janet emphasised the positive in her life and her marriage to Tony. When he read her autobiography, he was surprised to discover how kind she had been in regard to him.

Perhaps she was truly unaware of any early problems in their marriage, or just preferred not to acknowledge them in retrospect. He seems to have been acutely aware of their problems from an early stage, and in a sense that must have magnified them for him. While Janet made no mention of any kind of disintegration in the marriage up to this point in her autobiography, Tony's autobiography suggested that things were already bad for them by the time he made *Beachhead*. He wrote, 'Neither Janet nor I was the best of spouses, so we'd gotten pretty distant.'

He also wrote that while he and his leading lady from *Beachhead*, Mary Murphy, were mutually attracted, they both decided not to consummate the relationship – suggesting that at the very least they kissed and spent time together – because he 'didn't want to jeopardise my already fragile marriage'.

I don't think Tony lied when he wrote, all those years later, that he didn't know Janet was pregnant, but because of the way the memory becomes distorted in old age, and because of his own emotional turmoil which surrounded the miscarriage and the marriage, he became convinced she had kept it from him, and therefore she must have had some guilty reason to do so. Tony's sliver of schizophrenia must have played a part too.

His schizophrenia must have been diagnosed, possibly in 1980 when he was admitted to hospital with a complete emotional breakdown, or when he was in rehab in 1984 for drug and alcohol abuse, because he told me in 1985, 'I finally know now why, for a few seconds or minutes and for longer when I was freebasing, I heard voices.'

He also told me, 'I often heard them, if only for a moment. "She's cheated!" Or "She's screwed around behind your back." "You can't trust her." I'm fighting it, ya know?'

I don't think he ever accused Janet outright of being unfaithful – he just assumed it. She was in a fragile condition following the miscarriage, and he must have buried all his paranoia and suspicions just deep enough to keep going as if nothing but the miscarriage had happened. If the marriage was troubled, it was because Tony was troubled. And when he heard that she had miscarried, his troubled mind somehow convinced him that he hadn't even known she was pregnant, and the paranoia set in, and he believed the worst.

His private life was getting bogged down in all this emotional and mental turmoil, but his career was still gaining strength. *Beachhead* turned out to be a good picture, and Tony got his best notices to date. 'Tony Curtis and Frank Lovejoy are first class as the case-hardened sergeant and the ardent, bitter young marine,' said the London *Evening Standard*. 'This is a picture which deals with neurosis, brutality, bravery, lust, unselfishness and despite such a mixture it achieves a sense of truth. One hesitates to flog a word but this picture has integrity.'

Variety said, 'Curtis turns in his best job yet, giving an intelligent mixture of toughness and good humour.' The *News of the World* praised the film and said that it 'belongs to the two marines played by Tony Curtis and Frank Lovejoy'.

His next movie was *Johnny Dark*, a drama about sports car enthusiasts and their efforts to get a new model off the assembly line, and it cast him once more, and for the last time, with Piper Laurie. The *Hollywood Reporter* noted that the director George Sherman 'uses the pertness of Miss Laurie's profile and the good-natured persistence of Mr Curtis's personality in a way that will delight the public'.

While Tony's burgeoning career was still full of potential, he was discovering what it was like to be married, as revealed in a frank fan magazine article of the day. Janet was very fastidious, and he wasn't. She was always picking up his clothes and putting them away, leading to arguments. When she decided to let him take care of his own clothes, he turned up one day at the studio wearing odd socks, and when this was pointed out to him, he said, 'I got another pair at home just like them. Ask Janet!'

She was always quick to put anything of his away, and he became quick to tell her, 'Leave that right where it is,' and when she replied, 'But I was just putting it away. I know where it goes,' he insisted angrily, 'I *know* where it goes and *I'll* put it away.'

She led an efficient and systematic life in which every meal with carefully planned dietary needs, every outing and every invitation was recorded in a planning book. He never planned ahead and lived life on whims and spontaneity, and when he saw the planning and appointments book, he said, 'Honey, I love you, but that thing has got to go.'

He admitted at the time that his biggest adjustments in marriage were 'learning to live with a woman', and 'learning to accept responsibility'. He said, 'I'm a gypsy at heart. Janet plans ahead, but that's very difficult for me.' He confessed to not being 'very punctual; I'm very bad in this respect – in fact, I'm impossible.' He also disliked having regulated meals, claiming he had always been 'a confirmed muncher. I just like to munch all day long.'

Janet explained, 'He was working so hard at the studio, and his father was ill, and I was anxious for him to keep his strength up.'

Tony objected and told her, 'You're trying to make me eat and I don't feel like eating.'

Fans were reassured that the couple seemed to have come to a compromise by which Janet tried to learn 'not to have everything on schedule – and not to let it bother me'. But what fans didn't know is that they were already reading about the slow disintegration of their favourite Hollywood couple.

'I blow money whenever I get the chance, many times for things I don't even need,' Tony admitted in print. 'Like more shoes and shirts and records. And I buy pipe cleaners by the gross. I can't resist pipe cleaners. I wish I knew why. I don't even smoke [a pipe].'

Amazingly, they seemed happy to lambast each other in print about new-found revelations. 'He's cranky when he first gets up,' Janet revealed, 'and says things without even knowing he's saying them. A little later he'll ask me why *I'm* acting peevish.' (This was something that never changed, and when Tony was making *The Persuaders* in 1970/71, the series production manager Johnny Goodman noted that if he said 'hi' to Tony when he first arrived at the studio, Tony would reply, 'Fuck off!' When Tony emerged from make-up, he was once again all charm and friendly smiles.)

Of her, he said, 'Janet doesn't know how to relax. To her leisure means emptying ash trays, cleaning out the desk and bureau drawers.'

He believed that money was earned to be spent. She thought it was best to save it. He came from a background where a nickel earned or found was a nickel to spend there and then because it brightened up his dull, dark life in which money had long been scarce. He remembered how his father would come home with some kitchen gadget he had managed to purchase. 'Carrot-curlers, that type of thing,' recalled Tony. 'He would say, "Here, let me show you how it works," and it never worked! But this was fun and we would all laugh.'

Janet knew, before they married, that it wasn't going to be easy. 'There were all these great differences between our backgrounds and our personalities – great *chasms* – and I knew well that we would have to be unselfish with each other. I felt we could only try and see.'

Despite these light-hearted confessions about their domestic clashes, Tony was increasingly resentful about the way she was trying to change him. He said in 2008, 'Janet was bossing me around, just as my mother had bossed my father around, which only made my flashbacks to childhood more intense.'

But it wasn't all disharmony, and there was a lot of happiness – that was clear more from talking to Janet Leigh in 1984 than from ever talking to Tony Curtis. Unhindered by bitter memories of the marriage, she told me, 'I was hopelessly, passionately in love with Tony.'

One of the problems they overcame was that of their different faiths. God wasn't really a major factor in Tony's life, but while he had no strong religious beliefs as a Jew, he was extremely cognisant of his Jewishness. How could he not be? Since he was a child he had been called 'Jew boy', and had faced anti-Semitism at school, in the navy, and then in Hollywood.

Considering the number of studio heads and producers, and also directors and writers, in Hollywood who were Jews, it may seem surprising that there might be anti-Semitism among actors in Hollywood. Many actors looked down on studio heads, who they regarded as mere moneymakers, trading in the talents of the stars who were, after all, the ones who attracted audiences. In later years, stars from the studio system would bemoan the fact that those studio heads had been replaced by accountants who cared nothing for creativity and only for commerce. The moguls like Louis B. Mayer at MGM and Harry Cohn of Columbia loved movies, and they skilfully balanced creativity with commerce.

Many of Hollywood's greatest directors had been Jews who fled anti-Semitism in Europe, such as William Wyler and Billy Wilder. Most movie stars would have given countless eye teeth and right arms to work with directors like them.

But among actors, Jews were second class, and Negros less than that. Tony was acutely aware of it and, unlike many other actors who were Jewish, he not only refused to hide it but actively promoted himself in interviews from his earliest days in Hollywood as a Jewish boy from New York. The studio star system had tried to disguise his Jewish roots, as it had to Jeff Chandler and Kirk Douglas, and later to Paul Newman. Tony was so incensed by this that he made a point of giving frank interviews about his background to the fan magazines, knowing this was the way he would reach his biggest audience, so before the studio could prevent it from happening, millions of fans were reading headlines like 'TONY CURTIS SAYS, I WAS BEATEN UP FOR BEING A JEW.'

'I wasn't going to hide behind a mask,' he told me, 'and I wasn't going to try to make myself into some kind of Jewish symbolic figure. I was simply trying to say that I had come from nothing and got to where I was because I thought that was something to celebrate. I never lied about my background or about the times I was beaten up for being a Jew. I told it like it was. I'm pugnacious like that. I'm honest. But I guess some people took umbrage at that.'

Yet the dichotomy was that he had tried to bury his identity by changing his name. He once told me, 'I don't wanna be a Jew, but I *am* a Jew, so I wanna *be* a Jew as I can't *not* be a Jew – it's no wonder I'm nuts!'

He was acutely aware that there were factions in Hollywood society where he wasn't welcome because he was a Jew, and he felt there was bias against him for marrying a Gentile. But Janet had many friends among the Hollywood greats, and some of them accepted him. Despite mocking his accent in *Son of Ali Baba*, Debbie Reynolds was one of the first. A large section of Hollywood society revolved around her, including Gene Kelly and his wife, Henry Fonda and his wife, and Mr and Mrs George Sidney. But Tony never felt totally comfortable and was paranoid that his Jewishness, his poor upbringing and lack of education were all drawbacks, and he felt that Debbie and her friends simply accepted him for the sake of Janet.

Debbie Reynolds went on to marry Eddie Fisher, a Jew. Henry Fonda told me, 'I despise any kind of prejudice, racial or otherwise. I've always been a liberal. I'll not be counted among the right-wing Conservatives who don't like blacks, Jews or communists.' Gene Kelly invited Tony to his house a number of times to teach him some of his own stunt techniques. But still Tony couldn't always tell the anti-Semitics from the non-prejudiced movie stars he mingled with.

'I was still being held back by my background,' he told me. 'It was hard for me, you know? I had trouble keeping my equilibrium in those days. I felt there were people who didn't want me around them.'

To help maintain his equilibrium he smoked marijuana, a substance not then recognised as one which increased paranoia in a user who had a predisposition towards psychological dysfunction. And if anyone ever had such a predisposition, it was Bernie Schwartz/Tony Curtis, a man who was never entirely one or the other; he fought for years to become the latter, while the former never let him go.

'It [cannabis] was everywhere in Hollywood,' he told me. 'Later it would be cocaine, but back then it was dope. It wasn't addictive, and it wasn't harmful.' (Recent studies would dispute that.) 'I was having trouble winding down, or just getting calm, and someone [Robert Mitchum] said, "Try one of these." I knew what it was when I had it.'

Tony's co-workers often spoke about his use of marijuana, sometimes with humour, sometimes with disdain. Ken Annakin, who directed him in *Monte Carlo Or Bust* in 1969, told me with distaste, 'He smoked it all the time.' Sir Roger Moore remembered, with a smile, that Tony smoked a joint while they waited to shoot on the steps of 10 Downing Street for a short scene in *The Persuaders*. 'He's probably the only person to smoke marijuana at 10 Downing Street,' said Sir Roger.

I don't think Tony used cannabis heavily in those early days, and I think he may have stopped using it for a while when he became close friends with Frank Sinatra, who was so anti-drugs that when he discovered Peter Lawford and Sammy Davis Jr were using, he cast them both out of his presence for a time.

Tony had first got to know Sinatra when they did the Variety Club show in London in 1951, and then got to know him better through Dean Martin. The Curtises had begun to spend time with Dean and his wife Betty after their friendship with Jerry Lewis waned. Tony said he found Lewis was becoming unpleasant to be around and Lewis had told him, 'You think you're going to be a star? You'll never be bigger than me.'

Sinatra asked Tony to do him a favour by making a guest appearance in his film, *Meet Danny Wilson*, in which Sinatra played a singer, unsurprisingly, working in a club which attracted celebrities. Tony and Jeff Chandler appear as themselves, sitting in the club and listening to Sinatra sing.

Sinatra often invited Tony and Janet to come up to his house on Carolwood Drive. Sometimes Frank called close to midnight, telling Tony to come over but leave Janet at home. She seemed not to mind, so he would duly arrive at Sinatra's to watch a movie in his private cinema where there would be other guests, including some pretty girls. Tony would have a drink, and after the movie started he usually fell asleep. He'd wake up when it was over, have some food, flirt with the girls, then head for home for a few hours' sleep before getting up to go to work. He found being Frank's friend could be very tiring but was always fun.

He said of Frank, 'He wouldn't let anybody see a weakness in him. And if you saw something in him, he wouldn't just bawl you out, he'd say, "Get the fuck out of my face or I'll knock your head off." So I was never sure. But he liked me a lot, and that meant a lot to me. To be a friend of Frank's was a great help in those early days. I didn't abuse it or take advantage of it. I would just make myself available when he would call or want to go out to dinner.'

I once asked Frank Sinatra what he thought of Tony Curtis. He said, 'I love the guy. He was like me. He came from nothing and he went to the top and beat the odds. The odds were against him, but he fucking beat them all. I like that about him. I also like that he's a loyal friend and you can't say that about too many people in this business.'

The Curtises were not able to afford to throw their own large Hollywood parties at their home on Summit Drive. Besides, Tony didn't care for Hollywood parties, but Janet did and used them as a means of networking, which worked in her favour and his also. Her friends, whom she had known before she met him, invariably outnumbered his. One of them, Danny Kaye, made wisecracks about Tony's height and his background in the Bronx. Tony simply told him, 'Fuck you, Danny!'

'Danny Kaye was an asshole,' Tony said. 'But nobody's perfect!'

They were both from New York, and both Jewish. But the public didn't know Kaye was Jewish, and Tony had become aware that other Jews were often uncomfortable around him. They were closet Jews, and Tony was out, the first American movie star almost as famous for being a Jew as for being an actor. It was a chip on his shoulder that he dared the studios to take away from him, basically saying, 'Take it or leave it, it's who I am.'

But he was losing sight of who he was. Or perhaps he'd never really found out who he was, or thought he was. His paranoia was reaching a peak, and he admitted to Janet that he was scared. When she asked him what of, he said he didn't know but that even though he knew everything was going great for them in their work, he was jumpy all the time, and his moods had become erratic, up one moment, down the next.

He related to her an experience on the set of *Johnny Dark*. 'I'm standing on the set, and the fellow came up and sort of looked at me funny. So I said, "What's the matter, you don't like my clothes?" So he said, "I never said a word about your clothes." And I got furious. I said, "Don't you tell me that. You're looking at them like you don't like them. Now get outa here. Don't stare at me. Beat it." And then I found out he wasn't staring at me. He wasn't disliking my clothes or anything. He was just standing there, that's all.'

He could be extremely rude to people. Some directors, like Ken Annakin and Roy Ward Baker (*The Persuaders*), spoke of his sudden and surprising rudeness on the set. Others, such as Richard Fleischer (*The Vikings* and *The Boston Strangler*) recognised that he had demons. 'It was only at odd times when he suddenly became difficult, and then he would realise it and apologise. I came to realise, especially on *The Boston Strangler*, perhaps because of its subject matter, that he had a very dark and troubled side to his personality. I don't know what it was, but *something* made him do those things.'

When that sliver of schizophrenia came through and he needed to calm down, he smoked dope, and that way he somehow managed to survive – for the time being.

CHAPTER NINE

As Lew Wasserman had planned, the screen partnership of Curtis and Leigh completely overshadowed the old partnership of Curtis and Laurie when Hollywood's golden couple were cast in *The Black Shield of Falworth* at Universal. Tony was having reservations about them working together again. 'There are pressures on a movie,' he said. 'There are pressures at home. Sometimes it can be the worst thing to bring your home problems to work, or your work problems home. We decided we'd keep everything at work purely professional.

'We had a scene where I took her in a clinch and kissed her. It was our first love scene in the picture. We thought we were very professional and behaved like two actors screen kissing, but [director] Rudy Maté just shook his head in disbelief, and said, "No one would believe you are man and wife. Please, let's do it again, and try to look as though you really love each other."'

Perhaps Tony was simply having trouble maintaining the image of a happily married couple. Janet had no problem at all.

The workload was heavy with a good deal of night and day shooting, so for the duration of filming Tony and Janet lived in their bungalow dressing room at the studio. 'In those days you didn't just have a dressing room. You had somewhere you could actually *live*, it was so big and comfortable,' Janet recalled. 'It had trees around it and a sprawling lawn. The studio was called Universal City, and it *was* like a city, and so were all the major studios. All the big stars had big bungalows on the studio lots, and Tony and I were given our own which was really Tony's as he was under contract there.'

It was a physically demanding film for Tony, who had to ride horses, wield a lance, leap about and fight with real swords. 'Oh, those swords were as real as they could be,' he told me. 'Heavy, too. You could get hurt.' And he did, slightly.

Janet recalled, 'During one of the fencing scenes his opponent missed his timing and caught Tony's cheek and it drew blood. This was for a close-up so he had to do it. Dave Sharp was the name of Tony's stunt double. He was a sweet guy. He felt *he* should have done the scene, but Tony would always do as much as he could, no matter how dangerous. It wasn't a deep cut, but if the sword had caught him a quarter of an inch higher it would have caught his eye. They covered it up with plenty of make-up.'

She never gave any indication, in my interview with her or in her autobiography, that she thought anything was seriously wrong with their marriage during *The Black Shield of Falworth*, but Tony wrote that when they finished working on the movie, they both agreed to make an effort to behave in a way that didn't anger or upset each other, and thereafter settled into 'a functional but unromantic marriage'.

The film was hugely popular but, while the critics generally liked the film, some took delight in mentioning his accent, such as the *Monthly Film Bulletin*, which said, 'As the bold English knight, Tony Curtis reveals great athletic prowess and much determination, but, alas, his voice betrays him. Altogether, a straight-forward piece of hokum, with no pretentions and spoken in a variety of accents that only Hollywood could muster.'

TIME said, 'He is possibly one of the few belted knights in history to say "Mayhap" with a Brooklyn accent.' Ignoring the accent, the *Motion Picture Herald* said, 'Tony Curtis leads nimble vigour to his role of a young peasant.'

The Curtises moved again, into a spacious rented house at 2018 Coldwater Canyon, where there was a studio for Tony to paint in. It had a large patio with a pool, and their social life gathered momentum. Tony became good friends with actor José Ferrer, whose aristocratic polish and dramatic flair Tony hoped might rub off on him, and Sammy Davis Jr became a close friend. 'Janet and Tony were making it as big movie stars before I did, and I spent a lot of time with them,' Sammy Davis told me. 'They didn't care if I wasn't as big as them. They and Jeff Chandler were my best friends.'

Few friends were closer to Tony than Jeff Chandler. 'I always felt Jeff kept Tony's feet on the ground, or kept them from being too far off the ground,' said Janet. Sammy Davis told me, 'There was Janet and Tony and Jeff, who were all close buddies, and then there was me, the little black kid who'd made one record, and they accepted me because they had no prejudice. I wanted to be a big star like them. Frank Sinatra was the biggest, and a great friend, but Jeff and Tony and Janet never let me down.'

As Hollywood's most celebrated married couple, the Curtises were invited to a number of big parties, often to their utmost surprise, such as when Joan Crawford invited them for dinner. Janet recalled, 'Her children were in brief impeccable attendance.' Everything in Crawford's house was perfect, as was the party itself. Janet noticed Crawford was attracted to Tony, and by her own admission she felt jealous. Tony recalled, 'I couldn't even look at another woman without Janet making out like I was already getting her into bed.'

Another big Hollywood party they attended was at the home of Gary Cooper and his wife Rocky. 'I felt we were in the company of royalty, and that's when I realised *we* had become Hollywood royalty,' said Janet.

Although celebrated in fan magazines as everyone's favourite Hollywood couple, they became the target of the gossip columnists, who somehow got to hear about even the smallest of tiffs and wrote about them, adding strain on the marriage.

When Janet went to visit a friend in Tucson, Arizona, for a christening, one columnist wrote that they couldn't 'deny the rumours' any longer, without specifying what those rumours were. Tony was furious, especially when reporters began calling him to get a comment. He told Janet, 'They kept calling me and I keep telling them you're in Arizona for a baby's christening, and they think that sounds really phoney.'

A story appeared in a newspaper that Janet had kicked Tony in a fight. The reporter had seen Tony limping at a party and that was his evidence for the story. In fact, that was the time he had tripped over a cable when making *Houdini*. Janet threatened to sue, and the columnist issued an apology.

After one of many late nights, Tony was, as usual, grumpy in the morning, and there was an argument over breakfast. He went to work to do some dubbing, and later in the morning she called him at the studio to clear the air. Their conversation was overheard, and a story appeared saying the couple were fighting.

Columnists reported Janet was pregnant every couple of months. She remarked at the time, 'They say that so often that some day, when it's true, they'll be able to boast, "You read it here first."'

In 1954, Tony made *So This is Paris*, an unashamed rip-off of *On the Town*. Tony was one of three American sailors on leave in Paris, encountering girls, orphans, local society and gendarmes. The whole film was quickly shot on the Universal lot. Tony was put through a crash course by Gene Nelson, his co-star and the film's choreographer, who provided Tony with dance steps that looked good enough without being too difficult.

Gloria DeHaven, whom Tony had locked eyes with at the Hollywood Canteen, was the leading lady; very quickly there was a mutual attraction and they embarked on an affair, spending weekends together at the Beverly Hills Hotel. He fell in love with her but she put no pressure on him to leave Janet. They continued to see each other when the movie was finished until, as Tony put it, 'everyday life intervened'.

Tony proved himself to be a rather pleasant though untrained singer, and was never ashamed of what he accomplished in that movie. He told me, 'That was my first and only musical. I liked it, y'know. They make a big thing of musicals. One doesn't have to be that good a singer or that good a dancer. You gotta have flair and an attitude and a confidence about it. I never did coz that was never my bag. I never thought that was so desirable for me. It didn't mean that much to me.

'If I'd wanted to, in fact, I could have done that. I had a great opportunity at that age to start playing a guitar. I could've predated Elvis Presley by several years, ya know. Not that I would have been as good or as bad. That's immaterial. But the opportunity was there. I could've learned to sing. Singing is – what? Expressing what you have to say in another way. I mean, my voice was pleasant and if I'd continued it, if I'd had a bug in my head about wanting to be a singer like I had a bug in my head about wanting to be a movie star – a movie *actor* – I'd be a singer today.'

Next, Tony got what he most desired – a challenging role. In *Six Bridges to Cross* he got to flex acting muscles he'd never used. Gone was the charming, romantic, teen-idol image and in its place was a punk from the wrong side of the tracks, growing up to become a crime boss whose gang knocks off an armoured car and steals more than two million dollars. He's shot dead at the end.

It was based on the infamous Boston Brinks Robbery of 1950, described as 'the perfect crime'. Producer Aaron Rosenberg personally cast Tony as gangster Jerry Florea, and made the decision to film all the location scenes in Boston. Janet went too, but had to return to Los Angeles midway through production to begin work on her next movie, *My Sister Eileen*.

The film opened with a sequence featuring Florea as a young hoodlum. Aaron Rosenberg said, 'It made sense to cast a younger actor as the Curtis character when he was a boy. We needed someone who looked kind of like Tony. His mother wanted his younger brother, Robert, to play the part, and she was pretty persistent about it.'

Tony couldn't believe his mother thought that Bobby could even hope to be an actor with such a severe mental illness, but to keep her quiet he asked for some favours at Universal, and the studio had some photos taken of Bobby. 'We couldn't cast the boy because he was very troubled,' said Rosenberg, 'but we found a great young actor, Sal Mineo, and it kicked off his career.'

Helen blamed Tony for Bobby not getting the part.

Reviews were good. 'Curtis gives the character a good reading, rating a modicum of sympathy even though viewers know he is unregenerated and must die at the finale,' said *Variety*. The *News of the World* thought, 'The film belongs to Florea. And as that brash bandit is played by crew-cut Tony Curtis with his continual twisted smile I need say no more.'

Janet was still filming *My Sister Eileen*, usually working on Saturdays, when Tony finished filming and returned to Los Angeles, so he spent weekends with Frank Sinatra. Returning home one Saturday, he found a letter to Janet from Bob Fosse, who was choreographing the musical number in her film, which, in part, read, 'I can't wait to see you. When you're coming, please let me know.'

Tony's jealousy and paranoia kicked in. An involuntary image of Janet in bed with Fosse played over and over in his head, and he became increasingly upset and angry and probably schizophrenic. 'The times I heard, "She's cheated!" and "You can't trust her!"' he told me, and this must have been one of those times because he found no relief from his jealousy while Janet went to work with Fosse day after day until the film was finished.

He told me, 'It was like a movie running through my head. I couldn't turn it off. I tell ya, I figured I was going mad. I think I was. I think I had a mental breakdown. I was scared I was like my brother. I thought it had finally caught up with me.'

Janet recalled, 'He was sure I was having affairs, but I never did. I *could* have. But my marriage was too important to me.'

It's very likely that Fosse was enamoured of Janet and trying to instigate an affair. 'Janet was a beautiful lady,' Robert Wagner told me. 'She must have had any number of guys after her, but as far as I know she was always loyal to Tony.'

Tony justified the affairs *he* had by telling himself that Janet was being unfaithful. Convinced she was in love with Bob Fosse, he decided that he would have as many affairs as he wanted to without guilt. Desperate for some form of escape from the home he shared with the woman he considered to be a cheating wife, he took solace at the mansion of *Playboy* publisher Hugh Hefner in Chicago for a weekend, where he spent the time in the arms of sympathetic bunny girls.

Yet despite his jealousy, despite what he considered to be a broken marriage, he didn't attempt to leave Janet. And as far as Janet was concerned, there was no great problem in the marriage at that time.

Tony was back in swashbuckling mode for *The Purple Mask*, as a count who dons a purple mask to battle the villains in France at the time of Napoleon. He played the part with his tongue firmly in his cheek, as the *Monthly Film Bulletin* noted: 'Tony Curtis's evident decision to refuse to take seriously this ponderous piece of "period" writing was perhaps a wise one. The result is an engaging single turn which leaves the rest of the cast to their fate.'

Then he stepped straight into *The Square Jungle*, a fair boxing picture in which he played a young guy with no prospects who turns to boxing and becomes a champ. 'Curtis responds well to the directorial demands of Jerry Hopper as a young man who turns to the ring to raise bail money for his drunken father and goes on to become middleweight champion,' said *Variety*. The *Motion Picture Herald* noted Tony's improvement as an actor, saying, 'Tony Curtis piles up a telling score of points for himself as a performer in this trim tale of a boxer who learns more than the manly art of self defence from a trainer quite as tellingly played by Ernest Borgnine.'

Towards the end of 1955 Tony was reaching his limit of emotional endurance. He perceived his marriage to be in terrible trouble, and on top of all that he was plagued by his mother's constant complaining. He gave her the responsibility for renting out twelve garden apartments he had purchased, but she was constantly calling him about complaints from the tenants that he considered to be of her own making. He still had to support his parents and Bobby – Janet recalled that Manny had had another mild heart attack – and all the time Helen was increasing the pressure on Tony. Janet's own parents were, as she put it, 'at a low ebb in their war of attrition'.

He sank into a deep depression and confided all his problems to Bob Raines, head of casting at Universal. Raines recommended he see a psychiatrist and explained that his insurance would pay for it all. Tony took his advice.

Possibly as part of his therapy, he wrote a surprisingly frank account of his time in analysis for a fan magazine. 'I remember writing that,' he told me in 1980. 'I like writing. I always wrote things, like poems, even when I was a kid.' He published some of those poems in his first autobiography. His feature for the fan magazine was remarkably frank for its time, and also demonstrated an early effort by Tony Curtis to become a writer, a craft he never completely mastered.

> It was a beautiful day, clear and sunny, the kind of day that makes a person feel glad to be alive. I slammed the door of my car and stood for a moment, looking up and down the street. There were some kids playing ball in a vacant lot, a policeman passing the time of day with a grocer on the corner. The sound of laughter and juke box music coming from a bar; its door was open. A nice day for everybody, it seemed – except for me.
>
> Glad to be alive? I was anything but! Walking down the street was an effort. I looked at the buildings for the number, hoping I wouldn't find it. But there it was, just looking at me. I couldn't put off going inside any longer. My hand on the door knob was clammy. I pushed it open, and my heart started to pound so hard I could feel it. I, Tony Curtis, was going to see a psychiatrist.
>
> Well, truthfully, the first time I went I was scared stiff. But I wasn't going to show it – not me! After all, I knew pretty much about what went on in a psychiatrist's office.
>
> 'Where's the couch?' I tried to make the question sound

breezy, but I *was* surprised there wasn't a couch in sight. Everybody knew that was standard equipment – the place where you stretched out and bared your soul.

I tried to keep up the banter as the doctor waved me to a comfortable chair, and I sat down on the edge of it. 'What do I talk about?' I blurted. 'Sex?'

He smiled. 'If you like.'

[At that point in the article he related the story of when he was at P.S. 82 and going on twelve and had a crush on the cute little blonde who slapped him when he tried to put his arm around her, and how Ann, with the big scar on her face, taught him how to kiss.]

'Now isn't that exciting?' I asked the doctor.

'It must have had some meaning for you,' he replied, 'or you wouldn't have remembered.'

I leaned back in the chair. It was funny but I didn't feel nervous anymore. I felt relaxed and at ease as I hadn't felt in ages.

I mention this to show that my experiences with an analyst was not a long period of agony, as a lot of people say their 'treatments' have been. The relationship between the doctor and me was like an easy conversation between friends, with only a few periods when I became disturbed.

[He wrote about telling the analyst about being beaten up for being a Jew, and about the time, after being discharged from the navy, when he went looking for the German guy who had bullied him at school, hit him, and then cried.]

As I told my analyst about it, I looked down at the floor. But I couldn't hide the feeling of shame that I could feel was reddening my face. So I seized at a straw – an incident that was always a source of secret pride to me. I didn't realise that it was also an outburst of violence, this time directed at other things.

[There followed his accounts of further beatings, and about leaping across rooftops and from high buildings.]

My analyst pointed out that this feeling is not unusual, that people aren't normal who don't have a craving for achievement. But now I could see that I had used it as a protection against my terrible insecurity.

I went on to the analyst three times a week. His office became a pleasant, familiar place. There was a soft rug on the floor, and the colours were all restful. The sun streamed through the windows in the afternoon. But it didn't make it any easier for me to tell him all these things.

Sometimes, I'd come home shaken, as a result of having relived one of these experiences in our talks. Janet was wonderful – patient and understanding – though it must have been tough on her too. But gradually, from the analyst I was learning something very important – the great influences of a person's childhood experiences on his behaviour as an adult. Now I was beginning to understand *why* I did things I was ashamed of, in spite of myself. *Why* I had kept on running away from them – and myself – for so long. When I learned that it was merely a reaction set by events in my childhood, which I could not control because I didn't understand it, it was as if a great burden had fallen from my shoulders.

[He wrote at length about his discussion with the analyst about Julie's death, and the effect it had on him.]

A few weeks before the accident, a friend of mine named Mike [this 'Mike' is actually his Italian friend Frank] took me to services at his church. When he went up to the altar rail to take communion I did exactly what he did. He was horrified. 'You've committed a sin,' he said. 'Now something terrible is going to happen.'

I felt this was one of the reasons God took my brother away from me.

All in all, I'm glad that I did go through psychoanalysis, because the experience has helped me to understand the emotional and intellectual changes I have gone through in my life and up until now, and freed me from the fear and guilt that had made me miserable.

It is evident that even in the full and much longer version of this feature, he omitted any mention of his mother's violent personality, or any suggestion that he may suffer from bouts of schizophrenia. He went to see his psychiatrist three times a week for four years, and it cost him (or his insurers) $30,000 – those subjects *must* have come up.

He told me a little of what he left out of that fan magazine article, not to demonstrate why he didn't write about them but simply as an example of what he talked about with his analyst.

> I told him about my early sexual experiences, and about the first time I ejaculated in my pants when holding the hand of a girl in the cinema. We hadn't even done anything – just held hands. I had some problems in that area. I never knew when I was a kid when I would actually have real sex with a girl, and it never took much for me to ejaculate. When I had my first real experience with a woman she was a whore. I was in the navy. I knew I'd ejaculate straight away, so I went into the men's room first and jerked off so I would last longer, but when I was having sex with the hooker I still had an orgasm very quickly.
>
> I had to have sex all the time. When I got out to Hollywood I was having sex with every girl I met – well, *almost* every girl. They were starlets, extras, girls from wardrobe. I'd have them anywhere – the back seat of my car, or at the home of my friend Nicky Blair. I'd call him and say, 'Can I use your place?' and he'd say, 'Sure, I'll go out some place.' And he did that for me.
>
> It took a long time, a lot of visits, for me to tell the psychiatrist all that stuff. In a funny way, I enjoyed it. I *love* talking about myself. In the end I felt I had gotten all I could out of it and stopped.

He said he never really found the answers to the terrible guilt he felt about his brother's death. 'I started in analysis with the thought that somehow everything would come to me in a blinding flash. It didn't. There are still some answers I don't have.'

His guilt over Julie's death never waned. However, analysis helped him to become far more settled, considerate and determined to make his marriage a success.

CHAPTER TEN

Safari To Paris

Although he was bored being stuck in the mainly routine modestly budgeted movies Universal was churning out, Tony Curtis never refused a picture as he felt that he owed it to the studio to behave professionally. That was partly Lew Wasserman's influence. He told Tony to keep doing good work and he would get his reward in time.

Burt Lancaster was preparing to make a movie about circus life. He was one of a new breed of movie star who had come to Hollywood and signed a non-exclusive deal with producer Hal Wallis, then at Paramount, allowing him to make movies for other studios. Kirk Douglas and Charlton Heston had the same deal with Wallis. Lancaster had quickly become one of the more powerful actors outside the studio system by setting himself up as a producer in partnership with Harold Hecht and James Hill. They were about to make *Trapeze*, and Burt wanted Tony to co-star with him.

Trapeze was a labour of love for Burt, who played a famous trapeze artist injured and unable to fly in the circus. Lancaster thought that Tony, with his genuine athletic ability, would be perfect as the enthusiastic rookie who persuades the injured artist into teaching him to fly the trapeze. Wasserman negotiated a fee of $150,000 for Tony.

At first, Ed Muhl, head of Universal, refused to loan Tony out. Wasserman tried to convince Muhl that *Trapeze* would make Tony a bigger star and that would be good for Universal, but Muhl would not be moved, so Burt Lancaster got involved in the discussions. Between then, Lancaster and Wasserman finally persuaded Muhl to loan Tony out to Hecht-Hill-Lancaster.

Tony recalled that Universal warned him to steer clear of *Trapeze* because circus pictures never did well, with the exception of Cecil B. DeMille's *The Greatest Show on Earth*, which everyone thought was the ultimate circus film and couldn't be bettered.

Tony ignored the advice. 'In Hollywood, they all tell you you're making a mistake, whatever you do. As you usually are, they're onto a safe bet. But I did *Trapeze*, and I thought that, at the time, acting with real professionals like Burt and director Carol Reed, that if I was still working when it came out, I'd got it made.'

Trapeze was to be made in France in 1955 and, since Tony would be away from home for several weeks, Janet accepted a picture, *Safari*, to be shot in Africa and at Elstree Studios in England. She decided to give her mother a break from her domestic problems by taking her along. She could have gone with Tony to France, and he pleaded with her not to make *Safari*, fearing the separation would irreparably damage the marriage which he obviously thought was salvageable, but Janet wanted to work. She would be able to fly each weekend to be with him in Paris while she was in England. Her decision dented his ego, or maybe it was vanity – he often thought his wives didn't appreciate how attractive he was – and it hurt his feelings that she chose her work over him.

Many years later he admitted he had been a male chauvinist, and also that he was selfish and demanding. I think he simply sought to be loved in a highly demonstrative way to make up for all the love and affection he had been denied as a child and which he still didn't receive from his parents, particularly his mother, during his rise to stardom.

Tony again refused to fly so went by ship to France. 'Anywhere I went was by boat, train or pack mule,' he recalled. 'I never got forty feet off the ground. It was written into every contract that I had that I would not fly to a location. So if a studio wanted me bad enough, they'd take me without flying. I was even using that excuse as a club. It was one way of making it difficult for a studio; I would be saying, "Let's see how much they really want me."'

During his voyage to France, he called and cabled Janet every day. By the time he next saw her, they had been apart for two weeks. They both found the separation tough.

His fear of flying had nothing to do with heights, and he had no anxiety about working on a trapeze. He trained at the Cirque d'Hiver with his trapeze stunt double, Fay Alexander, who taught him to land properly in the net, and how to swing on the trapeze, time his release, fly and be caught by Burt. All this meant Tony could do many of his own stunts in close-up, while Fay Alexander performed the most dangerous feats in long shot.

Tony didn't get off to a good start with the film's Italian leading lady, Gina Lollobrigida. She disliked his trademark hairstyle and pressured Lancaster and Hecht to make Tony cut it. He reluctantly agreed, but he resented her for having his mop of hair cut to a crop. 'Tony only ever had one problem,' Burt Lancaster told me. 'He had a lot of vanity, but not enough ego. You got to have more ego than vanity, and I felt that held him back.'

When Janet arrived in London, she discovered she wasn't imme-diately needed, so she cabled Tony that she was coming to join him immediately. He went to meet her that night at the airport, and when told by a messenger boy that arrangements had been made so he could go on to the runway, he took off at a run with the messenger boy sprinting behind, waving a pad and calling for an autograph. Tony took the pad and signed it while on the run.

Discovering the plane wasn't actually due yet, he went to the lounge, dropped into a chair and took out a cigarette. Before he could reach for his lighter, a match was suddenly struck, and Tony looked up to see a GI offering the light. He thanked him, and then signed autographs and posed for photographs for the GI and a bunch of other homesick soldiers. The arrival of Air France Flight 279 from London was announced, and he was led by an airport official to the runway and watched the plane come in. Members of the press had been alerted and were hurrying to witness the reunion. Disembarking passengers gathered to watch Janet Leigh come down the steps and into Tony's arms, followed by Mrs Morrison, who found herself surrounded by reporters wanting to know what it was like to have Tony Curtis for a son-in-law.

Tony packed his wife and mother-in-law into a waiting car and they left the airport for 2 Rue Spontini, where he had an apartment on the fifth floor. After settling in, Mrs Morrison went to her room while Tony and Janet enjoyed a passionate reunion in their bedroom. He had a surprise gift for her; a diamond ring set in gold which he slipped on to the fourth finger of her right hand. 'Welcome to Paris,' he told her. He was making a huge effort to heal all marital wounds.

He suggested she take her mother on a tour of the art galleries as he was working in the morning. It was to be the first day of filming at the Cirque d'Hiver. She told him, 'Don't be silly, I came here to see *you*, not the art galleries.'

The next morning he went to work and Janet and her mother joined him later, arriving to find him working on the bars, under the instruction of trapeze artistes Eddie Ward and Fay Alexander. 'Tony really put everything into learning how to fly on the trapeze,' Burt Lancaster told me. 'When Janet saw him for the first time standing on the bars, she screamed. He just got onto the rope and descended like a real circus veteran. His dedication helped make that film possible.'

He kissed Janet and his mother-in-law, and found them seats with the best view, and then climbed back up again. Janet recalled the circus as 'a huge, rather smelly, flea-infested circus ring'. The large Klieg lights brought the temperature in the circus to almost 95 degrees. On top of the smell and the heat, she was growing more anxious as she watched Tony working so high up. 'My heart was in my mouth the whole time,' she said.

She felt a lot easier the next day when they filmed the big circus parade down the Champs-Elysées. Tony, Burt Lancaster, Gina Lollobrigida and Katy Jurado rode down the great boulevard of Paris on their float, dressed in their dazzling circus costumes, and behind them came the animals and chariots. Janet remembered thinking how handsome Tony looked with his hair now cut to a crop. She and her mother followed the parade in the comfort of a studio car through streets lined with spectators, most of which were American tourists come to flash their cameras at Hollywood royalty.

As the parade neared the Place de la Concorde, Tony looked back from his float and called to Janet to join him, but being so far back she couldn't hear him, so the message was relayed all the way, and she wound up travelling on the float for the rest of the parade as it wound its way back to the circus grounds. She stood at his side, waving to the crowd and throwing kisses. 'Those were happy – *very* happy – days for us,' she told me.

Tony's progress with the trapeze was rapid, and he amazed the professional artistes by flying without a safety belt. He had become what was called in the circus a 'yugo', because as an apprentice flyer he stood on the platform catching the bars and waiting for the command, 'Now next time, you go!'

Unsurprisingly, Janet watched all this with a great deal of trepidation. Tony often missed the bar and dropped into the net, and each time that happened, she literally leaped out of her seat and screamed. 'I couldn't help it,' she said. 'It was impossible not to.'

The following Sunday she flew back to London, and as the Monday was a French holiday, which meant there would be no filming, Tony went with her. He even found the courage to fly. He might not have remembered being desperately in love with her, but he must have been to take that short flight. 'We were really intense,' Janet told me. 'It seemed that when we were being separated and we had to find ways to be with each other, we were at our best.'

He watched her first day of filming at Elstree and, when she had a break, they found a haystack in a corner of the sound stage for a lusty roll. He returned to Paris, braving the short flight on his own, proving how determined he was to keep the marriage alive. She returned to Paris the following weekend and, at her suggestion, they moved into a sumptuous penthouse suite at the George V Hotel where the crew and supporting cast were staying, so that after she left for Kenya, he would always be able to find company with some of the film crew down in the bar or the other public rooms.

They were guests of Gina Lollobrigida and her husband Milko Skofic at a formal dinner at the exclusive Laurent restaurant. While most of the guests talked of little else but movies, Tony and Janet danced. 'It was like we would never let go,' she recalled. 'Tony was funny and romantic and danced me right outside.' They danced in the woods which shielded the restaurant from the Champs-Elysées.

Janet had a whole week to be with him before she had to set off to Africa, and as he had some days free too, they spent a lot of their time exploring. They hiked to the hilltop forest of Meudon and through the rustic villages of the countryside. She wore Bermuda shorts and one of Tony's old raincoats. He wore blue jeans and a striped jersey, and they avoided the inns and country restaurants, preferring to picnic. At the end of the week she left for Kenya, and they both promised to write letters and send cables.

Alone, Tony took the opportunity to inspect places frequented by artist Amedeo Modigliani, visiting his studio and standing where his mistress had jumped from his four-storey window the day after he died. 'I was lonely enough to relate to how she'd felt,' he recalled.

Filming in Kenya proved to be the most unpleasant experience of

Janet's career. The drive to the location through Mau Mau country was hair-raising as jeeps and trucks bounced along non-surfaced roads at an unsafe 60 miles per hour. On arrival, tents were set up for the cast and crew to live in. Janet's tent had a few luxuries – a bath, a wardrobe, two chairs and, to welcome her upon arrival, a bottle of whisky and a bunch of flowers. Her only true consolation was the presence of her mother.

She kept a daily diary of her activities and thoughts, most of which were of Tony (and were released for publication for publicity purposes). She wrote about the time a plane arrived one Sunday with three letters from Tony. 'I got so lonesome I started to cry at dinner. Pretty silly, but what are you going to do?'

On the Thursday she wrote, 'What great news. Found I had a day off and somebody used the wireless to arrange a call to Tony. How lucky I am to have a husband who loves me and lets me know it. His letters mean more than anything else to me out here.'

She was driven to the nearest small town for her wireless call. 'We waited at a hotel for the call to come through from Tony. I got so antsy-pantsy, and then finally it came. He hadn't received a letter for three days and was terribly worried. I was only sorry I couldn't reach out and touch the voice I was hearing. How I miss him.' The heat, the stress and a debilitating stomach bug all took their toll on her.

In Paris, Tony was enjoying the work, especially as Carol Reed was wringing out of him a really fine performance. He left each day's filming at the Billancourt Studios in Paris exhausted. After one evening's work, he decided not to bother changing out of his *Trapeze* clothes – striped jersey and old slacks – and just walked alone along Parisian streets. 'I found this little Italian place where you buy food to take out,' he recalled. 'I got a pizza and some fresh fruit, and ate them on the way back to the George V Hotel. Nobody even gave me a second glance. Except some Americans I ran into on the steps of the hotel. They gaped indignantly, obviously wondering how I got past the doorman!'

While Janet was lonely and thinking of him from her tent in Africa, he was keeping company with pretty French girls. He never saw his philandering as detrimental to his marriages. He told Dr Pamela Connolly, 'I was an excitable sexual guy. And why shouldn't I be? It's me. I'm not offending anybody if I found somebody who wanted to share it with me.'

He did miss Janet, but his feelings for her, his philandering and his jealousy over what he perceived to be her adultery all clashed and drove him into moments of depression, out of which he managed to clamber with the help of work, casual sex and reunions with Janet.

She had become increasingly unwell in Kenya, so producer Andy Worker gave her two weeks off to be with Tony in Paris. She wrote in her diary, 'I was so nervous and excited. The passengers couldn't get off fast enough for me and then there HE was. We started talking in the car and didn't stop the rest of the day. The apartment had surprises all over – flowers, candy, perfume and all of it was lovely. After everyone left, we had a little dinner and then went to bed. What a day!'

She was not fully recovered from her illness when she returned to Africa, but insisted on working all the same. With a further two weeks to go and with no sign of improvement in her health, she was sent to the Hospital for Tropical Diseases. Her illness proved to be a kidney infection, which was treated with antibiotics.

Tony was able to phone her regularly when the *Safari* unit returned to London for a final week of interiors. 'Tony called me three times today,' she told her diary. 'It is so horrible not to be able to help him – he really is miserable. Not too long now.'

When *Safari* was finished she flew to Paris, and recorded that the first thing they did was have a drink with Carol Reed 'and then came home. We necked the whole time in the car. Thought I was back in high school.'

They moved into a new apartment at the Elysées Park Hotel, 2 Rue Jean Mermoz. Mrs Morrison had returned to Los Angeles so they had their new temporary home to themselves. Janet was kept busy with publicity work while Tony filmed. She paid a visit to a doctor at the American Hospital in Paris and on 18 November it was confirmed, as she had hoped, that she was pregnant again. She broke the news immediately to Tony, and they decided to keep it secret. A few days later Carol Reed congratulated Tony on the set, telling him, 'You really didn't think you could keep this confidential, did you, dear boy?' They never discovered how anyone knew.

Because of the previous miscarriage, they agreed she had to rest and not work at all, and she needed to get back to full health after her kidney infection.

Tony celebrated impending fatherhood by buying a gullwing Mercedes, 300 SL model in metallic grey with red leather. His plan, when the picture was over, was that he and Janet would drive to Italy to board the ship to take them home. Janet was furious that he had spent so much money on the car, but to him money was for spending, and he loved cars. This was the fatal flaw in the delicate fabric of their marriage.

On 30 November 1955, all their belongings, packed in countless cartons and trunks, were loaded into a plane to Genoa in Italy, to arrive ahead of Tony and Janet, who got into the Mercedes (which she called the 'spacemobile') and set off for Italy. She was convinced the car looked like it had come from Mars.

They crossed into Italy just before San Remo where the people, recognising them, cried out in excitement, 'Jawnet Lee-egg-a and Too-ne Coor-tis!'

They drove through the large industrial city of Genoa, and at Sestri took the road through the mountains and on to Pisa, before taking the freeway to Florence, and then to Rome. But it wasn't the idyllic journey it may sound. They were both tired and irritable, and when they talked they bickered, and when they were not bickering they drove in icy silence.

They finally arrived at the Hassler Hotel at the top of the Spanish Steps in Rome, and almost the moment they settled into the suite they had an almighty argument about the car, which Janet hated and Tony loved. After a long night's sleep, they felt refreshed and less inclined to quarrel, and enjoyed four days relaxing and taking in the culture and the many sights. They drove to the villa of Gina Lollobrigida and husband Milko, just off the Appian Way, where they spent a wonderful day that included an exploration of the villa's ancient tombs and urn altars.

United Artists took the opportunity to throw a cocktail party for the Curtises, which attracted a great deal of publicity for *Trapeze*. They finished their Roman sojourn in good spirits, and then had to backtrack to Genoa in the car that Janet hated, to embark on the *Cristoforo Colombo* on 11 December. The liner docked at Naples for six hours, giving Tony and Janet time to tour the preserved remains of the ancient city of Pompeii.

It was a long voyage home, finally docking in New York on 20 December. Their joy at returning home as well as at the expected baby only masked the splinters in their marriage, which was slowly being eroded by their different values and attitudes. But Janet was optimistic, writing in her diary on the train to Los Angeles that during the five months they were away from home, and often apart, 'the most important lesson has been our added knowledge of each other and life – and I hope we never lose the little progress we'd made'.

When released in 1956, *Trapeze* proved to be Tony's most successful film so far, liked by the public and critics. The *Sunday Times* found 'Tony Curtis most engaging'.

'Curtis had to overcome the fact that he is a very handsome young man,' noted the *Hollywood Reporter*. 'He has done it so that his appearance is now secondary to a talent and vitality that mark him as one of the most important young stars.'

Variety called the movie 'high-flying screen entertainment. Reed's direction loads the aerial scenes with story suspense for even more thrill effect, and male stars Burt Lancaster and Tony Curtis simulate the big top aristocrats realistically.'

MCA negotiated a new seven-year contract for him with Universal, raising his salary to $25,000 a week. Tony and Janet even formed their own production company, Curtleigh Productions. 'We wanted to be independent, like Burt and Kirk [Douglas] were,' said Tony. 'It's easier said than done.' As for going into partnership with his wife, he said, 'We were trying to make *everything* work at the same time – our marriage, our careers. And we didn't feel we *had* to be in the same movies. We could produce movies for other actors, or I could be in one, Janet in another, but, ya know, what everyone else wanted were movies starring Tony Curtis and Janet Leigh.'

Janet had a different approach and outlook. 'We set up our own company so we could try and have more of a say in the movies we did, and maybe we could make some extra money for ourselves, and give us the chance to make more movies together.'

In early 1956 they bought a bigger house, at 1152 San Ysidro Drive in Beverly Hills. It was a French country-style house, with a guest cottage, which would be ready for them to move into before Janet's due date of 1 July. To pay for the kitchen, they both signed to do individual TV movies for the *Schlitz Playhouse of Stars* series; Janet's was *Carriage from Britain* in 1957 and Tony's was *Man on a Rack* in 1958. He also made two other TV dramas, *Cornada* in 1957, and *The Stone* in 1959, both for the *General Electric Theatre* series.

While the house was being decorated and made ready, Tony made *The Rawhide Years*, a Western in which he played a man falsely accused of murder and bent on clearing his name. The *Hollywood Reporter* enthused about his performance: 'Tony Curtis, as the young gambler-turned-honest, is very good, showing a flair for comedy that has seldom been exploited and the ability to carry his own in an outdoor, rough-

and-tumble western. The young actor can apparently do anything in the way of parts and his name is always potent box-office for the younger set.'

The *Monthly Film Bulletin* was less enthused, though it liked the movie overall, which it thought 'an energetic and sharply-paced melodrama, in which the emphasis is mainly on straightforward and sometimes unnecessarily violent action. Performances are standard with Tony Curtis presenting a decidedly modern appearance as the misunderstood Ben.'

Sammy Davis Jr and Kim Novak were regular visitors to their house. They couldn't be seen in public because not only did many white Americans object to a black man dating a white girl, but Columbia Studios head Harry Cohn, to whom Novak was under contract, also objected. Tony knew that Cohn was 'well connected with men who would gladly have broken Sammy's legs'. So Tony and Janet allowed them to stay at their home, in the guest house.

Janet restricted her appearances during her pregnancy to guest spots on TV variety shows. The day she was to appear on *The Rosemary Clooney Show* she was five months pregnant and experiencing backache but hadn't told Tony because she didn't want him worrying. As she sat sketching for a new batch of Janet Leigh dresses, she felt a surge of pain, but ignored it and left for the TV studio. She was in agony but managed to get through the recording without letting anyone know.

By the time she and Tony went to bed that evening, she was in so much pain she finally had to tell him. He called the doctor and was told to take Janet straight to St John's Hospital in Santa Monica. He eased her into his Cadillac convertible, then sped all the way to the hospital and arrived at 1.30am. He helped her out of the car, up the steps and into the marbled foyer, which was empty except for a switchboard operator and the admission clerk, to whom he explained that Dr Pearl had told them to come right away.

A nurse took Janet to a private room, leaving Tony alone and anxious. Janet recalled that as she sat in bed, a nun came in and said, 'Your baby is going to be all right. We are praying for you.' The nun smoothed back the wet hair from Janet's forehead and pressed a small medallion – the Sacred Heart – into her hand.

Dr Pearl finally arrived, gave Janet an unhurried examination and diagnosed a kidney infection. The next day X-rays showed that the foetus was pushing the kidney against the pelvis, and she needed to remain in hospital for treatment. For the next four days Tony 'was a basket case', Janet recalled. Because of her previous history, Dr Pearl insisted that she needed a few days in hospital and would only be allowed home if she rested completely when she got there.

When Tony told the doctor they were going to be moving into a bigger house in a few days, the doctor made it clear that Janet was not to lift so much as a carton; knowing how stubborn Janet could be, he said, 'Maybe it would be best if on the moving day Janet went to the movies.'

Janet didn't need to go to the movies. Tony moved into the house while she was still in hospital, and on the day she was discharged, he collected her and pushed her in a wheelchair towards the elevator, accompanied by a nurse. Waiting by the elevator was the nun. Janet said, 'Thank you,' to her, but she said nothing and just smiled and nodded. It was just a curious thing that Janet always remembered.

On 17 June her contractions began, and Tony got her to the hospital. He was ushered into the waiting room while she was taken to delivery. He waited anxiously for the phone in the waiting room to ring, but 12 hours and 16 minutes passed and no call came. He eventually saw Janet being wheeled down the corridor, and as he rushed out he was met by Dr Pearl, who was on her way to inform him that they had a little girl who weighed six pounds, six ounces.

Janet was very groggy when he went in to see her. They told a fan magazine that he whispered, 'Honey, we've got a little girl.'

'Yes, I know,' she feebly responded.

'Do you know what she weighs?'

'No.'

'Six pounds and six ounces.'

'That's a nice price,' she said, and fell asleep.

He went to the nursery to meet his daughter, Kelly Lee Curtis, named by her godparents Jerry and Jackie Gershwin. He later admitted that, although he felt thrilled, he had expected some kind of sudden overwhelming sensation of love for his child, but it didn't happen. 'It didn't hit me right away,' he told me. 'Maybe it was my upbringing, or maybe that's just the way it is, or just the way I am. Or maybe I had just been so worried we would lose her, and I was overcome with relief. Just too many emotions to deal with at one time. And I really didn't feel like the baby was mine in a curious way – I hadn't been there at the birth. You couldn't do that then. I think a father has to be there, for that magic moment when you see the life you helped to create come into your world. It was only when I got Janet and Kelly home that I really felt Kelly was mine.

'I'd sit in the chair while Janet rested, and I'd be holding our baby. And when Kelly was in the nursery, I'd hear the faintest sound and I'd get into the nursery as quickly as I could. I was afraid of I dunno what. But that little baby was so precious to me.'

He took so many photographs of his little girl that Janet recalled, 'Tony singlehandedly supplied all the business for the camera shop!'

The arrival of Kelly Lee Curtis seemed to bring a sense of serenity to Tony and Janet that had long been missing. They were at their happiest, and Tony seemed to have overcome, for now at least, a lot of the paranoia and stress he had been suffering. But there was still the pressure of being Hollywood royalty, and they continued to be targeted by gossip columnists.

They were at a nightclub one evening when a girl approached and asked Tony for an autograph. He smiled and signed his name for her, and she went away, but Janet was annoyed, and it was obvious to onlookers that she was unhappy. The next day a story appeared in columns that Tony had shown interest in another girl and Janet had been furious. That kind of unwanted and unwelcome media attention raised anxiety in Janet, and anger in Tony. They were both happy to cater to the fan magazine market, but they detested the gossip columnists.

She always thought it important to play the part of Hollywood royalty to the hilt by attending the premieres, the parties and all the big events, whereas Tony tried to avoid what he called 'the bullshit of Hollywood', which included all those things Janet felt were important to the job and which she enjoyed. That took them in different directions, and added to the strains.

His career was still accelerating, although he had to fight for some of the films *he* wanted to make, such as *Mister Cory* in which he played a young man from the slums of Chicago who becomes a big-time gambler. For once on a Universal picture, Tony had the bonus of a good script and slick direction, both coming from Blake Edwards, as well as a good supporting cast including Martha Hyer and Kathryn Grant.

Tony was attracted to Kathryn Grant but she was engaged to Bing Crosby. Martha Hyer was spoken for and scared that her lover, Al Hart, the president of City National Bank, and also a personal friend of Tony's, would find out if they had an affair, which (according to Tony's second autobiography) would result in her losing her house in Palm Springs.

Mister Cory and Tony's performance both received respectable reviews. 'Curtis can carry this type of role perfectly,' said the *Hollywood Reporter*. 'He is one of the few young stars of major value who has that contained recklessness, insouciance and bubbling good humour that regrettably has been lost in the current substation of soiled T-shirts for the Byronic Collar. Curtis can play the earthy parts too, but he is not limited.'

'Curtis gives the title role a good ride and pleases,' thought *Variety*.

His next picture, *Midnight Story*, offered him a solid dramatic role as a traffic cop who independently investigates the murder of a parish priest. 'With each successive film Tony Curtis proves again that he must no longer be regarded as a mere "pretty boy" but as a serious actor,' said *Today's Cinema*. 'He puts in here a performance of considerable dramatic depth.'

The *Monthly Film Bulletin* concurred. 'The acting, particularly of Tony Curtis as the priest's avenger and Gilbert Roland as the murderer, is accomplished, and the whole production evidences a purposeful sincerity.'

His next movie would allow him the chance to get his revenge on the gossip columnists who were plaguing his and Janet's lives, and would result in one of the very best performances of his career.

CHAPTER ELEVEN

A Sweet Smell

Because Tony had been such a success in *Trapeze*, Harold Hecht talked to Lew Wasserman about making another film with him, and told him about a movie property owned by Hecht-Hill-Lancaster. *Sweet Smell of Success* was an original screenplay by Ernest Lehman that exposed the corruption in the world of press agents and newspaper columnists. It was a daring subject to tackle because Hollywood and the gossip columnists lived off each other – or, as Tony put it, they 'bled off each other'.

Tony was offered the role of a press agent, Sidney Falco, who will do anything – literally *anything*, illegal, immoral, it didn't matter – just to get his clients a mention by the powerful and ultimately dangerous columnist J.J. Hunsecker, who had fewer morals than Falco. Hunsecker wants to break up the romance between his sister and a jazz musician and gets Falco to deal with it by planting drugs on the musician.

Universal were unhappy with Tony's decision to make a movie that was likely to make enemies in the newspaper world, but Tony ignored all and any advice in order to make a movie that would, he hoped, lift him out of the league of lightweight stars in which he had been stranded. And he loved the idea of playing a heavy instead of a squeaky-clean good guy. Orson Welles was originally going to play Hunsecker, but because he was no longer a name to bring in an audience, Lancaster decided to play the part himself. 'As soon as we began shooting I realised Burt was a great choice,' said Tony.

Tony and Janet wanted their own production company to be involved, although their participation was largely symbolic. It was the first Curtleigh production, but the main power behind the movie was the partnership of Burt Lancaster, Harold Hecht and James Hill.

British director Alexander Mackendrick, famous for Ealing comedies such as *The Ladykillers*, was the surprising choice to helm *Sweet Smell of Success*. 'It was an inspired choice,' said Tony. 'Sandy Mackendrick brought to that film a style that I don't think even an American director could have given it.'

Mackendrick wanted the film to have a distinct, if unreal style of speech, so he brought in Clifford Odets to write the film's unique style of dialogue, which bristled with now classic lines. 'Cat's in the bag, bag's in the river.' 'I'd hate to take a bite outta you. You're a cookie full of arsenic.' 'Watch me make a fifty-yard dash with my legs cut off.'

It was filmed in New York early in 1957, and Janet and Kelly came too, as well as the baby's nanny, all living for the duration in a lush apartment. Tony poured his heart and soul into his role, and something amazing and possibly even unexpected began to take shape in front of the cameras as he created a character that was unlike anything he had played before. He said he didn't find it hard to play Falco. 'I wanted success all my life. So *Sweet Smell of Success* was something I understood the fabric of.'

Mackendrick was a perfectionist and allowed no interference, not even from Hecht, Hill or Lancaster as they tried to object to his often time-consuming and expensive techniques. He shot many scenes by moving the camera far more than was usual, and this meant more rehearsals with the camera and actors than normal as each had to hit the right spot at exactly the right time. Cinematographer James Wong Howe worked as fast as he could to light the difficult and challenging angles Mackendrick sought, but it took longer to do and ran up the costs. (These days such shots would be achieved quickly using Steadicams, but back then cameras had to move on tracks. Cameras then needed more lighting than today's and a moving camera presented its own problems.) Mackendrick's eye for detail was demanding, and sometimes (arguably) unnecessary, such as when he insisted cocktail drinks be a certain colour, even though the film was in black-and-white.

Tony believed that because Mackendrick took so long to make the movie, Lancaster and Hecht never forgave him, and he didn't work again in Hollywood for six years. That isn't the case, because two years later Hecht and Lancaster assigned Mackendrick to direct *The Devil's*

Disciple, and it was on *that* movie the producers clashed with him and fired him. After that Mackendrick directed *Sammy Going South* in 1963 and *A High Wind in Jamaica* in 1965, but his reputation in Hollywood had suffered, not because of any revenge by Hecht and Lancaster, but because *Sweet Smell of Success* was a box-office disaster.

The film was savaged by newspaper editors and columnists like Walter Winchell, who berated it for its attack on their moral standards. The publicity hurt, as did some of the lukewarm reviews in the American press. *Variety* seemed to give grudging praise, noting how it 'captures the feel of Broadway and environs after dark', yet carped, 'Flaw in *Success* concerns the newspaperman's devotion to his sister.' It noted that Tony Curtis 'comes through with an interesting performance, although somehow the character he plays is not quite all the heel as written.'

The public stayed away, unaware that they were missing what was to become one of the great noir classics of American cinema. 'You could say *Sweet Smell of Success* is the greatest failure my company ever made,' said Lancaster. 'I don't think they understood the background and the incredible Clifford Odets dialogue. It's the best acting I've ever seen Tony do. He should have got an Academy Award for it. Really he should have.'

But there was to be no American Academy Award nomination for Tony or the film. He was nominated, however, for a British Academy Award, though he didn't win, and the British press gave the movie and Tony deserved praise. 'Curtis, foxy eyes set in a little boy face, has never done anything better,' said the *Daily Herald*. 'His performance is some-thing to goggle at.' The London *Evening Standard* said, 'The playing, particularly that of Tony Curtis, has an attack and authority that drive a melodramatic plot at a pell-mell pace.' And the *Sunday Express* thought, 'Tony Curtis is astonishingly persuasive as a sickening agent prepared to slide through any slime for a fast dollar.'

Tony was baffled by the American reviews. 'I was thinking to myself, what do I have to do? Just what do they want from me? I didn't know that over a long period of time my performance and the movie would be recognised.'

Licking his wounds, he placated Janet by trading in his 300 SL gullwing for a more conventional white Mercedes, which she much preferred to the 'spacemobile'. He also bought her a new pet poodle, called Mercedes, who hated Houdina so much that Houdina had to move in with Manny and Helen Schwartz. Around this time Bobby Schwartz's behaviour had become increasingly erratic, so it was left to Tony to have him put into therapy and also to pay for it.

By May 1957 Janet had recovered from giving birth and was ready to go back to work. Curtleigh joined forces with Kirk Douglas' Bryna Productions to make the epic *The Vikings*. Through Lew Wasserman's negotiating skills, Tony and Janet earned a cool million dollars between them.

Kirk Douglas played the bloodthirsty Einar who kidnaps Welsh princess Morgana, played by Janet, and enslaves Eric, played by Tony. Eric escapes with Morgana and falls in love with her, and eventually he and Einar fight to the death, unaware that they are half-brothers.

Tony had previously met Kirk Douglas at a party; Burt Lancaster introduced them. Tony made some joke which Kirk took umbrage to and he made a move as if to knee Tony in the nuts. Tony didn't flinch but kept on talking, and Kirk, realising Tony couldn't be intimidated, took an instant liking to him. They remained friends for the rest of Tony's life.

In June 1957, Douglas and director Richard Fleischer took their cast and crew all the way to Norway, where cameraman Jack Cardiff was to capture many beautiful and spectacular shots of the long ships sailing up the fjords. The 70-foot-long vessels, based on authentic designs, had been constructed and were rowed by two hundred enthusiasts from Norwegian and Danish rowing clubs.

Still refusing to fly, Tony went by train to New York to meet Janet, Kelly and their baby's nanny, who had flown. They settled into their three-bedroom suite on the *Ile de France* and set sail for England. The crossing of the Atlantic was enlivened by having dinner at the captain's table, playing the gambling tables, enjoying cocktail parties and spending time with Boris Karloff and his wife, who were on their way to England.

Disembarking at Plymouth, they took the train to London and settled into the Audley Suite, a penthouse apartment at the Dorchester Hotel. Tony had grown a suitably rugged beard for his role in *The Vikings*. He recalled, 'Kirk had told every man in the cast to grow a beard to look like authentic Vikings. So I grew mine, and every man in the cast did too – all except Kirk. He stayed clean-shaven. He knew exactly how he was going to be noticed among this big cast of strong men.'

Tony and Janet had costume fittings, met the press, managed to socialise with numerous friends, and caught Howard Keel's show at the

London Palladium. On 3 June they celebrated Tony's thirty-second birthday, and then their sixth wedding anniversary the next day. Their neighbours at the Dorchester, in an even bigger suite, were Elizabeth Taylor and Mike Todd, who threw a party for them, inviting Debbie Reynolds and Eddie Fisher, Michael Wilding, Kirk and Anne Douglas. Among the many other guests was Noel Coward, who greeted Tony by saying, 'Hello, you bearded beauty.'

They moved from one social event to another, meeting so many Lords and Ladies that at one point Tony wearily shook the hand of a peer whose name he had missed and said, 'Nice to know you, Lord.'

On 14 June, Tony and Janet joined Ernest Borgnine on a five-day goodwill tour of Scandinavia. Tony found the courage to fly with them to Copenhagen, Denmark. He was highly nervous and somewhat shaken by the time they landed, but he was revived by the tremendous welcome they all received from the entire population of the village of Frederikssund, which turned out in full Viking regalia with ancient instruments to entertain the movie stars at the airport.

Their goodwill tour created tremendous publicity for *The Vikings* ahead of filming. Luncheons and banquets were laid on for them in Stockholm; in Oslo they were taken to the Viking museum, resulting in much coverage in the Norwegian newspapers.

The final stop was at the Olympic ski jump at Holmenkollen, where they took a lift to the top of the hill for a magnificent view over the entire city. From there, Janet returned to London to finish her wardrobe fittings while Tony and Borgnine joined the rest of the cast and unit in Bergen on the Norwegian coast, where a complete Viking village had been constructed, as well as a coffee hut, make-up huts, wardrobe huts and dressing rooms, some of which had a lean-to for a toilet.

It rained so much that after waiting days for it to stop, director Richard Fleischer decided to film in the rain. 'It was a pretty miserable experience,' Tony recalled. 'We didn't film for days. One day Kirk was sitting on a rock, looking very gloomy, and when I sat next to him, he looked at me and said, "Wanna buy a film company?"'

When Janet arrived at the location a week later, she was greeted with a huge banner on the side of a hill that read 'WELCOME JANET'. Fleischer recalled, 'When Janet Leigh arrived it was like a real splash of Hollywood glamour, which cheered the company up.'

Janet recalled that Tony was happy to see her. His recollection was, 'I really would have preferred to have had another leading lady. Janet's a wonderful actress, and we worked well together. But, ya know, things weren't great in the marriage by then.'

No matter how happy Janet appeared to be, or how happy she thought her marriage was at the time they made *The Vikings*, Tony felt his marriage had become a trap.

To lift the spirits of the unit, Janet produced a show for the whole unit. Tony, Kirk and Ernest Borgnine sang a risqué song. Tony and Kirk performed a terrible juggling act while Janet performed a striptease behind them to rapturous applause. Even Richard Fleischer, producer Jerry Bresler and cinematographer Jack Cardiff did a sketch, but the star turn was a sketch about the making of a movie. Tony played himself, Kirk his stand-in, Fleischer the movie director, Cardiff the cameraman, and Janet the script girl. Every time Tony was supposed to do something physical, Kirk was called to be hit in the face with a pie, soaked with water, hit over the head with a stool, and locked in a trunk, while the movie star received all the credit and adulation. It all got out of hand and everyone got covered in custard pie and water. It was a tremendous success. Kirk thought everyone would work well after that celebration.

The next day the Norwegians playing the Vikings went on strike. Kirk was enraged. When another storm held up filming, Douglas, Bresler and Fleischer decided to abandon Norway and the striking Vikings. The unit moved to Dinard, France, to film at an authentic coastal castle, Fort La Latte.

During the battle scene, an arrow hit Tony in the eye. By luck he had his eyes closed when it happened, and of course it was only a stage arrow with a blunt tip, but his eye was severely bloodshot and bruised, and he was badly shaken. So, too, was Kirk Douglas. Janet recalled, 'Kirk got into such a terrible state of anxiety and shock that Tony gave him the sedative he was supposed to take. A few days later, Tony was really ill with shock and had to be put to bed and tranquillised, and his eye was all bandaged up. That started rumours that Tony had been blinded and was in a coma. Then I went to pieces. I was sick and dizzy and crying all the time. Kirk must have wondered if he'd ever get his movie finished.'

Tony recovered for the final scene, fighting Kirk on steep steps at the very top of the castle. It was dangerous to shoot, but both stars performed most of the sword fighting themselves. Janet recalled, 'The stunts they did in that movie made me sick with worry.'

Richard Fleischer always felt that he 'survived making *The Vikings*'. He told me, 'It was difficult, really tough, and worse because Kirk was the producer. He had promised me that he would let me direct *The Vikings* and he would just play the part. But sometimes I'd set up a shot, and he'd want to change it because *he* had to be in the centre of any grouping of characters.

'We had a shot of him sitting in a big chair, and after we'd done it I was happy, but he said he could do it differently. He asked if his right arm should cross to his left or his left arm cross to the right. It made no difference to me. Then he said he liked it one way, and I said we'd shoot it that way, and then he said it was uncomfortable that way, so I said, "Kirk, what the hell do you want from me?" and he said, "Forget the whole fucking thing," and walked off the set. I never knew what would make him happy.'

Tony learned the secret of keeping Douglas happy. 'Kirk doesn't trust people he is working with. He was always trying to get the advantage on the set. But I had learned how to make guys like him love me. And he trusted me. I could give him whatever he wanted. He was like a little kid asking me to give him what he had already.'

Tony refused to do one scene as written. He was to knock out a captured older Viking, played by Ernest Borgnine. 'We rehearsed the scene, and everything seemed fine,' said Fleichser, 'but when we came to shoot it, Tony said he wouldn't do it because it was bad for his image. I said, "Tony, this guy has been chasing you with a whole pack of vicious Vikings who are going to kill you if they catch you, so your fans will love it when you hit him." But he said he wouldn't hit an old man.'

Borgnine recalled, 'Tony was worried about hitting me, and I said, "Come on, Tony, hit me. I won't mind." In the end he hit me.'

'Tony Curtis was eager to please everyone,' said Fleischer. 'He was just anxious and still very young, and he wanted to give his best.'

Filming continued in Munich from 30 July. A minor crisis arose for the Curtises when they got a call that Kelly, back in London at the Dorchester Hotel with her nanny, was sick. It turned out to be a minor throat infection and she was treated with penicillin, but as soon as she was well enough, they arranged for her to join them. Kelly, along with Kirk's young son Peter, appeared in the film as Viking children.

Bobby came to visit for a week, adding to Tony's stress. He drove Tony crazy, asking him, 'Are you my brother?' and when Tony assured him that he was, he asked, 'How do I know you're really my brother?'

Unable to connect with Bobby, and feeling as though his marriage was becoming too much to cope with, he turned to Kirk Douglas. Although Kirk was very demanding at work, Tony found him to be very kind and considerate, and Kirk quickly became 'a brother figure'.

During a break in filming, Tony and Janet visited the island of Herrenworth to have dinner at Herrenchiemsee Palace. When asked to sign the guest book, they saw among the signatures those of Hitler and other top Nazis, which the manager was extremely proud of.

Tony wrote in the guest book, 'I am a Jew, signing this book that Hitler also signed, in a place owned by a Nazi. What does it mean? Are these people not even true to their own disgusting beliefs?'

On 5 October 1957, after four months, *The Vikings* wrapped.

When released in 1958, it was a spectacular box-office hit, taking nearly $6.5 million in America, and around $13 million worldwide. 'It is rough, riotous and wholly enjoyable,' said the *Daily Express*, while *Variety* called it 'spectacular, rousing and colourful', which summed it up.

Lew Wasserman recognised that Tony was sought after as a co-star by big-name stars like Kirk Douglas and Burt Lancaster, and with each picture outside Universal Studios he was being given the chance to expand his acting range. Just as importantly, Wasserman was able to get Tony top fees for those major pictures. He was smelling sweet success.

CHAPTER TWELVE

Boinie and Francis Albert

When *The Vikings* wrapped, Tony and Janet sailed to New York. From there Tony caught the train to Los Angeles while Janet and Kelly caught the sleeper flight to California.

He arrived home seemingly happy to be back. But he felt he needed a break, having spent almost the entire past four months with his wife. He just wanted to get away for a bit, and was becoming influenced by the way Frank Sinatra was living his life, footloose and fancy-free, and he increasingly sought Sinatra's company.

'He called me "Bernie" but with a strong New York accent – "Boinie" – and I always called him "Francis Albert",' Tony said of his friendship with Frank Sinatra.

He spent time at the Cal Neva Lodge, the hotel casino Frank owned in partnership with his silent partner, Mafia boss Sam Giancana. Tony recalled, 'I was there and one night he had a party and we were standing with some people and suddenly Frank said to me, "Come on, Tony, come with me," and we walked away from these people – that's how it was with Frank; he had all these friends but with me he was very easy and would give me his time and his values. And we went to one of the bungalows up there – there were a lot of bungalows where people stayed only some were bigger and better than the others, and we went to one of these bungalows and there was Sam Giancana. I was shocked, ya know? I'd heard the name and knew a bit about what he was – Frank never said anything like "Sam runs the Mob in Chicago", or anything like that. He just introduced me to his friend Sam Giancana, and I was struck by how small he was. Just 5 feet 1 inch or 5 feet 2 inches, no more, and very immaculately dressed. But forget about Marlon Brando's *Godfather*, this guy was tiny.

'He said to me, "Tony, I love your movies. Keep 'em going." We talked a while, and then Frank made a gesture like we should go, and we left.'

Tony didn't expect to see Giancana again, but another time he was at a club in Reno, he was invited to see Giancana privately. Tony was in for a shock. 'Giancana wanted to "manage" me, whatever that meant,' he told me. 'He asked me if I felt I was doing OK in my profession, and I said it was OK, could be better. He said he could make it better, and I remembered that I'd heard that these guys sometimes did favours for stars and then wanted favours in return, and I didn't want any of that in my life. Peter Lawford had said a few things, so too did Sammy [Davis Jr]. Frank never spoke about it, but I knew that when he was having a tough time and he wasn't making records or movies, these guys were giving him work in their clubs, and maybe they got him a movie or two – who knows?'

Tony told Giancana, 'Thanks, but no thanks.' But that wasn't the end of it. Tony ran into 'one of these guys' – Giancana's mob guys – who tried to persuade him to let Giancana's 'Hollywood agents' represent him. He turned down the offer, but he was approached a number of times, and as each time he turned them down they became increasingly 'intimidating in their manner', he began to worry where it would end.

Finally he confided to Sinatra what had been happening, and Frank 'almost exploded'. Tony recalled, 'He was pretty angry coz I'd not gone to him before. He said he could fix things, but I told him I could handle it. He thought I was crazy. Maybe I was. I didn't quite realise what these guys might do to me. I just kept saying "no" to them, until they gave up. I knew how to tough up. I never allowed anyone to intimidate me.'

Sinatra came to feel very protective of Tony. 'He was my kid brother,' said Sinatra. 'He might have been a Jew, but he was an Italian at heart.' That was a compliment.

Sinatra figured he owed his life to Tony. 'He told me I saved his life,' Tony told me. 'I don't know that I did, but if he chose to believe it, what was I to say?'

He told me the story:

He was ill one night and called me. His voice was kind of

slurred, and all he said was, 'Bernie' – or 'Boinie' – 'get over here, will ya?'

So I got over there, and he was really sick. Hot, perspiring, said his head hurt like hell, kind of out of it. His heart was racing. I called a doctor who came over, took his temperature, checked his heart, his head, everything, and said he had to go to hospital. He said he was seriously ill and needed full-time care and treatment. Frank didn't wanna go, so the doctor said to him, 'If you don't you could die.' That made Frank even more determined *not* to go coz he didn't want his picture being taken while he was dying in some hospital bed and it ending up in some trash rag. He just wouldn't go, so I said I'd stay and take care of him. I didn't have a single clue what I was doing.

The doc gave him some shots and pills, and told me to stay with him, and if I thought he was getting any worse to get him straight to a hospital. I said, 'What if he refuses to go?' He said, 'He won't be in any condition to refuse because if he's alive he'll be in a coma, and if he's not in a coma he'll be dead.' So that was reassuring!

I called Janet and she came over, and she didn't know what she was doing either, and the next day she had to go to the studio, so I was there alone with Frank, and I was thinking about how I was going to explain this to everyone if he died, ya know?

I didn't sleep. I was mopping him down all night, trying to keep him comfortable, cool him down. I figured he had meningitis or something. But whatever it was, he was sick for the next two days till his fever broke. The doctor came back to check on him, but he was still out of it by then. The doc just shook his head slowly, went 'tut tut!' and left.

The first thing Frank said when he came round was, 'What the hell you doin' in my home?' I said, 'Francis, you were sick. The doc said you coulda died.' He said, 'Where's the doc?' I said, 'He isn't here. It's just me.' He said, 'You took care of me?' I said, 'Sure.' He said, 'You saved my life.' I said, 'Sure I did.' He said, 'I owe you big time.' I said, 'I'll say.' He never forgot. He never mentioned it again, but he always said, 'I owe you, Boinie. Whatever you want . . .'

Frank Sinatra's next movie was *Kings Go Forth*, a World War Two drama, playing a GI who meets and falls for a French girl but loses her to his best friend who, upon discovering she is half-black, unceremoniously dumps her. Sinatra wanted Tony for this part, and demanded that the producer Frank Ross and director Delmer Daves cast him.

'Nobody's bigger on the set than Frank,' Tony told me. 'Not the producer, not the director. If he didn't want to work, he just didn't show up. But that never happened on *Kings Go Forth*. He never took a day off.'

The film offered Tony a good part, playing a charmer who turns out to be a racist bigot. But he knew of Frank's reputation for being difficult, and was prepared for trouble. 'I had heard all these stories about him, not all of them true, and I was nervous about being in that picture with him when we started. But he had always been nice to me.'

He hoped Sinatra would still be nice to him when they worked together. He was prepared to do all he could to make his screen partnership with Sinatra go smoothly. 'I knew that he liked to do everything in one take, so I knew at the very start I would have to give my best in the first take, which wasn't always easy, but I'm a very spontaneous kind of actor when I need to be. So that worked fine between us, but sometimes he would get his lines wrong a little – never too much – but he'd never do them again. I found myself having to carry the weight and to sometimes cover any way I could for his mistakes. He made the whole process of making a movie very complicated.'

Kings Go Forth would be his only movie with Sinatra – and it was by Tony's choice. 'When it got too difficult for him, he became very bad-tempered. I mean, *oh*, just keep out of his way. He was never that way with me, but it made things very uncomfortable. So I decided I'd never make another movie with Frank, even though I loved him and we've always stayed friends.'

He found working with Natalie Wood, playing the half-caste French girl, a delight, and they went on to make three movies together in all. 'Natalie was a lovely and very wonderful actress,' he told me in 1985, four years after her death from drowning. 'I was so sad when I heard she'd died. She was incredibly pretty. I completely understood why RJ [Robert Wagner] was so in love with her. She was very intelligent, and very cute and funny, and had very sexy eyes and a sexy mouth. That's why the camera loved her. A close-up of Natalie was like a bright shining diamond. You just wanted to kiss it. Kissing her was nice. I liked doing that.'

When Sinatra insisted that United Artists premiere *Kings Go Forth* in Monte Carlo rather than Hollywood, simply because he was already there and didn't want to return immediately to America, Tony had to get on an aeroplane and fly from New York to Monte Carlo. He was terrified throughout the entire flight, but he did it for Frank Sinatra.

The film was a modest success, and there were a few good reviews. 'By sheer insouciance Curtis makes this intriguing and repulsive individual completely believable because each of us recognised in him some of the human enigmas encountered in life,' said the *Hollywood Reporter*. 'Sinatra is superb as a man with great capacities of devotion and little self conceit. Curtis is equally fine as the reckless show-off who arouses pity by his very shallowness.'

Variety was not impressed. 'Curtis has had experience acting the heel, and he does a repeat, though this is a tough character to swallow. He's best when acting the charm boy.'

Tony found himself a member of the legendary Rat Pack. Sinatra often called him to ask if he wanted to go to Vegas for the weekend. He would pick Tony up in his Karmann Ghia and the two of them would head for Vegas to meet up with Dean Martin, Peter Lawford, Sammy Davis Jr, Joey Bishop and other friends who hung out with the pack.

Tony recalled, 'We used to sit in the lounge at the Sands after the guys worked, and have drinks. I was a very light drinker, and I passed out, and Frank and Dean and Carl Cohen picked me up like a Viking, like Kirk Douglas when he's dead in *The Vikings*, and walked me solemnly through the casino out to the pool and threw me in, and left.'

He could forget his troubles when he was with Sinatra and the clan. 'I had fun with those guys, and I still love Frank,' Tony told me in 1994. 'He's like my older brother.' (Tony collected 'older brothers' – Sinatra, Lancaster, Douglas.) Tony had a special assignment which he had a great gift for – rounding up showgirls from other casinos and bringing them to the Sands where Sinatra threw extravagant parties for his buddies. Peter Lawford recalled, 'Frank would ask him to go and find a few girls, and he'd come back with a whole dance company.'

Even as cracks were appearing in the marriage, in January 1958 Tony and Janet starred together in *The Perfect Furlough*, produced through Curtleigh and directed by Blake Edwards. It was a fast-paced comedy with Janet as an army psychologist who arranges a competition for the servicemen on an isolated Arctic base to win the ideal leave indicated in the film's title. Tony played the corporal who wins and then heads for

Paris with film star Sandra Roca, played by Linda Cristal, while the psychologist, along as chaperone, falls for him.

Janet felt she and Tony 'functioned smoothly as a screen team', and they developed a close friendship with Blake Edwards. 'They were a sweet couple,' Edwards told me. 'I saw them at their best together. I didn't notice Tony having any kind of problem working with her.

'Janet helped me out when I needed a close-up of Tony reacting to seeing the girl he had taken to Paris appearing in only a sheet. I wanted it to be spontaneous and unrehearsed, so I enlisted Janet to stand by the camera in a robe and nothing on underneath. Tony had no idea. I had the camera running and as she caught his eye, she opened the robe and, well, I certainly got the reaction from Tony I needed. We had fun. It was easy to work with them.'

There was obviously still life in the marriage because in March 1958 Janet discovered she was pregnant again.

Tony felt that with *Sweet Smell of Success* and *Kings Go Forth* he had established himself as a dramatic actor and told Lew Wasserman to find him something that would stretch him further. Wasserman came up with *The Defiant Ones*, the story of two convicts on the run, one a Negro, Noah Cullen the other a Southern racist, John 'Joker' Jackson, chained to each other. It was a dynamic and bold project, produced and directed by Stanley Kramer, who kept the screenplay hidden under lock and key and the whole project a secret from all but those he wanted to bring on board.

Before Tony joined the project, Kramer had secretly met with Sidney Poitier, who had been in films since 1950 but had not yet headlined a picture although he was recognised as a considerable talent. Kramer set him up with the writers, Nedrick Young (a blacklisted writer credited as Nathan E. Douglas) and Harold Jacob Smith, to give his input as a man who had faced discrimination all his life. Kramer and Poitier made a deal to go ahead with the picture if financing could be secured.

While Poitier was in New York, Kramer, in a shrewd and creative move, approached Lew Wasserman to try and interest Tony Curtis, knowing that his name was likely to secure finance from United Artists. Kramer had been immensely impressed with Tony's performance in *Sweet Smell of Success* and felt that he had hidden depths as an actor yet untapped.

In a rather underhand fashion, Kramer implied that the Cullen role had not yet been cast, and he agreed to give Curtis approval of the casting of that part. Tony wanted to give the role to his friend Harry Belafonte, but Belafonte's name wasn't on a list of names United Artists would approve. Poitier's was, and Kramer steered him in that direction, and then arranged a meeting between Curtis and Poitier. Tony gave his approval.

Poitier said that he immediately warmed to Tony. 'He was terrific. He was full of life – bubbly – bubbly – all the time.'

Tony was enthused because of the quality of the script and because he knew only too well what it was like to be on the receiving end of racial discrimination. He also loved the idea of playing the film's heavy, a pretty despicable character who, towards the end of the movie, redeems himself. He wanted to cover up his famous good looks and chose to have an ugly bridge built for his nose that had a remarkable but subtle effect. He still looked like Tony Curtis, but somehow more threatening and no longer boyish.

Although the film had the backing of United Artists, Stanley Kramer needed to find an extra million dollars, and when he was unable to secure it, he told Tony that the movie would have to be shut down. Tony went to his friend Al Hart, president of the City National Bank in Los Angeles, to ask for help. Hart, a Hungarian Jew, was eager to become involved, and he found the million dollars from a number of different investors.

The credits were going to read, 'Tony Curtis in *The Defiant Ones* co-starring Sidney Poitier'. Tony insisted that Poitier be given equal billing. 'It was the first time a black actor in America got top billing,' said Tony. 'Ya know, that makes me feel good. That represented what the movie was about. It could have been an Arab and a Jew. In our case it was a black man and a white man because at that time that was the dilemma on our planet.'

'That was a wonderful thing Tony did for me,' Poitier told me. 'Any other star I can think of would have kept the billing as it was but Tony said, "Sidney is not a supporting actor in this, he's one of the stars and you're going to bill him above the title with me." That was generous and considerate, and I love him for doing that for me.'

The Defiant Ones was filmed during the spring of 1958 in the Kern River Valley in California. For a scene in which the two characters had to cross a fast-moving river while still chained together, Kramer wanted stunt doubles to stand in for Curtis and Poitier. Poitier didn't swim so he was glad to allow his stand-in to take over, but Tony insisted he do the scene himself. Kramer objected on the grounds that it was too dangerous, but Tony's regular stunt double Davey Sharpe assured the director that Tony could do it, and so he did.

Tony was always adamant about doing his own stunts. 'I feel that they are integral to the part. It's like asking someone else to do your voice. When an actor can do as much of his own action stuff, his body language is the same. A double can't double that. You can't do everything. You can't fall out of aeroplanes. You can't get hurt.'

Poitier said, 'Tony's enthusiasm was contagious. I felt we worked well together, and we never had a cross word.'

Between scenes, Poitier told Tony about the racial abuse he had suffered throughout his life. Tony realised that Sidney had suffered far more than he had. They both tried to speak out against racism in print but only obscure black magazines published what they had to say, and no national television talk show would allow Poitier on. Tony was offended, but rather than speak out on his own, he decided to allow the movie to speak for itself.

The Defiant Ones was released in September 1958. *Variety* gave it a rave. 'The performances by Tony Curtis and Sidney Poitier are virtually flawless. [Poitier gives] a cunning, totally intelligent portrayal that rings true. [Curtis] delivers a true surprise performance. He starts off as a sneering, brutal character. When, in the end, he sacrifices a dash for freedom to save Poitier, he has managed the transition with such skill that sympathy is completely with him.'

'In each picture recently, Tony Curtis has been proving that his bobbysox past is a long way behind him,' said the *Evening Standard*. 'And with *The Defiant Ones* he achieves his best yet: a performance of corrosive and devastating power.'

The Defiant Ones was one of the top ten grossing films of 1958 (despite being banned in Alabama). Yet Tony became depressed and felt that the critics refused to take him seriously – an odd attitude considering the rave reviews he and the film got. He said he was convinced critics had not recognised that he had just done some of his best work in *The Defiant Ones*.

Lew Wasserman understood Tony's foibles and paranoia, and may have even known about some of the demons that tormented him, so he took him to the library to borrow a book on acting by Stanislavsky, knowing Tony had no belief in the Method, and then to the offices of the *New York Times* to look up old reviews of movies starring James Cagney, Cary Grant and Clark Gable. He told Tony, 'If you still feel depressed after reading those notices, you can start reading the book.'

Tony was amazed to discover that those great stars he idolised, and who were now considered to be among the screen's finest actors, had all earned lousy reviews in their younger years. The next morning Tony handed back the book on acting, unread.

Perhaps the psychology worked for a brief spell, but his personal problems were always simmering. He felt trapped in his marriage. Janet was expecting their baby in November 1958, and after *The Defiant Ones* had finished filming they got back to trying to have some superficial fun. Dean Martin and wife Jeanne conspired with Tony to throw a huge shower party for Janet. She thought they were just going for a casual intimate dinner but arrived to discover around sixty people shouting, 'Surprise!'

In August 1958, she and Tony were at a party at Peter Lawford's beach house in Santa Monica. When it was over they piled into a car with Dean Martin and Sammy Cahn, followed by friends David and Patricia North in another, and bringing up the rear was Frank Sinatra.

A man called Robert Seddon sat in a parked car outside Lawford's house. Convinced his wife was hiding in North's car, he revved up and rammed North, and ricocheted into the first car, sending six-months pregnant Janet into a screaming frenzy. While Tony, Dean Martin and Sammy Cahn tried to calm her down, Sinatra got on his car radio and called for the police and an ambulance.

Janet was still hysterical when the ambulance arrived. Sinatra was standing in his car calling 'May-day! May-day!'

Seddon was arrested and charged with 'assault with a deadly weapon'. Janet was rushed to hospital where doctors confirmed the baby was unhurt. She was allowed to go home.

Not long after this incident, Tony began drifting away from the Rat Pack. He reflected, 'It was terrific. I felt like a man. To be included in this circle was a wonderful feeling. But I didn't feel comfortable for some reason.'

With a second baby on the way, the Curtises moved to a bigger house, just a block and a half away from where they had been living, to 1151 Summit Drive. Downstairs it had a huge living room, a study and dressing room for Tony, a master bedroom and sitting room, a den and bar, kitchen, breakfast room, and a dining room big enough to seat thirty. Upstairs were four bedrooms and another kitchen. Outside was a large pool with changing rooms. Sammy Davis Jr was in awe of their movie-star mansion and spent hours, sometimes days, there. 'Sammy was there all the time,' said Janet. 'He lived in that house. He said to me, "Some day I'm going to buy this house." And he did.' He was unable to afford it until 1970. Janet recalled, 'He called and said, "Guess what? I bought 1151."'

When *The Defiant Ones* premiered in September 1958, Tony was making the film for which he would always be best remembered. But it was also the cause of many of his worst troubles.

CHAPTER THIRTEEN

Too Hot To Like

One afternoon, while walking down Beverly Drive, Tony bumped into Harold Mirisch, who had produced *Beachhead*. Mirisch invited Tony over for dinner and to watch a movie, and it quickly became a regular occurrence. With his brothers Walter and Marvin, Harold had formed a new independent film production company, Mirisch Brothers, working out of rented office space at the Samuel Goldwyn Studios, with a deal with United Artists for finance and distribution.

Tony recalled, 'Harold Mirisch used to run movies at his house, and I'd go, and one day he said, "Come by a little earlier than usual, Billy Wilder wants to talk to you." So I got there early and Billy took me to a little room and said, "Tony, I'm gonna make a movie about two musicians, both guys, who see a murder and have to dress up as girls and join a girls' band so they don't get killed."'

Some Like It Hot was inspired by a 1951 German movie called *Fanfaren der Liebe* (*Fanfares of Love*) about two out-of-work musicians in Berlin who get jobs in an all-girl band.

According to Tony, he was immediately cast and would have played either of the two musicians. 'Billy said he was going to get Frank Sinatra to play one of the guys and Mitzi Gaynor to play Sugar,' said Tony. 'About a week later he called me in and said he wasn't going to do that because he felt Frank would be too much trouble.' Wilder had arranged a meeting with Sinatra to discuss the movie, but Frank had failed to show up.

Wilder offered the part to Jack Lemmon, who said, 'Felicia [Farr, his girlfriend, soon to be his wife] came with me to Billy, who told me, "If you take the part you're going to be in drag for eighty-five per cent of the picture. Do you want to do it?" It took me two seconds to decide and said, "Yes!" He said, "OK, I'll send you a script when it's finished," and when we got outside Felicia said, "Why did you say yes without a script?" and I said, "Because it's Billy Wilder, that's why, and now he knows I'm going to play that part he'll write it with me in mind."'

Wilder and his regular writing collaborator I.A.L. Diamond always began with a complete script, but during the filming process they developed scenes and ideas and dialogue to suit the actors they had cast as they went along. This was their method of making the writing fresh and pertinent to the story and characters. Tony said, 'Billy felt that writing was like ninety per cent of the film and directing was just a chore he had to do to make sure it was the way he wanted it.'

Lemmon recalled, 'Quite a long time passed and then about sixty pages of the script arrived, and I sat down with a cup of coffee and began reading it, and I was laughing so much I spilled my coffee and fell off the couch and the script went all over the room. I went to see Billy and said, "This is the funniest sixty pages I have ever read," and he said, "The rest of it we'll finish writing while we film."'

Marilyn Monroe's husband, playwright Arthur Miller, encouraged her to approach Wilder, who directed her in *The Seven Year Itch*, to cast her as Sugar, the singer in the all-girl band. She really didn't want to play another dumb blonde and was only interested in good dramatic roles, but Miller thought it would help take her mind off the miscarriage she had suffered in 1957. She called Wilder, telling him she would love to work with him again and so Wilder cast her as Sugar.

The first thing Curtis and Lemmon had to do was be transformed into females. 'We had to look like we could reasonably pass for women,' said Tony. 'These gangsters are looking to kill them, so that puts a frame around the environment that doesn't allow you to *not* try to pass as a woman because you *have* to be believable enough as a woman or they're gonna kill us. That's why I think the film is so good.'

Tony as Joe had to become Josephine. Jack as Jerry had to become Geraldine – although he chooses the name Daphne because he never liked the name Geraldine!

Lemmon remembered, 'We had make-up tests which were drudgery because we went through a week of sitting there, side by side, Tony with his make-up man and me with mine, and after four days I began to realise that with the bee-sting lips which I wanted, I was getting more and more to look like my mother.'

Tony was also looking frighteningly like his mother.

Recalled Lemmon, 'On the fifth day the two make-up men said, "We think this is great," so I said, "What do you think, Tony?" and he said, "I'm happy," and I said, "So am I. Let's go and see Billy." He said, "Wait a minute, I got a better idea. Let's go to the ladies' room in the commissary and see what happens. See if they know it's us or two guys, or if we can get away with it."

'So we walked down to the commissary and into the ladies' room and stood at the mirror and we put lipstick on over our lipstick and were chatting in our phoney voices and girls came out, would look in the mirror and say, "Hi!" and we'd say, "Hi! How are you?" and not one of them batted an eyeball.'

Tony recalled it slightly differently. 'I took Jack Lemmon to the ladies' room. We were dressed as girls. I said, "Come on, Jack, let's try it out." He said, "I'm not going in there." I said, "Oh yes you are!" So I pulled him into the ladies' room – it was at the studio and they had mirrors there – and I'm standing in front of the mirror putting my lipstick on. He's standing next to me. Through the mirror I can see girls going in and out of the stalls. Nobody said nothing. I finished with my lipstick, put it away, we walked out, I said, "Well Jack, how'd you like that?" He said, "That worked." I said, "I'll say it did." Just then a girl coming out of the toilet says, "Hi, Tony!"'

According to Jack Lemmon, he and Tony went straight from the ladies' room to Billy Wilder's office and told him that none of the girls recognised them as guys, and Wilder said, "That's it, then! Don't change anything. Leave it the way it is."'

Tony admitted, 'I didn't feel comfortable dressed up like a woman. I felt very awkward. I came out very prim, very proper, beautiful but very aloof, while Jack came out like a three-dollar pretzel.'

Celebrated dress designer Orry-Kelly was assigned to dress Lemmon, Curtis and Monroe. Tony recalled, 'He took measurements of us and they started making the dresses, and he was measuring Marilyn around her bottom, and he looked up at her and said, "You know, Tony Curtis has got a better ass than you." So she opened her blouse and said, "He doesn't have tits like these!"'

In 1983, Tony told me, 'I loved the idea of working with Marilyn in a movie. It was exciting, I can tell you. I was nervous too. There'd been something special between us all those years back. I didn't know how I would feel about seeing her – being with her – again.'

He wrote his thoughts and initial feelings about working with her in his *Some Like It Hot* memoir. 'Would all the old feelings resurface? I was married. She was married.' He had told me, 'My marriage was in a bad state, and I had no idea what hers to Arthur Miller was like, but I had this insane idea that maybe something would happen between us while we were making the movie.'

Marilyn was prone to ectopic pregnancies. 'Those problems caused her to miscarry a number of times,' said Tony. 'The last one [in 1957] made her very depressed. They had her on all sorts of pills to make her sleep.' Early in 1958 she overdosed on barbiturates and had to have her stomach pumped, although Tony commented, 'She wasn't in a bad way when she started work on *Some Like It Hot*.'

She was seeing her phychiatrist in the morning, and her acting coach, Lee Strasberg, in the afternoons. Strasberg's wife Paula had become Marilyn's friend, confidante and mentor, and Tony felt that Marilyn came to depend upon her and Lee Strasberg more than anyone else. 'They exploited her,' he said. 'They told her she didn't need to play the dumb blonde in movies any more and she could be a great dramatic actress, but they somehow made her feel she needed *them* to do that, and she didn't think anyone else but those people could understand her or see how intelligent she was. And she *was* very bright. She was very perceptive about people, I can tell you. But she didn't have a clue about anything to do with her own issues, so she was in constant need of reassurance. And there were those people there to give her all the reassurance she wanted, and nobody else counted.'

Because she didn't want to play any more dumb-blonde roles, she nearly didn't sign to do *Some Like It Hot*. She asked Lee Strasberg if she should make the movie or try for another baby. Strasberg told her to make the movie.

Filming began on Monday 4 August 1958 at the MGM studio where, on Lot 2, they had a standing set of a train station. Tony recalled, 'On the first day of filming we did the scene in the station, and Marilyn was supposed to come trouncing down looking for the band, and Billy Wilder was standing on the side, and Paula Strasberg was standing on the other side, and Marilyn never took her eyes off Paula. She finished the take and instead of looking to Billy to see what he had to say, she looked at Paula to see what she had to say.

'Then we did another take, and at the end Billy yelled, "Cut!" and he looked at Paula and said, "How was that for you, Paula?" And Paula almost fainted, and that was the end of that bit of trouble for Billy.'

After a week at MGM, the unit moved to the Samuel Goldwyn studio to film interior scenes on board the train, and things went smoothly.

'I was enjoying being with Marilyn,' Tony told me. 'When I walked on to the set and saw her sitting in her chair, our eyes would catch each other, and I swear to you I was in love with her all over again, and her with me.'

In his second autobiography he wrote that when they looked at each other, 'I felt like I had had a whole love affair with her before I even sat down.' In his memoir about the film he noted, 'So much emotion would pass between us in those moments.'

The chemistry between them was still there – both sexual and romantic. He told me, 'I would go to her dressing room, just to visit. "Hi, Marilyn, it's me." "Come in, Tony. Sit down."'

When he visited her dressing-room trailer, parked on the sound stage, he just sat and watched her reading her lines until they were called to the set. He wrote, 'I really liked those moments we had together. They meant a lot to me, and I could see she enjoyed them too.'

This was only a hint of what was happening between them. Tony told me, 'Every time I saw her, I felt like I did in those early days when we were first seeing each other.' They had been in love, and it seems those feelings were resurfacing. And she hadn't forgotten a promise he had made to her. 'She kept reminding me that I had said I would marry her when we were both successful, and there we were, successful, and I was married to Janet and she to Arthur Miller, and whenever she smiled at me and said, "Let's get divorced and then get married," a little thought went through my head of, "Yeah, that might be nice." And then I would remember how miserable marriage had made me, and I put it out of my mind. But whenever she said it, I always told her, "Let's wait and see," and she took that to mean we probably would.

'I don't know why I didn't tell her straight, "It's not going to happen, Marilyn." Maybe it's because in some small way I loved the idea that it *could* happen, *if* I divorced my wife and she divorced her husband, so I might have led her to believe it might happen after we finished the movie. I don't know what the hell I was thinking.'

He was very forthcoming with his feelings about Arthur Miller and the kind of relationship he had with Marilyn. 'He was a brilliant playwright with a brilliant mind and so much older than she was and hardly an Adonis. She didn't marry good-looking men her own age. She married men who would be her father. But she came to resent him and ended up humiliating him, like the teenage daughter who wouldn't do what her father said. Maybe that was her game – to be the bad daughter of a well-intentioned parent. But as a lover, what was he to her? I don't know that she had that many lovers her own age. I don't mean the one-night stands. She let enough men use her, but they never loved her.'

But he did, and he was sure she loved him too. 'I honestly think I was the kind of guy Marilyn needed at that time, when we made that movie. Miller began hanging around the set, and when he was there she was different. She didn't smile at me. But when he wasn't, when we were on our own, she smiled, and when she smiled, her eyes were just so sweet and needing and giving, and her body was perfect – she had the perfect figure, the most perfect figure I ever saw – and she'd squeeze my hand and say, "Remember your promise."'

'We kept those moments private, in her dressing room. Nothing happened, and yet everything was happening.'

Tony decided to get on with making the movie and worry about what might or might not ever happen between them when it was finally complete. 'The work had to come first,' he said. 'I didn't know what might happen when it was over.'

It seemed a happy and creative first few weeks of filming for all concerned. Marilyn wasn't needed for the third and fourth weeks of filming while Tony and Jack Lemmon worked on the opening scenes in the speakeasy, shot at MGM. The two actors developed a close bond and friendship. 'It was a happy experience,' recalled Jack Lemmon. 'Tony and I worked great together.'

Tony said, 'I loved working with Jack. He never did anything just to make himself look good at the expense of the other actor.'

The unit returned to the Goldwyn studio to finish the interior scenes on the train involving the three stars and all the girls playing the band. Tony observed that Marilyn 'was sweet to those girls. She didn't have a lot of women friends.' He didn't consider her secretary May Reis or Paula Strasberg 'real friends'. He noticed how Marilyn 'went out of her way to make those girls comfortable', and he would see them 'huddled on the set, whispering and giggling'.

He became protective of her, and when he saw she was struggling with her lines because there was too much noise going on around her, he would call for more quiet on the set. 'I felt she trusted me and looked to me for some kind of guidance and reassurance,' he told me. 'We would be doing a scene, and she would suddenly say, "How's my make-up?" and I'd say, "It looks good to me," and then she just carried on with her lines. Wilder kept the camera running when everything else was working because he would edit around her unscripted moments.'

He began to notice Paula Strasberg coming out of Marilyn's dressing room and knew she was still coaching Marilyn out of Wilder's sight and sound.

In September the unit moved to the Hotel de Coronado, a Victorian beach resort in Southern California, to shoot all the beach scenes and exterior shots of the hotel. Tony recalled, 'We shot all the exteriors of the hotel, and the picture was a lot of fun then. There was no trouble with Marilyn, no trouble with anybody.' And Jack Lemmon said, 'It was great fun and it was all going perfectly. The only problem we had was there was an airbase nearby and the jet planes were flying over all the time and we just had to stop and wait for them to pass over each time and then continue filming.'

When they came to the scene where Tony had to disguise himself as a mild-mannered millionaire who encounters Sugar on the beach, Wilder told him to find a different voice. 'You can't speak like a musician from Brooklyn,' Wilder told him. Tony took that to mean Wilder thought he couldn't manage a Boston accent or a mid-Atlantic accent.

'I took umbrage at what Billy said to me,' he told me. 'I was still very self-conscious about what people had to say about my accent. That was just a sample of the kind of madness I had at times. I felt like people were still saying, "You're not good enough," and I thought for a while that's what Wilder was saying to me.' His obsession that everybody else thought he wasn't good enough was a reflection of his own belief that he wasn't good enough. And his paranoia about all that surfaced that September when *The Defiant Ones* opened while he was still in the middle of filming *Some Like It Hot*.

Fighting down the hackles on his neck, he thought hard about what kind of accent he could manage. 'I got desperate so I decided to use the Cary Grant voice in an exaggerated way because I could imagine Cary playing that part. After we did the scene I asked Billy if the accent was OK, and he said, "What accent?" I said, "I was doing Cary Grant." He said, "If I'd wanted Cary Grant, I would have gotten Cary Grant." That's all he said, but since he didn't say *not* to do the voice, I stuck with it, and

I enjoyed playing that part much more than I did playing in drag. I did the Cary Grant voice as much out of desperation as anything.'

Despite Wilder's reticence about the Grant impression, and Tony's desperation to come up with some kind of non-New York accent, it was to become one of the enduring elements of the movie that helped make it such a classic.

While Tony and Marilyn were filming the scene, she was relaxed and doing well, making a few mistakes and relying heavily on his support. 'I would feed her lines when she couldn't remember them, and Billy just kept shooting and edited around my prompting her. It was very nice. Billy was happy because Paula Strasberg wasn't around for that scene, and Miller wasn't on location with us. Between takes Marilyn and I sat together, and she was really wonderfully relaxed without those people to put pressure on her.'

She was so relaxed that at one point she leaned towards Tony and whispered, 'Come and see me tonight.'

That night, in her hotel room, they made small talk and had a drink, and she asked him his advice about her role, and how he thought it was going. She seemed to distrust Billy Wilder's direction but Tony assured her that Wilder was doing what was best for her and the movie. 'The old feelings were still there,' he told me, 'and I stayed the night.'

He had told me in 1983 about his night with her, but didn't make it public knowledge until he wrote his memoir about the making of the film in 2009. He hadn't mentioned it in his 2008 autobiography, or even hinted at any such relationship in his 1994 autobiography. And when, in 1994, I broached the subject of his night with Marilyn, which he had told me about eleven years earlier, he was quite vehement in replying, 'It never happened. I wouldn't do that.' While promoting his first autobiography he refused to even discuss Marilyn in TV interviews. It was a very sore subject, and the consequences of that night haunted him almost as much as the death of his younger brother did.

He was desperate not to be discovered coming out of her room, so he didn't dare wait until morning. 'It was a wonderful night. She told me she loved me and more than anything wanted to have babies with me. That made me feel awkward. My wife was expecting our second child. It wasn't a marriage I wanted to stay in, but I didn't want to get divorced at that time because I thought that was the wrong thing to do. But Marilyn wanted to divorce Arthur Miller if I divorced Janet.'

He admitted, 'It was such a romantic wonderful night that I was seriously thinking about it for five minutes. I was kind of mixed up with feelings that it would be a mistake to get a divorce with my second baby on the way. I couldn't think straight about it, but Marilyn had made up her mind. I didn't want to ruin the moment by telling her it wasn't going to happen, which maybe I should have, but nobody's perfect, as they say.'

Their night together ended with her apparently believing they would get married and he knowing they probably wouldn't. Their situation was unresolved.

The next day, Thursday, they worked together with 'no awkwardness', he wrote. He was surprised that she behaved as if nothing had happened between them. He was relieved, too, because Janet had arrived with Kelly. After he finished his scenes he took Janet and Kelly to their hotel. He wasn't called for the next day so he drove them back to Los Angeles.

Back on set on the Friday, problems suddenly surfaced. Marilyn was two hours late, by which point the sun was too high and it was too hot to work on the beach, so Wilder postponed shooting until after lunch. She was late coming back after lunch, by which time the sun was getting too low for a master shot so they worked only on close-ups of her and Jack Lemmon. Lemmon recalled, 'Marilyn would say "Cut!" in the middle of a scene because it wasn't right for her.'

She had been taught a relaxation method by Paula Strasberg which was to shake her wrists. It became something she did to excess, either before every shot, or when she stopped in the middle of a scene, and it became a sign that she was losing focus on her work. When Wilder asked if she was ready, she shook her hands.

Jack Lemmon said, 'She'd just stop in the middle of a scene and shake her hands each time, and she wouldn't be ready until she had shaken her hands and found some kind of sense that she was ready, and sometimes we would be waiting for ages.'

That evening Arthur Miller called her from Roxbury, Connecticut, and they argued about text he had written for an article about her in *Life* magazine. Unable to sleep, she took some sleeping pills, had a drink, accidently took more pills, and was sick. She called Paula Strasberg and May Reis and they summoned a doctor. Early that Saturday morning she was rushed to Cedars of Lebanon Hospital, and when the press found out they were told she was undergoing tests for a mystery illness.

It was assumed by her colleagues that she had been so upset over her argument with Miller that she had taken an accidental overdose. It might well have been the case, but in his *Some Like It Hot* memoir, Tony said he was worried that Marilyn had taken an overdose because of 'what she and I had done at the hotel a few nights before'. But that only told half the story of what made him so anxious. 'I think she coulda been upset because I wouldn't say I would marry her,' he told me. 'When Marilyn wanted attention, she took desperate measures.'

Arthur Miller arrived on Sunday, and production on *Some Like It Hot* was shut down. The unit returned to Los Angeles as Wilder seriously considered replacing Marilyn with Natalie Wood, Carroll Baker or Mitzi Gaynor. He told Tony, 'This is not the story of Sugar Kane. This is the story of two musicians who have to dress up like women, and one of them happens to fall in love with a beautiful girl singer.'

Wilder decided not to recast. While Marilyn recovered in hospital, he worked around her. After she was discharged, Wilder took his unit back to the Coronado on 28 September to film the day-for-night scenes (shot during the day but with filters to make it look like night) of the motor launch and exteriors of the hotel. Arthur Miller came too, keeping a close eye on her. And with Tony came Janet and Kelly.

On her first day back at work, Monday 29 September, Marilyn had a nine o'clock call for shots of her on the beach. She finally emerged from her hotel room at two-thirty in the afternoon. Tony immediately noticed that she was very different from before. She no longer smiled or even talked to him. Miller was constantly at her side, and Tony thought it obvious that Miller was keeping her away from him, and he began to fret that Marilyn had confessed about their night together.

They filmed the scene where they kiss goodnight and he climbs the facade of the hotel to get back to his room. He told Wilder he could do the stunt himself, but Wilder insisted that his stunt double do it. Tony ran across the veranda, leaped on to the facade of the hotel, climbed up to the balcony, and then climbed down again. Wilder agreed he could do it.

On Monday 6 October, the unit returned to the Goldwyn studio in Los Angeles. Almost all the scenes to be shot involved Marilyn, and it quickly became apparent that it wasn't going to be easy. Tony recalled, 'She was having trouble with getting there on time, getting her make-up right, and Billy Wilder was so kind to her. He told her, "Every time you get it right, I'm going to print it, so you don't have to worry."'

Tony noticed that she seemed a little heavier and wondered if the sleeping pills were causing her to retain fluid. He sometimes heard her vomiting from inside her dressing room, and both he and Jack Lemmon felt sure she was drinking wine or vermouth from a thermos flask she had May bring to her.

On Saturday 18 October, Tony was at home with Janet when columnist Hedda Hopper called him and asked if Marilyn was pregnant. He didn't want to discuss it, so she threatened to print a story about him and a 'girl in Laurel Canyon'. It was the kind of blackmail he had exposed in *Sweet Smell of Success*. He told her, 'Marilyn's tits are enlarged. That's all I can tell you.'

It was all she needed to know. A few days later she wrote in the *Los Angeles Times*, 'Marilyn Monroe's closest friends believe she's pregnant. If true, I hope she'll be able to carry this baby.' When Marilyn read it in her dressing-room trailer, Tony heard her yelling, 'That fucking old bitch!'

She was barely able to work after that. Wilder shot eighty-three takes of one simple shot of her saying through the door, 'It's me, Sugar!' She would forget to say her line on cue, or she would say, 'It's Sugar, me,' or 'Sugar, it's me,' or any other variation of just those three words. They spent two days on the scene until she finally got it right.

She had the same problem with the line, 'Where's the bourbon?' Curtis and Lemmon were in agony standing in their high heels through eighty-one takes.

The next day, Marilyn stayed home sick, and so did Billy Wilder, who was suffering a bad back and stomach pains brought on by the intense stress he was under. When they came back to work the following day, Marilyn remained in her dressing room until after lunch, and when she finally emerged, Wilder began shooting another angle of the 'Where's the bourbon?' scene. Marilyn's lines were written on cards and placed all over the set. This time she had no problem saying the lines as written, but she kept demanding retakes because she didn't feel they were right.

Wilder was on the verge of a nervous breakdown when Miller finally confirmed that Marilyn was pregnant and insisted that he let Marilyn go each day at four-thirty. Wilder told him that he was never able to get his first shot of her until around three even though she was called each morning at eight. He asked Miller what she did all morning. Miller said she left their hotel at seven each morning. Wilder revealed that she didn't arrive before eleven-thirty and never appeared on the set until mid-afternoon. Miller was at a loss to explain where she was between seven in the morning and almost noon. When Wilder asked her outright where she was all those hours, she said, 'I got lost and couldn't find the studio.' Wilder found her behaviour contemptible and disrespectful to her co-workers.

Tony stayed out of the arguments, as did Jack Lemmon. Working with her became a nightmare for both actors, although Lemmon said, 'It was far worse for Tony because he had all those scenes with her.'

When someone asked Wilder why he put up with Monroe's behaviour, he said, 'I could get my auntie and she'd come to work on time and maybe even remember her lines. But the public wouldn't pay to see my auntie.'

Tony recalled, 'I had a scene with Marilyn on the boat, which we shot in the studio, and she had to look at this big fish and say, "What is it?" and I say, "It's a member of the herring family." She couldn't get that one line right. We spent a week and a half shooting that scene. She'd say, "What is it?" and then she'd turn to Billy and say, "Is that what I say?" and Billy said, "Cut! Yes, Marilyn, that's the line. Now let's do it again." We'd start again and she'd say, "What does it do?" and Billy yelled, "Cut! The line is, *What is it?*" And this went on for take after take and she got very flustered and said to me, "Tony!" "Yes Marilyn?" "What's my line?" "What is it?" And she said, "That's what I said, what is it?" "I said, "That is the line." "What's the line?" "What is it?" "Yes, what is it?" Oh! It got frightening, I'll tell ya.'

Finally, there were just two major scenes involving Marilyn to film. The first was the scene which took place on the yacht where Joe, disguised as Junior with the Cary Grant voice, insists women leave him cold, and so she proceeds to kiss him.

That day, Marilyn invited Tony to her dressing room for a glass of champagne to 'get a little loose' before the scene. She was in good spirits, and, said Tony, 'looked incredibly sexy with that white ball gown which was so see-through she had to wear little pieces of cloth to cover her nipples, only she had removed the pieces of cloth'.

He had one glass of champagne, wanting to keep a clear head for what was a key scene. Marilyn had a second glass. He asked her how she felt. 'Oh, I don't know,' she said. 'I think about things.'

'Like what?'

'Oh, about you.'

He asked her what she meant and she replied, 'If only it could be like what we had before.'

He gave her a long kiss. She responded, relaxed, and, in his words, 'never looked more sexy and beautiful. I'll tell ya, I would have given her anything in that moment.' 'Anything' possibly meaning a wedding ring. 'That's what she wanted,' he said. 'Later, after the scene, she made it clear.'

On the set, Wilder asked her to kiss Tony so he could set up the camera for the close-up. She said she would only kiss him when they shot it. Wilder gave in to her, and they shot the scene and it went perfectly. So well, in fact, that for Tony, 'It was the most intimate moment I ever shared with a hundred people all standing and watching on the set.' When she kissed him, he had an erection 'which would have killed an ordinary man', he joked, and she purposely ground her body against him.

Wilder said, 'Cut!' and she slowly pulled away, smiled at Tony and said, 'I got you this time, didn't I?' And then she showed him her finger which would usually have had her wedding ring on it – it had to be removed for all her scenes – and she whispered, 'Very soon this will have our ring on it.'

Tony admitted, 'I really liked the idea of coming home every day from work to be greeted with a kiss like the one I'd just had.'

The next day Wilder continued with the scene, but this time Marilyn was 'not relaxed, not warm, and very anxious', Tony said.

Jack Lemmon recalled, 'I came on to the set one morning to watch Tony and Marilyn shoot the scene where he's doing the Cary Grant voice and she's kissing him. We sat around for two hours before she would come out of her dressing room, and when she did she was saying, "I'm sorry," and flapping her hands.'

Her whole demeanour had changed and so had the atmosphere on the set. It didn't help that Arthur Miller had come to watch. They began shooting, with Tony pouring her a glass of champagne which was really ginger ale, and after just a few lines, Marilyn stopped and asked to do it again. They restarted the scene. She stopped again, closing her eyes, biting her lip and shaking her hands. 'She wasn't blowing her lines,' said Jack Lemmon. 'She just felt it wasn't going the way she wanted it to go, and she had to get it right *for her*. It drove Tony nuts.'

When she stopped again during the thirty-eighth take, Tony lost his temper and shoved the glass of ginger ale at her. She deflected it and it smashed to the floor. Arthur Miller flew out of his chair at Tony, who pushed him to the floor. Marilyn flew at Tony and he shoved her away. People rushed in to restore the peace, and Wilder called for a break.

Distressed, Tony returned to his dressing-room trailer. He could hear Miller and Marilyn arguing in her trailer. An hour later Arthur Jacobs, Marilyn's publicist, came to Tony's trailer and asked him if he would go and talk to Marilyn and Miller. Thinking he was simply being asked to apologise and try and smooth things over, he agreed to go to her trailer.

When he got there, he quickly apologised, but Miller remained hostile. 'Don't you want to accept my apology?' Tony asked him.

'Only if you'll apologise for sleeping with my wife,' Miller said.

Marilyn had confessed. Tony felt 'a heaviness in my chest and arms. I tried to breathe.' With a pepper-dry mouth, he tried to explain that he and Marilyn 'have a special feeling for each other'. He said it had started many years before and that when they were alone, 'it came back. I'm sorry.'

Miller threatened to 'beat the hell' out of Tony, although he probably wouldn't have stood a chance, but it didn't happen because Marilyn cried, 'Stop it! That won't fix it.' Tony wanted to know what there was to fix. Marilyn told him, 'I think the baby is yours.'

Tony was stunned. He hadn't even considered her pregnancy was a consequence of their one night together. He asked her what made her think the baby was his. Miller cut her off before she could answer.

When I asked Tony if she really was pregnant, he replied, 'Well, of course. Everybody knew it. But it couldn't have been Miller's coz he wasn't up to the job any more. Marilyn made mention to me that he wasn't able to make love to her. In my opinion he had begun to feel inadequate because she was so desirable and he was so undesirable, and she was always around handsome Hollywood leading men. That musta drove him so crazy, he just couldn't compete.'

Tony asked Miller and Marilyn what he could do about it. Miller said the only thing he could do was to finish the film and stay out of their lives. Tony returned to his dressing room and locked the door. Now Wilder had both the leading lady *and* the leading man refusing to come out, so he sent everyone home.

Tony said in 1983, 'She wanted me to marry her, and she thought she could trap me by saying she was having my baby.'

The day after the confrontation between Miller and Curtis, columnist Walter Winchell wrote that the two had got into a fight. That was Winchell's revenge for *Sweet Smell of Success*. Marilyn didn't come to the studio that morning, apparently sick, but was on the set the next day, surprisingly arriving early for a change. They began filming where they had left off, with the champagne glass, and she got it in one take.

Then they did a shot where Tony had to nibble on a piece of pheasant – only they used chicken because pheasant went off quickly under the hot arc lights. It took forty-two takes for Marilyn to get it right, and Tony felt so sick he didn't eat chicken for years after.

Curious to see how the scene on the yacht looked on film, Tony went to view the rushes. He quickly realised that Wilder had printed the scenes in which Marilyn was good but in which he had begun to wear down. On top of this, he was getting angry about obscene remarks some of the men were making about Marilyn's breasts.

At the end of the screening Tony said something that was to haunt him for the rest of his life. He said that kissing Marilyn Monroe was like kissing Hitler. Tony spent years denying that he ever said it at all. In a 2001 documentary, *The Making of Some Like It Hot: Nobody's Perfect*, he said, 'Once that scene was done the rumour came out that I said kissing her was like kissing Hitler. I never said it.' He never made any mention of it at all in his first autobiography.

He hoped to bury that old chestnut, but Jack Lemmon heard him say it. 'When we watched the rushes of that scene, Tony said something which he really didn't mean, and if I was him I might have said the same thing, but when the rushes ended and the lights went on, Tony stood up and said, "It's like kissing Hitler." I said to someone sitting next to me, "Jesus, he didn't really just say that, did he?" "Yeah, he said it."'

In his second autobiography, Tony made an attempt to explain himself. His version of the event was that when the lights had come up, one of the guys in the screening room had asked, 'What was it like kissing Marilyn?' Tony thought that was such a stupid question, he replied, 'Kissing Marilyn is like kissing Hitler.'

But I think the truth lies more in what he told me in 1980:

People always say to me, 'Isn't it terrible what happened to Marilyn?' I can't lie. I didn't like her. They say, 'But she was a legend.' Why do I have to listen to all this legend bullshit? She treated men like shit. She pushed them around, every man she was ever with. Lew Wasserman was my agent, also Marilyn's, and I saw how she treated him. He came on the set one day and waited for her while she was working, and as she walked by he said, 'Hiya, Marilyn, how are you?' She didn't stop, didn't say, 'Hiya, Lew,' didn't even acknowledge his presence. This was the man who helped her end up with seven and a half per cent of the gross of *Some Like It Hot* and a great up-front salary. And she treats him like this? Not just him. All people. Billy Wilder – she walked all over him because he asked her not to be late. Jack and I would get to work each morning at 7 a.m. to get into our trusses, skirts, heels, and all the make-up and all the hair, and by 9 a.m. we were ready, but she wouldn't turn up until 11.30 a.m. Made no difference to her. 'Fuck 'em,' she thought. 'Piss on 'em.'

Billy Wilder said, 'Now listen, you guys, you'd better be good in every take, because when she gets it right, that's the one I'm gonna print.' So there's Jack maybe with a finger up his ass, and me with a finger in my ear, and we look terrible in the shot but it's suddenly, 'Cut! Print! Next shot!' because it had to be good for Marilyn. That's what the woman was. When I said it was like kissing Hitler, it was [because of] the way she treated everyone.

Tony rarely spoke about Marilyn, but when he did it was with disgust. He loathed her behaviour and, even as late as 1994, he felt she didn't deserve the term 'legend'. Joan Collins, who appeared in an episode of the TV series *The Persuaders* in 1971, told me, 'I find it odd that a man like Tony Curtis should find it necessary to still talk with such hatred about Marilyn Monroe so many years after her death.'

This attitude puzzled people. Much of it was, of course, due in part to the intense difficulties of working with her, but it was also about their personal dilemma. They loved each other, they talked about marriage, they slept together, but whether they could have actually resolved all of that remains unanswered because it all came to a shattering end when she became pregnant with a child he believed was his. Did she really intend to trap him with her pregnancy? It's possible.

During the first week of November 1958, he and Marilyn filmed their last scene together in the movie. It was the scene, to be shot over two days, when they, Jack Lemmon and Joe E. Brown as Osgood escape in the motor launch. It was a process shot, filmed in the studio. Marilyn worked well, although Tony had most of the lines between them. The final moments in the film, with dialogue between Lemmon and Brown, were scheduled to be shot the next day.

Tony remembered, 'The day we shot in the motor launch in the studio, we finished the scene, and she had behaved well all day, and at the end of the day, we were on our way to our trailers, and she said, "Tony, I'm having our baby, and now you *have* to marry me." My wife was having a baby, and now Marilyn was having my baby, but then I figured it was just her way to get me to marry her. She was kinda desperate because she wasn't happy. She figured I could make her happy. We had all that history. It really got me thinking, ya know?'

At the end of that day's shooting, the new pages for the next day were printed out and handed to the actors. For days, Wilder and Diamond had agonised over what the final line of the film should be. In desperation, Diamond suggested that when Gerry finally tells Osgood he's a man, Osgood could respond, 'Nobody's perfect.' Wilder didn't think it was funny but they agreed to try it. When Marilyn saw for the first time that she didn't have the last line in the movie, she literally packed up her things from her dressing room, left the studio and didn't come back.

In the morning, Marilyn's stand-in took her place on the rear seat of the motor launch with Tony. He obscured her face while the camera focused on Lemmon and Brown and the final line was delivered, 'Nobody's perfect,' and Wilder called 'Cut! Print!' It was a wrap.

The very next day, Saturday 8 November, Marilyn was rushed from the Bel Air Hotel to Cedars of Lebanon Hospital with a suspected miscarriage, but it was a false alarm.

The film had become torture for Wilder but he had managed to stave off a complete nervous breakdown. The original fifty-day shooting schedule had stretched to seventy, costing an extra $600,000 on top of the original $2 million budget.

While Wilder was cutting the film, Tony was dealing with more emotions than he could cope with. He had been considering what part he should play in the life of the child Marilyn was having. He didn't like the idea of his child being raised by Arthur Miller, and he decided he would try and work out some kind of arrangement with Marilyn. Possibly even marry her. And yet, he had another child of his own – and Janet's – due very soon.

On top of all that, he was distressed to see his father become seriously ill. Manny's heart was weakened, he was under doctor's orders to give up all the rich and wonderful foods he had come to enjoy, and he was told to give up smoking. Despite having had a lung removed he had remained a virtual lifelong smoker and found it almost impossible to give up. The lung cancer had returned. Several times Tony caught him disappearing for a secret cigarette.

Tony had quit cigarettes in 1957 after smoking a pack and a half a day. 'I was thirty-two when I quit. What convinced me was that I had been to my dentist, and he was cleaning my teeth, and he said, "I'm getting tired of cleaning the tar off the inside of those teeth of yours." And he said, "I notice some white spots on the back of your gums. I think you ought to quit." He explained how one can get cancer and where it comes from, and that scared the hell out of me.'

He might have given up tobacco, but he hadn't given up marijuana. He told me he smoked it heavily when he was making *Some Like It Hot*. When he saw how often Manny was in pain and desperate for something to smoke, he made the decision to offer his father a marijuana cigarette. Manny said, 'Are you crazy?' and refused to take it.

'He thought I was a habitual drug taker,' Tony told a fan magazine in 1970. 'It was difficult to convince him that I did not smoke marijuana and that I had procured it only to try and help him. I told him, "Dad, you know cigarettes are cutting your life short yet you can't give them up. What harm can there be in trying to smoke this type of cigarette? I'm desperate. I don't know what to do to alleviate your suffering. Who knows? Maybe an occasional one of these cigarettes can help."'

Tony left his father alone with the marijuana cigarette, and later noticed that his dad was calm and his eyes no longer had the desperate look that had been there since trying to quit. Tony knew his father had smoked the joint, and he gave him all the marijuana cigarettes he had.

Manny never actually asked Tony for more marijuana but relied on him to get him some, and after that first time Manny never smoked them without Tony being there with him.

'I'm sure that someone reading my story will say that I was wrong, and that I went beyond the limits of filial love. Maybe!' said Tony in his interview, continuing:

I know that marijuana helped my father to live his last days in tranquillity and this is enough for me.

Naturally, my father realised that the calm he experienced was artificial and only temporary. He never deluded himself by thinking it was a cure for his illness. Once, after he accepted a cigarette, he said, 'You know, Bernie, things are much better with your mother now that I'm more calm. She worried too much about me and I had to make her happy, especially now as I feel my life slipping away day by day.'

I don't want to tell this story to advertise marijuana. I decided to tell it only in hope of convincing some smoker to give up cigarettes to avoid running the risk of having ten years of suffering like my father.

The article concluded with Tony saying, 'If you love someone who is a heavy smoker, for heaven's sake try to persuade that person to give up at all costs.'

When I saw Tony in 1985, I showed him a photocopy of the article and asked if it was true. He didn't hesitate and said, 'Why hide it? I've smoked dope a lot in my life, and I knew the medicinal benefits and I knew it would help my father. Marijuana is a narcotic. Like any pre-scribed drug. It should be available for medical conditions. I no longer believe it should be recreational.'

Tony completely gave up marijuana in 1984, along with the harder drugs he had become addicted to, but he didn't regret giving his father marijuana. 'It worked for him when nothing else would. What can I say? Dope made him feel better. But in the end he became too weak to smoke any kind of cigarette.'

On 16 November, Bobby phoned Tony and said, 'Daddy has gone to sleep.' Tony knew that meant his father had passed away. He called Jeff Chandler to ask him to come with him to his parents' house, and they found Manny lying dead on the bedroom floor. Tony never forgot Chandler's kindness and friendship. 'When my father died of a heart attack Jeff came, rushed down to their apartment with me and we sat shivah. He organised the funeral and all of that. That made me feel good, that I had somebody to rely on.'

Janet recalled that Jerry Gershwin and his wife Jackie also arrived to give support.

Manny was buried two days later. On 22 November 1958, Janet gave birth to Jamie Lee.

Manny's death created a huge hole in Tony's life, and perhaps that's partly why he found it so hard, in the following years, to feel as close to Jamie as he did to Kelly. His death and her birth almost coincided, and when she was born Tony was in mourning. He was also worried about what to do concerning the baby Marilyn was having.

Janet knew nothing about the Marilyn situation, but she was resentful that he was putting the needs of his mother and brother before her and their children. He had obligations to Helen and Bobby Schwartz, and he had no choice but to see to their needs. Bobby's circumstances were especially difficult, and Helen continued to make demands on Tony, and with Janet unable to hide her jealousy, the pressure piled up on him.

Shortly after Jamie Lee was born, she was discovered to have a swelling on her right side. A doctor diagnosed a hernia and Jamie, just two weeks old, needed surgery. Janet, trying not to panic, called Tony and he met her at Cedars-Sinai Hospital, where the hernia was successfully repaired.

Wilder had *Some Like It Hot* ready for its first preview in December 1958. It was a disaster. Nobody laughed. The audience had come to see *Cat on a Hot Tin Roof*. The Mirisches demanded Wilder cut 15 minutes from the film, but he ignored them and previewed the film the following week in Westwood where the audience was largely made up of students from UCLA. Lemmon recalled, 'When Billy told me they were having another preview, I asked him, "How much did you cut?" He said, "Sixty seconds, and if they don't like it, that's too bad for them."

Tony described for me the scene they cut. 'Jack and I are in the same berth. He thinks I'm Marilyn because I've taken her berth and she's gone to sleep in my berth. And Lemmon sneaks outta his bed and climbs in Marilyn's bed and climbs on top of me. He says, "I've got something to tell you, Sugar." So I try to get up again. He shoves me down. He says, "You know that before I was telling you about the birds and the bees? Well, I wanted you to know I'm a man." With that he whips his wig off and he starts to unbuckle his belt. And I said, "I'm gonna punch you right in the mouth," and he puts his wig back on and says, "You wouldn't hit a girl, would you?" They cut that scene coz they thought it was a little salacious.'

Lemmon said, 'Bill took that one scene out. On its own it's a terrific scene, but Billy said, it was "gilding the lily". It was one scene too much on the train.'

That second preview at Westwood was a huge success.

On 14 December, Marilyn was again in hospital. Two days later the news was released that she had lost the baby. It was said to be a miscarriage, but Tony had his doubts. 'They said it was a miscarriage because she had had miscarriages before,' he told me in 1983. 'But what I later found out was she had taken sleeping pills and washed them down with sherry on an empty stomach, and *that's* why she was in hospital. And I'll tell you what I think. I think she had an abortion. I can imagine Miller putting on the pressure and she gave in and that was that.'

Believing the baby he and Marilyn had created had been aborted, that on top of everything else he had been trying to come to terms with created an emotional maelstrom. Writing in 2009, he said that the news of the miscarriage coming on the heels of his father's death 'caused me to sink into a depression'.

This period of deep depression must have delivered the fatal blow to his marriage, even though it lingered on for a couple more years, and it coloured his whole attitude towards Marilyn Monroe for decades, and also towards the film that he is probably best remembered for, preferring not to even refer to it for many years.

'I had no idea *Some Like It Hot* would become such a classic,' he told me in 1994. 'It was just a nightmare for me, and I couldn't see the quality of it for a long, long time. I came out of it feeling like I'd been through a war, and although it was a big success at the time, it kind of got forgotten about for some years, and suddenly here we are in 1994 and everybody loves *Some Like It Hot*, and I'm realising what a great thrill it is to be a part of that movie. But for years I didn't think about it too much.'

On top of everything else, he had one more blow to his fractured ego. Billy Wilder didn't like his voice when he was playing Josephine so he had that whole performance re-voiced by actor and impressionist Paul Frees.

It must have been the final indignity.

CHAPTER FOURTEEN

Roller Coaster

n autumn 1958, Universal saw an opportunity for Tony to be a part of what the studio considered to be its most important movie of the decade. Kirk Douglas and Eddie Lewis were producing *Spartacus* for them. The Roman epic about the gladiator who led a slave revolt against Rome had big sets, a cast of thousands, and an impressive line-up of stars, headed by Kirk himself as Spartacus, Laurence Olivier as Crassus, Charles Laughton as Gracchus, Peter Ustinov as Batiatus and John Gavin as Julius Caesar. A German actress, Sabina Bethmann, was cast as Varinia, the wife of Spartacus (she was later replaced by Jean Simmons).

Tony had one version of how he came to be in the movie, and Kirk Douglas another. Tony's version was that Universal, who were financing the movie, wanted him in it, playing the role of Antoninus, a poet and a slave who runs away from his master to join the slave army. It was a short role that would only take 12 days to shoot. When he read the script, he found it nothing special, just an 'adventure movie in the mould of *Ben-Hur*', he said.

Kirk Douglas told me, 'Tony asked to be in it, so we created the role of Antoninus, which isn't in the book by Howard Fast. He wasn't in the original screenplay. I thought he was wrong for this kind of movie, but he was enthusiastic.'

It's more likely that Universal insisted on Tony being in the movie because he was still a magnet for the teenage market, and since Antoninus was written into the screenplay by Dalton Trumbo just for him, the version of the script he read was an early draft. It's likely that the likes of Olivier, Ustinov and Laughton had not been cast at that point, so Tony had no concept of the quality that was going to wind up on the screen. It was a big movie at Universal, and the studio needed him in it. His role was an important cameo, and he believed his relatively few scenes would be filmed in twelve days. In actuality, however, he was working on it, on and off, for a year; the difficulties of making such a big movie that took almost a year to film caused schedules to change constantly, and Tony found he had to be available throughout. He wasn't there when the first scenes were shot in January 1959, in the scorching heat of Death Valley, but instead was having a wonderful time filming *Operation Petticoat* with Cary Grant off Key West.

Tony said, 'Universal were so happy with me they asked me what I wanted to do after *Some Like It Hot*. I told them I wanted to do a service comedy with Cary Grant set on a submarine, and they gave me *Operation Petticoat*.'

Operation Petticoat, a World War Two comedy about a damaged submarine, was especially written by Stanley Shapiro and Maurice Richlin as a vehicle for Tony and Jeff Chandler. The two friends couldn't agree on who would take first billing. Friendship was one thing, billing another, so Chandler was dropped, and Tony was asked whom he would like to have as his co-star. He named Clark Gable or Cary Grant.

Gable had just made a submarine picture, *Run Silent Run Deep*, so he declined, but Cary Grant was happy to sign on to serve with Tony Curtis, who said, 'To be accepted by Cary was a great *Mitzvah*; a "great thing" when he chose to be in the movie.'

Grant liked Tony personally, but he never allowed friendship to get in the way of work, and he demanded first billing. Tony might have demanded billing over Jeff Chandler, but in this instance he accepted second billing just for the chance to work with his idol. Grant also insisted that Universal erect a permanent bungalow on the studio lot for him to live in during production. One was duly built. Star power had many advantages.

Tony also had star power, and he approved the choice of his friend Blake Edwards as director. Grant played the captain of the damaged submarine that gets painted pink because it's the only paint his lieutenant – played by Curtis – who has a gift for scrounging, can acquire. The submarine takes on board a party of stranded army nurses, leading to all sorts of sexual situations and problems.

Much of the film was shot at sea off the coast of Florida in January

1959, where, between takes, Grant and Curtis found ample time to lounge on the deck of the submarine as it drifted through the blue-green waters off the Gulf of Mexico, rolling gently in the swell off Key West, some 2,500 miles from Hollywood.

Tony roasted to a deep bronze as he sat fishing off the back of a launch while Grant sat nearby, looking incredibly handsome and fit for a man of fifty-five years. When Blake Edwards asked for his stars to take their positions, Tony left his fishing rod and joined Grant before the cameras. They did the scene and then returned to fishing and basking. 'It was just about the easiest picture I ever made,' said Tony, who was paid a hot $700,000. He had come a very long way from when he earned just $75 a week just a little over ten years earlier.

Tony was never far from Grant's side. He watched and studied his every move. Back at the studio, he haunted Grant's bungalow and dressing room. He told me, 'I've had such nice times with Cary. I sought out that relationship with him because I admired him so much, ya know. And he never took advantage of our relationship in the sense that he never grew tired of me as, shall we say, a fan.

'Whenever I needed him or wanted to ask his advice, he always made himself available, and I tried to be a good friend to him. There was a time when he wanted to spend time with his daughter, Jennifer, so I invited him to stay at this huge house I owned where he could spend quiet moments with his daughter without the press or anyone else hassling him. That meant a lot to me, to extend my home to a man I've admired all my life.'

Janet joined Tony at Key West while Jamie and Kelly were looked after by their nannies at home. Janet and Tony needed time alone after 'the epidemic of traumas had left us a trifle limp', as she put it. She said it turned out to be 'a glorious second honeymoon', and that 'the electricity flowed anew with each look or touch'.

Tony remembered it differently. 'I needed that time alone with Cary coz I had so much that was troubling me, and it was kind of a relief, ya know, to get away from home, from my wife, from Hollywood.'

Operation Petticoat was a huge success, grossing a staggering $23.3 million just in America (and probably as much again in the rest of the world).

In February 1959, both Curtis and Poitier were nominated for the Best Actor Oscar for *The Defiant Ones*. It was also nominated for best picture, direction, editing, screenplay and photography, and also for best supporting actor (Theodore Bikel) and best supporting actress (Cara Williams).

Janet remembered that 'the Academy Award night was nerve-wracking suspense'. As they walked up the red carpet, hand in hand, she noticed how cold and clammy Tony's hand was. He had told her that he didn't expect to win because he and Sidney would cancel each other's chances.

Oscars for best screenplay and best black-and-white cinematography went to *The Defiant Ones*. Theodore Bikel lost to Burl Ives for *The Big Country*, and Cara Williams to Wendy Hiller for *Separate Tables*. *Gigi* was named best picture, and it also took the best direction award. Curtis and Poitier both lost to David Niven for *Separate Tables*. Tony said bitterly, 'I only got nominated as the token Jew and Sidney as the token Negro, and they gave the award to a white Englishman.'

Curtis and Poitier were also nominated for Golden Globes and BAFTAs. Poitier won the BAFTA.

Tony never received another Academy Award nomination. 'It hurt not to win,' he told me. 'I thought I should have been nominated for *Sweet Smell of Success*.'

Trying to prove himself as an actor would become a lifelong battle. Jerry Lewis said, 'Of all the actors in Hollywood, I think he is the most underrated, without question. I mean, here's a guy that stretched from *The Defiant Ones* to *Some Like It Hot*. I mean, there's not a lot of actors who can say that.'

Despite his resentment, he was at the peak of his profession, had received great reviews, had been nominated for an Oscar, and the movie was among the year's top ten biggest moneymakers.

On 29 March 1959, *Some Like It Hot* was premiered at Loew's State Theatre in New York. The reviews were lukewarm and the first week of the run was disappointing. But the few who saw it loved it, word began to spread, and it became a huge hit, earning $7.5 million in North America and a further $5.25 million everywhere else. With reissues, TV showings, video and DVD sales and rentals, it's estimated it may have taken as much as $30 million by now, a huge profit for a film costing $2.6 million.

Tony didn't attend the premiere. He never explained why, but just said he was unavailable. I think he was avoiding a film he had come to detest, and he was also trying to deal with the emotional turmoil that had engulfed him.

He was soon dealt another blow. MCA bought Universal, and Lew Wasserman became the studio's top executive. He continued to be Tony's agent, but his time running the studio meant he had little left to guide Tony's career, although he assured him that his career at Universal would be better than ever.

Tony talked frankly to a fan magazine about the loss of his father, and recalled in great detail a morning, four months after his father's death, when he stood at his bedroom window, looking out at an April sky 'with the first glow of dawn'. He remembered the scent of wet earth that was carried in a light wind from the rain that had fallen during the night.

He had been unable to sleep. He was unable to cry but wanted to. He looked over at Janet asleep in their bed and decided there was something he had to do. 'Death, with all its finality, was the hardest thing in the world for anyone to understand.' (He wasn't admitting it, but he was mourning two deaths – that of his father and that of Marilyn's baby.) All he wanted was 'some comfort, some understanding from God, and [to] try with all my heart to talk with God'.

He got dressed in a bulky woollen sweater and a worn pair of khakis, went down the hall and stopped at the nursery where Kelly lay 'all huddled in a heap on the bed'. Then he looked in at the nursery where 'Jamie curled up in a white, rosebud-trimmed crib . . . all pink and beautiful'.

He needed, he said, to go off 'all alone, to the little place Janet and I found, the hideaway in the hills only a few miles away, the quiet glen with the tall trees and the big boulder rocks'. He left a note for Janet in the kitchen, 'Going for a drive. Be back soon.' Then he got in his car and drove.

Later, sitting on a cold rock in the chilly glen, he smoked a cigarette. (He had given up smoking cigarettes in 1957, so either he had relapsed, or this was a marijuana cigarette, which isn't a detail he would have given to a fan magazine.) He recalled that 'blackbirds rustled through the treetops'; otherwise he was all alone. He peered up through the dark branches of the trees and asked God for help. For four months his father had been dead, and all the wishing and hoping and praying couldn't bring him back. He related that the sun rose in the 'white April sky – a strange ghost of a sun'.

According to the article, memories of his father ran through his mind, as did the principles of his Jewish faith. But he must have been thinking about many more things. His career, his marriage, the children, Marilyn, the baby he believed was aborted.

Whatever it was that he needed to resolve, I doubt he was able to. The only clue the article gives is that Tony told himself, or to God if He was listening: 'I must teach my children gentleness and patience, a kindness for strangers, and the beauty of family ritual.' (Tony would later condemn himself for his failings as a father as he went through further marriages that resulted in more children, and divorces, and being an absent father for some of the time. But if a man is the sum total of his parts, then Tony was, according to his children, even if they only knew it in later years, a better father than he gave himself credit for.)

He drove to the cemetery where his father was buried and stood over the grave and said, 'If only you could have lived to see Jamie.'

And then he finally cried and even managed a silent prayer that he remembered from his Bar Mitzvah. Then he got in his car and went home. The article said he had found peace. But clearly he hadn't.

In late spring 1959, he and Janet were paired one more time – and the last – in *Who Was That Lady?* He played a college professor caught kissing a student by his wife, played by Janet. He enlists the help of his friend, played by Dean Martin, who concocts the wild story that he and Curtis are really FBI agents and that the kissing was all in the line of duty. Foreign agents believe their story and go after them. It was a wacky and highly enjoyable comedy farce.

'So long as it doesn't happen too often there is nothing more cheering in the cinema than a film which is palpably, madly, wittily, mercilessly and deliberately absurd. *Who Was That Lady?* fits this description,' thought the *Sunday Express*.

Tony claimed he found little joy in making the film, which he said had such a ridiculous plot that even Bob Hope turned it down. He felt he and Janet had been faking their marriage for years by this time, and he disliked having to work with her again. At home there were constant arguments, not helped by the fact that Janet's father had become her business manager and 'a constant thorn' in Tony's side.

Contrary to Tony's perceptions about making the film, Janet wrote, 'I hope the audience had as much fun as we did.' She recalled Tony having trouble keeping a straight face in some scenes, and they enjoyed water fights which began with paper cups and progressed to water guns. Clearly, Tony had become adept at hiding his true feelings. They tended now to socialise separately, she going out in the evenings to see her friends, he to see his.

He went to work on *Spartacus* to find that the movie's director Anthony Mann had been replaced by Stanley Kubrick, the thirty-year-old maverick who had directed Douglas in *Paths of Glory*. Very quickly Tony began to realise the movie was a lot more than a sword-and-sandals adventure, and credited much of its quality to Kubrick. 'It has a lot [more] subtleties and flair to it than most Roman epics. It was a most entertaining movie. It holds your interest, it moves nicely and it's got such a lot of good stuff in it. Stanley Kubrick gave that film a style it wouldn't have had if someone else had directed it. I'll tell ya, he was diligent in his approach and attack.'

For Tony, the highlight of making *Spartacus* was working with Laurence Olivier, who played his master, General Crassus. 'Olivier taught me a lot about acting. He said to me, "Tony, clothes maketh the man." He taught me that you choose your clothes and you put them on and you finally become that character. He didn't just put on any costume that was given to him. He chose what was best for the character he was playing and showed me how that helps to take the character into another dimension. I learned that from him and always used it. So he gave me tips on acting and I gave him tips on body-building. I took him behind the set and said, "On your face." Then I showed him how to do press-ups properly, and it helped to get him into good shape.'

They shared one notable scene in which Crassus attempts to seduce Antoninus while taking a bath. But the scene was cut by the censor. 'That was madness. It was a wonderful scene,' said Tony. 'Maybe they'll put it back in the movie some day. You never can tell.' They did, when the film was fully restored in 1990. By then the soundtrack to that scene had been lost and Tony was called in to re-record his dialogue, but Olivier had died in 1989 so Anthony Hopkins provided the voice of Crassus.

Because of the film's restoration and subsequent reissues, and video and DVD sales, Tony found himself enjoying a new public image as the one who first uttered the immortal line, 'I'm Spartacus!' and he found that when he was recognised in public people would often call out to him, 'I'm Spartacus!' to which he would reply, 'No, I'm Spartacus!'

Midway through production, he was injured playing tennis at the home of Kirk and Anne Douglas. He had lunged for the ball and severed an Achilles tendon. He had surgery at Cedars-Sinai, and his leg was put in a cast for six weeks. Kubrick had no problem shooting around him, but Tony squirmed and fussed impatiently, eager to get well and go back to work.

In August the family had another scare when a swelling was found on Kelly's side. At the hospital, the swelling was diagnosed as the same kind of hernia Jamie Lee had, and it was concluded that it may have been genetic. Surgery solved the problem, but it was another stressful period of time.

Spartacus was a massive success. In its first release it earned $10.3 million in America and around $21 million worldwide. (By 1998, it had earned a staggering $60 million worldwide.) Just being in the movie earned Tony extra kudos, although some critics were unkind about his accent yet again, but his delivery of the poem *Blue Shadows and Purple Hills* is poignant and wistful and remains one of the movie's standout scenes. 'In some ways the most subtle performance in the film comes, very surprisingly, from Tony Curtis,' said *Record Show Mirror*. 'This may not be the most spectacular of Curtis's screen roles but it is perhaps his cleverest portrayal all the same.'

While Tony had been making *Spartacus*, Janet had been making Hitchcock's thriller *Psycho* and shocked audiences by dying in a horrific knife attack in a hotel shower just thirty minutes into the movie. Despite her brief performance, the movie was to become her most memorable.

Tony enjoyed making *The Rat Race* in the spring of 1960. He played a musician sharing an apartment with a dance-hall hostess, played by Debbie Reynolds. Tony actually mastered playing the saxophone and flute, and sometimes went over to Sinatra's to practise. When Frank noticed that he was playing a cheap flute, he bought him a new and very expensive one, a priceless gift that Tony cherished to his final day.

There was a good chemistry between Curtis and Reynolds. Director Robert Mulligan recalled, 'It was my second picture, and it gave me the chance to learn. I had a good time working with Debbie Reynolds and Tony. They were both pros, and there was never any of the star crazy stuff.'

Tony spent time with Debbie in her dressing room and believed 'the sparks flew between Debbie and me', but he found her 'a hard nut to crack' because she had developed a tough shell, having been in show business since she was a child. His attempts to romance her came to nothing. At the wrap party, she presented him with an art set, and he gave her a modern painting of a trumpeter.

The film netted $3.4 million Stateside, and once more Tony proved he was much more than a pretty face. 'A delightful and increasingly subtle actor' is how the *Financial Times* described him.

He was one of a myriad of guest stars in *Pepe*, an attempt to make Cantinflas, the Mexican actor from *Around the World in Eighty Days*, a major star in America.

Tony and Janet were introduced by Sinatra to Jack Kennedy, who was a big movie fan and loved meeting the stars, especially the beautiful women. Through Peter Lawford, Kennedy's brother-in-law, the future President of America began a secret affair with Marilyn Monroe; when that was over, Bobby Kennedy had an affair with her. For many years Tony insisted that those affairs couldn't have happened. 'By then Marilyn was unkempt, untidy – to be honest, just plain dirty,' he told me in 1994. 'They wouldn't have gone anywhere near her.'

He said he did once see Marilyn and Jack Kennedy together, 'but I couldn't tell for sure whether they had any sort of relationship'. By the time he wrote his second autobiography he reluctantly accepted that Jack Kennedy had had a relationship with Marilyn because 'everyone says they did'. But it was obvious he never wanted to believe it.

He often played touch football with Kennedy's younger brother Robert, and was friendly with the family patriarch, Joe Kennedy, who told him he loved Janet Leigh 'because she had a great chest'. When Tony and Joe Kennedy were at a movie premiere together, Tony introduced him to all the girls he knew there.

In September 1960, Tony and Janet, at the behest of Pat Lawford, Jack Kennedy's sister, hosted a luncheon in the grounds of their Hollywood mansion to kick off Jack's campaign to be President of the United States. Hundreds of buses and cars ferried guests from all over America for the event at which Edward Kennedy spoke and Sinatra, Martin and Davis entertained.

Tony was absent from some of the rallies to support Kennedy, because he was making *The Great Imposter*. It was based on the life of Ferdinand Demara, who changed identities, going from job to job, joining the navy and becoming a doctor in Korea, and generally running everyone ragged. It's an engaging, entertaining film, and he gave a dazzling performance. 'Demara's many facets afford Curtis a rare opportunity to demonstrate what movie acting is all about,' said *Saturday Review*.

TIME noted, 'Mr Tony Curtis, by now one of Hollywood's most versatile and accomplished actors, works wonders in holding the film together with his performance as Demara.'

Tony was now enjoying the most successful period of his career so far. He played Ira Hayes, the Native American who was at the raising of the American flag on Iwo Jima and hailed a hero. The film was *The Outsider*, (the story has been retold more recently in Clint Eastwood's magnificent *Flags of Our Fathers*). There were many in the business (and among his peers as well as the critics) who initially thought that playing Ira Hayes was outside his capabilities. He knew there were doubters yet set about preparing himself for the role with dogged determination, cutting and styling his hair to an Indian fringe and adding a bridge to his nose to give him a more authentic Native American look.

'It was something very different for me,' he said, 'to play an Indian boy. I used Olivier's trick of adding putty to my nose to give me a different look, but more than that I could empathise with what Ira Hayes went through, the kind of pain he felt because he was truly an outsider. I know how that can feel.'

Janet joined him in Arizona where he was filming, and together they met Ira Hayes's family on the reservation. They were shocked by the conditions they lived in. Several family members lived in a two-room house set in a barren wasteland with no running water, while immediately outside the reservation the land was green and irrigated.

When the unit moved to the marine base, Camp Pendleton, Janet and the girls stayed with him in nearby Oceanside. Her PR man, Warren Cowan, turned up to persuade her to make a bid for an Academy Award for her role in *Psycho*. She was hesitant, but Tony urged her to do it, and she allowed Cowan to begin placing advertisements urging Academy members to nominate her as best supporting actress.

Tony's performance as Hayes was worthy of an Oscar nomination, but it was an outstanding performance in a film that was no more than moderately good. As *Saturday Review* rightly noted, 'He brings the film alive and gives it a sense of urgency beyond either the script or the direction.'

After making *The Outsider,* Tony hit the JFK campaign trail again, and he and Janet joined Frank Sinatra on the podium with Kennedy for his New Jersey speech. Then they helped to attract thousands to the Shrine Auditorium in Los Angeles, where the crowds were so big they were unable to fit inside and filled the streets outside.

On the day of the returns, 8 November 1960, Tony and Janet hosted a party at their house, with guests including Sinatra, Sammy Davis, Gene Kelly and his wife, and Barbara Rush, to watch the results as they came in, but the party finally broke up at 4am as Richard Nixon refused to concede defeat. After a short sleep the Curtises and the rest of America woke up to find John Kennedy was the 35th President of the United States.

Christmas 1960 arrived. Tony and Janet were growing ever further apart. Janet, with typical professional aplomb, reported to a fan magazine how the Christmas spirit prevailed in their home. She told how Kelly was writing a letter, and she asked her daughter, 'What are you doing, honey?'

'Writing to Santa.'

'Better hurry. It's only two weeks to Christmas.'

Tony overheard and said, 'Some kid we've got. She gets eight days of Chanukah with presents every day, and then she writes to Santa for more.'

Kelly asked, 'Mommy, when will Santa get my letter?'

'If we mail it tonight, extra special delivery, he'll get it tomorrow after church.'

'Oh,' said Kelly. 'What church does Santa go to?'

That was the cute Curtis Christmas story that the fans read about, which no doubt reflected the kind of innocent ignorance of childhood amid the turmoil of a disintegrating marriage, but it was an effort to lay the rumours of a troubled marriage to rest.

Tony didn't entirely blame Janet for their problems, but it didn't help that she had been overwhelmed by the media attention her role in *Psycho* had attracted, especially now that she was campaigning for an Oscar nomination. She had begun to drink quite heavily because, Tony believed, she was frustrated that she couldn't compete with bigger movie stars like Elizabeth Taylor, which is something he understood because he always wished he could compete with Marlon Brando.

When she had too many drinks, she became, Tony said, 'belligerent, accusatory and downright nasty'. To avoid the arguments, he began staying away from home. He made visits to the Playboy mansion to 'fool around with one of Hef's bunnies'. He never felt guilty about his extramarital affairs, having long been convinced Janet was also having relationships with other men. He believed, 'She clearly didn't love me any more.'

How did he come to this conclusion? Janet appears to have been happy and optimistic by the end of 1960 and seemed to have no reason to suspect their marriage was actually coming to an end. She was to say she believed that 1961 'had all the elements of being one of the best of our lives'.

His jealousy and distrust was driven by his paranoia, although what exactly set it off is anyone's guess. This must have been a schizophrenic stage. Clearly, his life was a roller coaster which he wanted to get off.

CHAPTER FIFTEEN

An Emotional Tumour

After Kennedy won the 1960 presidential election in November, Peter Lawford asked Tony and Janet to host a luncheon for Jackie Kennedy at their home. Feeling intimidated by the new First Lady's elegance, Tony barely spoke to her. But he was now much liked by the Kennedy family and was invited by Joe Kennedy to stay at his home in Palm Beach in Florida.

Tony and Janet took part in the Presidential Inauguration Gala show on 19 January 1961, which also featured Gene Kelly, Milton Berle, Nat King Cole, Harry Belafonte, Ethel Merman, Jimmy Durante, Ella Fitzgerald, Peter Lawford and Frank Sinatra among many others. After the one and only rehearsal, heavy snow prevented Tony and Janet from returning to their hotel to change for the event, traffic was almost at a standstill, and the gala was two hours late starting. But it went ahead and was a huge success, after which Joe Kennedy threw a lavish party at a Washington restaurant for his family and all the gala stars.

Because the day of the inauguration was so bitterly cold, Tony and Janet remained in their hotel room to watch it on TV on 20 January, but they attended all the numerous inaugural balls held that evening at which the President and First Lady were present.

The next day the Curtises witnessed the investiture of Robert Kennedy as Attorney General, and then attended the luncheon at Robert's house that followed. After that they were flown in the Kennedy family aeroplane to Joe Kennedy's Palm Beach home. The Curtises had become valued and trusted friends of the Kennedy clan.

On 27 February, while they were staying at the house they owned in

Palm Springs, Janet received a phone call telling her she had been nominated for the best supporting actress Oscar. She immediately called the country club where Tony was playing golf with Frank Sinatra to give him the news.

It was the season of awards in Hollywood, and Tony and Janet were at most of them. They joined Jack Lemmon to perform some comedy skits at the Writers Guild Award Dinner in February, and on 16 March they attended the Golden Globes ceremony where Janet won best supporting actress.

The Academy Awards ceremony was on 17 April, and Tony and Janet were among the many star presenters. Janet lost out on the Oscar to Shirley Jones for *Elmer Gantry*, but despite her disappointment, she had to get back on stage to perform the *Triplets* song-and-dance sketch with Tony and Danny Kaye, which, along with her disappointment, had to be the cause of some marital unrest because, while Janet loved Kaye, Tony loathed him.

He would later recall of his marriage to Janet, 'We had a nice time together. It started falling apart near the end of it because, I feel, Janet's problem was beginning to overwhelm her. Sweet Janet started to drink a lot, and [was] taking a handful of pills. I felt bad for her, you know. I liked her, I liked her a lot.'

He admitted, 'Any problems I had at home [with Janet] I just buried and didn't pay any attention to them. There were a lot of difficult times and it was no one's fault but mine.'

Kelly believed that the problems came when, as sometimes happened, 'Jeanette sort of met Tony, or Bernard met Janet, and I think that dynamic was grist for some of the trouble they had in their marriage.'

Janet would acknowledge that 'an emotional tumour was growing, infecting the tissue of our marriage'. Among their problems was their conflicting attitude to money. When Tony told her he was going to buy a Rolls-Royce convertible, she objected because they were already financially overextended, and a furious argument ensued. He went ahead and bought the car anyway on credit. And yet despite her worries about money they spent a fortune throwing the biggest party they ever gave to celebrate their tenth wedding anniversary, with over 250 guests.

When Fred and Helen Morrison came asking for a loan, Janet agreed to it but Tony told her, 'Oh, *now* it's OK to spend money.' She burst into tears, so did her mother, Fred left in a foul temper, and Tony reluctantly agreed to help them out.

There was terrible news for Tony when he heard that one of his best friends, Jeff Chandler, had died. Chandler had hurt his back while making *Merrill's Marauders* and he had undergone surgery for a herniated spinal disc on 13 May. In the process, an artery was damaged and Chandler haemorrhaged. Surgery continued for a further seven and a half hours to try and repair the artery while he was given 55 pints of blood. Further operations followed and he had his entire blood volume replaced several times, but he died on 17 June 1961. Tony was among the pallbearers at his funeral.

'It really made me think,' he told me. 'Life is so fragile and can so easily be snuffed like a candle light. You only have to breathe too hard on a candle and out it goes, and when Jeff died, it was as though someone had just breathed too heavily. I miss him still.'

When Joe Kennedy asked Janet and Tony to attend Princess Grace of Monaco's International Red Cross Ball, Tony said he couldn't go, so Janet went on her own. They had quarrelled again before she left, so he phoned her at her hotel in Monaco and tried to patch things up. She was in such despair during the ball that she broke down in the ladies' room, and was discovered two hours later by Peter Lawford, who helped her into a car to take her back to her hotel.

The next morning Tony called. According to Janet, he said, 'Your dad died last night. He committed suicide.' As Janet understood it, a friend of her father's had been trying to reach him at his office and finally called the police and Tony. Empty bottles of sleeping pills were found, as well as notes taken away by the police, which included a scathing letter written to Janet's mother, although an aunt and uncle made sure Helen Morrison never read it.

Tony's account differs considerably. In his version, Helen Morrison called him, saying she had been trying to reach Fred all afternoon at his office. He wrote that Janet was attending a film festival in the south of France (his memory was at fault on this point), so he called the police and then drove over to Fred Morrison's office and found him slumped dead over his typewriter in which was a note. It read, 'I hope you're satisfied, you bitch!' (This, presumably, is the scathing letter Janet's relatives hid from Helen.)

Tony pocketed the note and then called Helen Morrison back with the news that Fred had died. The police arrived, and an ambulance took the body away. According to Tony, he never revealed the existence of the letter, and the police concluded that Morrison died of natural causes. However, the news went out that Janet Leigh's father had committed suicide.

After receiving the dreadful news, Janet flew home and, by her own account, was met at the airport by Tony who held her and comforted her, and 'was tender and compassionate'.

On their way to the funeral, on 15 August 1961, their car stopped at a traffic light opposite a newsstand which ran the headline, 'JANET LEIGH'S DAD WRITES NOTE, DIES'. She was devastated by her father's suicide and was unable to comprehend why he had taken his own life. She was distressed that he had not even left her a personal note.

With his wife in this state of mind, and with arguments raging between them, Tony and his family headed for Argentina in September 1961 to make *Taras Bulba*. He was playing the son of a 16th-century Ukrainian Cossack leader, played by Yul Brynner, in a spectacular production based on the famous Nikolai Gogol novel. It was largely filmed in Argentina because production costs were low, and the Argentinean Army provided several thousand men and horses to play all the Polish cavalry and Cossacks. The film's original budget was set at $3 million.

Still too terrified to fly, he, along with Janet and the girls, caught the train from Los Angeles to Miami, there to board a ship to Argentina. In their hotel room in Miami, Janet and Tony got into an argument, fuelled by alcohol. Janet described Tony, at that time, as 'preoccupied, edgy and restless'.

He wrote that she complained of being forced into taking the boat instead of an aeroplane by his neuroses, and that as she screamed at him and threw things, Kelly and Jamie looked on. It was then, he decided, that the marriage had to end.

The next day they boarded their ship and headed down the coast to Argentina. Tony spent much of his time with Kelly and Jamie, swimming in the pool and generally having fun, perhaps feeling subconsciously that this might be the last opportunity he would get to spend this kind of quality time with his girls.

They were put up in a splendid house in Salta, complete with a major-domo, maid and guards. Next door lived the Brynners.

'I liked working with Yul very much. I really did,' Tony told me. But he didn't like working with him at first. Brynner was unhappy that Tony was billed before him, even though Brynner had the title role. He told me,

'The picture was called *Taras Bulba*, not *The Son of Taras Bulba*. Tony Curtis had fought for top billing and won. Over *me*! So when we started I thought he was an upstart and wanted to teach him a lesson.'

Brynner told everyone that Curtis wasn't a good enough actor to be playing his son. Even Mrs Brynner made her feelings clear on the matter when she would bring a huge pitcher of orange juice to offer to everyone on the set but Tony.

'Yul liked to demonstrate his power over people,' Tony told me. 'He had this long cigarette holder, and when he took it out and placed a cigarette in the end of it, he had a man whose job was to rush over immediately and light it. And he better be there. Yul tried to assert his power on the director J. Lee Thompson, and he'd say something like "I think it would look better if the horses came from the other direction," and then he would take out the cigarette holder and wait for his man to light it.'

Tony was so disgusted by this behaviour that he brought an eye dropper, filled with water, on to the set, and when Yul put his cigarette in the ashtray, Tony sneaked up and squeezed a few drops of water on to the end of it. When Yul lifted his cigarette he was puzzled to find it dead.

After three days of this, Brynner was so mad at his servant that Tony stepped up and admitted he had been responsible for extinguishing his cigarette. Brynner laughed, and from that moment on they were great friends.

'Getting on with the people you work with is important to me,' Tony told me. 'A stranger comes in and everything that makes them strangers is eliminated, like knowing your name and where you come from is all you have to know. You don't have to know what kind of person it is, because you sense it. So right away you're on great terms. Right away you look like you have a great relationship when you hardly know each other. It's only because both people have been completely free with one another and opened the doors to allow each other the privilege of exchanging looks and not being concerned where the camera is, how they are photographing you. And this was such a good part for Yul. It was right down his alley, right out of his background. He wasn't asked to play anybody except a Ukrainian Cossack. That's all he had to do. He looked wonderful with that piece of hair sticking out of his head.'

J. Lee Thompson recalled, 'When we began *Taras Bulba*, Yul seemed to want to get everyone to hate him. But it was all an act. I could see through it, and I think Tony saw through it, and they got on well. They had a wonderful chemistry as the father and son. The most effective scene in the whole movie was when Yul has to shoot Tony Curtis, and because of the way they played it, it was a very emotional scene.'

The film is a sort of *Romeo and Juliet* with Tony's Cossack falling for a Polish lady, played by Christine Kaufmann. She was a sixteen-year-old German actress who had begun making movies at the age of seven in Germany and Italy, and had just made her American film debut opposite Kirk Douglas in *Town Without Pity*. She had a considerable intellect for one so young. She was fluent in Italian and English and her reading ranged from novelists like Dostoevsky and Mann, to poets like Heine, and philosophers like Descartes and Lin Yutang. She said, 'The more I learn, the more there is to learn. One lifetime is not enough.'

Tony was excited by her intellect. By now he was reading a diversity of subjects, and his interest in art was shared by Christine. He believed Janet was only interested in being a movie star. He was also excited by her beauty and fresh sexuality. Just sixteen years of age when *Taras Bulba* began filming in September 1961, she was, in the words of Yul Brynner, 'a child-woman'. At the age of just fourteen, she had played a romantic leading role in Sergio Leone's 1959 version of *The Last Days of Pompeii*.

Tony believed, 'She was very childlike and amused by me. She was a very beautiful woman.' From the moment he set eyes on her, he was smitten. J. Lee Thompson told me, 'It was obvious to everyone on the set that Tony was becoming very fond of Christine.'

She would later admit, 'When I met Tony my head was in the clouds.' Overwhelmed by his good looks, his movie-star status, she fell for him. Tony seemed to think nobody had noticed as he and Christine found opportunities to slip away for secret romantic liaisons. 'When I first met Tony I thought he was shy and sensitive. Handsome, yes, and important. He was mature, and boys my own age bored me. They either talked about hobbies or sport while they tried to get up the nerve to embrace me.' Tony didn't spend time finding the nerve. 'I was feeling like a woman, all woman, and that's what I wanted to be, not a film star.'

She said of herself, 'I was like an overdeveloped child, completely retarded in one respect, and yet too developed.' She admitted more than ten years after meeting him, 'I never did love Tony, not as I'd think of loving a man now, but what I felt for him was the kind of love a teenager has for an older man like a teacher. He was gentle – a gentle man and a gentle lover. I never hungered for the strong kind of man, muscles and rough, that kind of man. It's better to go with someone gentle.'

She said that a wise old woman once told her, 'The only real duty of a man is to make beautiful babies.' Said Christine, 'I looked at Tony and wondered if I would want his child. I decided, yes, he would make beautiful babies.'

The off-screen romance affected Tony's work, according to Yul Brynner. 'He struggled between giving a performance and romancing Christine Kaufmann. What he had going for him was his chemistry and charm, and I felt our scenes as father and son worked well because we had respect for each other and a liking for each other.'

To counteract rumours of an impending divorce that always pervaded, Janet gave upbeat interviews to the fan magazines.

I'm always hearing divorce rumours about me and Tony. But it doesn't bother me. We just ignore them. We've been married ten years and every year they come up with more stories. We're just two people and in these years I promise you, we've had fights, but we're not going to get divorced just because of a fight.

We were on location in Argentina with Tony, and did we have our share of problems! First Kelly came down with the measles. Then Jamie fell and broke her clavicle. Then one of our maids had an attack of appendicitis and had to be rushed to hospital. After that, the wife of Tony's stand-in had a baby, and Tony had a hard fall and was all bruised. Now don't you think that's stretching things too much? But other than that, the trip was wonderful.

Jamie had broken a clavicle when Tony took her to a park to play, threw her in the air and dropped her. He felt terribly guilty, and on top of that Janet felt unwell much of the time with colitis.

Janet wasn't on the set often but spent time horse riding with a general and his wife. She could tell Tony was relieved when she and the girls left for Rio de Janeiro to do work for the United States Information Agency, visiting hospitals and schools. On 22 November 1961, Janet and the girls returned to America.

Tony had few good memories of making *Taras Bulba*. 'That picture got a little out of hand in the making of it. Director J. Lee Thompson and the producer Harold Hecht had many disagreements. There was a lot of tension on the set. My marriage with Janet was split and I was in a very close proximity with Christine Kaufman.

'It wore unnecessary strains on everybody. It provoked relationships that shouldn't have been provoked. That picture is a haze to me because it was a tough movie to make. *Oh, tough!* We went down to Salta, Argentina, we did all that stuff, went all the way back to California to finish it up. It was a very hard picture.'

J. Lee Thompson had not finished filming the climactic battle scene when Harold Hecht pulled the plug and ordered the unit back to Los Angeles. Thompson told me, 'I had a hard time editing enough film together to complete the story. Frankly, it ruined the film.'

He was also suspicious about why they suddenly didn't have the money to continue filming in Argentina. 'It was cheap to film there, which is why we went in the first place, but suddenly the producer said we were out of money and had to return to California. I believe it's what they call "creative accounting". The money was going somewhere but not necessarily on the film.'

Janet was waiting at the dock in New York with placards and banners to welcome Tony off his ship. She recalled, 'A different person came off that liner, someone distant, removed, polite but not in touch.' He barely spoke to her on the train journey to Los Angeles.

Filming continued at Universal Studios where the interior scenes were shot, and at the Disney Ranch where Tony and Christine filmed their major love scene and kissed for the first time for the cameras. 'When we shot at the Disney Ranch, and Tony and Christine did their big love scene, nobody was in any doubt they were in love,' said J. Lee Thompson.

Janet began hearing the rumours but instead of accusing him outright, she turned up at the studio and asked him to introduce her to Christine. He didn't. By the time the movie was finished, the Curtis marriage was unsalvageable.

As for the movie, it was ruined by bad decisions, not taken by the director. Being unable to finish all the location work in Argentina affected many of the action scenes, and filming at Universal meant cut-price sets. When Thompson had completed his film it ran around two and a half hours and had an intermission. United Artists decided to cut it by half an hour. J. Lee Thompson told me, 'Tony had some brilliant scenes that ended up on the cutting-room floor. So did Yul. Yul blamed me for ruining his performance.'

The film split the critics. *Variety* commented that 'the panorama of fighting men and horses sweeping across the wide steppes provides a compelling sense of pageantry and grandeur', but of Curtis' performance it said, he 'was seemingly neither inspired nor irritated sufficiently enough [by Yul Brynner] to do more than kiss and kill on cue'.

The *Daily Mail* praised the film for its action and said, 'What Tony Curtis does would have left even Fairbanks Senior breathless.'

The final budget came in at $7 million. Somehow an extra $3 million had been spent, and not all of it on what went on the screen. Tony claimed that Harold Hecht was flying to Buenos Aires to deposit money that should have gone on living expenses in private bank accounts, and cheated him out of the profits he should have earned. The film took only $4 million in America but did well in the rest of the world, more than doubling the domestic box-office figure. Had the budget been kept to $3 million, it would have made a good profit.

With filming complete, Christine went back to Germany, where she was contracted to make a picture, and Tony sank into a depression. Janet was drinking heavily. Unable to stand being around her when she was drunk, he stayed often at Hugh Hefner's house or with Nicky Blair. In March 1962, he told Janet he was leaving, packed a few things, and left as she stood at the doorway holding Kelly by the hand and Jamie in her arms. He said that when he saw the two girls, 'my heart was torn apart'.

He moved into a three-room bungalow dressing room at Revue Studios to live for a while and prepared to make two films under the banner of his new company, Curtis Productions. The first was *40 Pounds of Trouble*, a remake of the old Shirley Temple film *Little Miss Marker*. The second would be *Monsieur Cognac*. Both were for his old studio, Universal. He was immersing himself in his work to help him overcome his complicated personal problems.

He turned to the man he most admired for consolation, Cary Grant. He arrived at Grant's home and for three hours unburdened himself of all his frustrations, inadequacies and inabilities. 'I just talked and let out the garbage,' he said. 'Again, I needed someone to talk to, and this time I didn't want to do it to a head-shrinker.'

40 Pounds of Trouble was Tony's first film where he had creative control. To direct it, he chose Norman Jewison, a young Canadian whose previous experience directing had been for TV, and who went on to direct *The Cincinnati Kid*, *The Thomas Crown Affair* and *Fiddler on the Roof*.

Tony played a Lake Tahoe nightclub owner who finds himself the unwilling guardian of a little girl, played by Claire Wilcox. Playing the casino boss was Phil Silvers, whom Tony had known for years. He once introduced his father to Silvers, saying, 'I want to introduce you to Mr Schwartz.' Silvers put on an air of indignation and demanded, 'Why do you call yourself Mr Schwartz? Isn't Curtis a good enough name for you?'

Much of the film was shot at Sinatra's Cal Neva Lodge at Lake Tahoe where, one evening, Tony caught an act that intrigued him. Hypnotist Arthur Allen seemed able to put people in a trance and make them do anything. Tony arranged to meet with him and asked if he could cure him of his fear of flying. Allen said he could.

In Tony's hotel suite, Allen told him to sit back in a chair and proceeded to put him in a trance. His eyes open, and perspiration running down his face, Tony recalled that someone had once told him, 'Be careful. You may go up high, but you can come down in flames.' He kept repeating the words, 'Down, down in flames. Red, glowing flames.'

He had seen those red glowing flames the night an aeroplane engine caught fire when he and Janet were flying to Germany. Allen told him, 'There is no logic for your fear of flying. It is nothing more than a subconscious phobia [of] one day falling from grace in Hollywood.'

Tony had always feared that every ounce of success he had fought for would be taken away, and Allen helped him to understand that when he saw the aeroplane engine on fire, it wasn't so much his life he feared losing but the success he had battled so hard for. He said, 'I was afraid people in the industry were trying to ruin my career. I was suspicious of everybody. I was certain someone was trying to bust my contract or steal parts from me. I had nothing but my career and therefore it made me frightened.'

When Tony came out of that room, he said to his public relations man, Len Kaufmann (no relation to Christine Kaufman), 'Do me a favour, Len. Rent a plane. I'd like to go for a ride.' He spent the next three hours soaring over the mountains of Nevada in a rented Cessna light plane. When he had to return to California to complete filming at Disneyland, Tony flew.

He became enamoured of his leading lady, Suzanne Pleshette, and admitted that if he hadn't been in love with Christine, he might have fallen in love with Suzanne. She told me, 'I always liked Tony a lot. We did two films together (*40 Pounds of Trouble* and, later, *Suppose They Gave a War and Nobody Came*). He has a lot of charm and is very handsome, and any woman would be tempted. I let him flirt with me, and I flirted back, but that was all. No harm in flirting; we were having a lot of fun.'

Tony had problems finding time to see his children, although he had often been away from them for months at a time before he became an officially absent father. Kelly recalled, 'My father moved out and I remember I missed him. He was an active father. He used to take us to the beach. I missed going to the beach with him. I remember those moments really clearly.'

He treated Kelly and the film's mini co-star Claire Wilcox to a day out in Disneyland. Jamie didn't go, for reasons never explained.

40 Pounds of Trouble was a good movie, and did well at the box office. *TIME* said, 'Tony has had better material but he has never made more of less. He skitters through his best scenes like a cat in patents. When he does a slow burn you could fry an egg on his deadpan. Cary should approve.'

Having just finished *40 Pounds of Trouble*, he was asked by director Richard Quine to appear in a few scenes in *Paris When it Sizzles*. Quine's star, William Holden, had checked into rehab because of his drinking, and Quine needed Tony to fill in for just a few scenes. He enjoyed working for a week with Audrey Hepburn, and then he flew to London, where he bought a Jaguar coupé. He went by ferry to France, and then drove the Jaguar to Munich where Christine was working on *Tunnel 28* for producer Walter Wood. Wood had got Christine at the bargain price of just £9,000. Tony and others thought Christine was worth a lot more money, maybe as much as £40,000, but her mother had made the deal. Mrs Kaufmann was Christine's agent, manager and public relations officer.

It hadn't yet become public knowledge that Tony and Christine were an item following his separation from Janet, and in an effort to throw the press off the scent while *Tunnel 28* was being filmed, Sam Wood got his publicity people to plant a story that Christine had a boyfriend waiting for her in Munich. When her mother, who had not been consulted about the story, read about it in an American gossip column, she demanded an explanation from Wood, who tried to assure her that it was a wise move because people were beginning to blame Christine for destroying Tony's marriage. He wanted to 'take the heat off Christine'.

'I don't care,' Mrs Kaufmann raged. 'What matters is that Christine has no boyfriend in Munich.'

Harold Hecht had compared Christine's rise with that of Sophia Loren: 'Sophia Loren and Carlo Ponti met by chance, leading to her eventual triumph. Nobody doubts Ponti was her Pygmalion. But Christine doesn't need a Ponti. She's got mama.'

A crew member on *Tunnel 28* remarked carelessly to one reporter, 'Where once Mrs Kaufmann's purse contained her knitting, today it bulges with newspaper clippings, photographs of Christine, letters, telegrams and drafts of new contracts. She thinks nothing of calling Hollywood on the spur of the moment to talk to Christine's agent.'

While he was in Munich, Tony discovered that rags had been jammed into both the exhausts on his Jaguar in what was a clear attempt to kill him with carbon monoxide poisoning. He could only guess that somebody working on the film had done it because he was a Jew in love with a German actress.

Before he returned to Los Angeles, Janet gave him a one-day Mexican divorce on 14 June 1962, and married Bob Brandt the very next day. Tony gave her the houses they had in Los Angeles and Palm Springs. He was determined not to fight over money, and wanted to make sure he supported his two girls. He agreed to pay a third of all Janet's expenses, which included everything Bob Brandt spent too.

Tony wondered if she had been seeing Brandt behind his back. In her autobiography Janet wrote that Jeanne Martin had introduced her to Brandt and implied it was after Tony left. She also wrote that after he proposed, she asked herself, 'Did I dare rush into another involvement after only six months?' They married just three months after Tony left, so if her sums were correct it would appear that she had been seeing Brandt for three months before Tony left her.

Tony found it difficult when Brandt moved into the house that he had bought with his hard-earned money – although it was also bought with Janet's equally hard-earned money – and he struggled to accept that Brandt had become his daughters' stepfather. He conceded that Brandt was a good man, who proved to be a good father to Kelly and Jamie.

He resented, though, having strict limits to the amount of time he could spend with his girls, and when he brought presents to the house for them, Janet or Brandt made sure he left after his allotted time. He found it difficult to have to ask for permission to see the girls, and before too long he found it was just too difficult, so gave up. He became, he said, 'the worst father of all time'.

CHAPTER SIXTEEN

Order Out of Chaos

uddenly broke with hefty monthly maintenance payments to make, Tony Curtis accepted every film that was offered to him, including *Lady L* for MGM. When the picture was delayed, he became desperate for money, so Lew Wasserman advised him to turn up for work on the movie every day according to the starting date on his contract. He did, and MGM had to pay him $50,000 every week for ten weeks until the picture was finally shelved (and later filmed with Paul Newman).

Tony accepted second billing to Gregory Peck in the excellent comedy-drama *Captain Newman M.D.* It was really just a secondary role but he enjoyed the challenge of combining comedy with human tragedy. Peck had the title role of a dedicated military doctor at an air-force base. Tony was Corporal Laibowitz, working among the patients and providing some of the movie's effective comedy moments.

Gregory Peck recalled, 'I don't do comedy well, but Tony does, and he can do pathos too, which is a combination very few actors can. He's very good at making the other actor look good in comedy, and I've always hoped we might make another comedy together.'

The film's producer, Robert Arthur, wanted Tony to play his part overtly Jewish, which he wasn't comfortable with, but he gave it a subtle touch in that direction. Although Bobby Darin as a decorated hero who believes he is a coward won an Oscar nomination for best supporting actor (losing out to Melvyn Douglas for *Hud*), Tony walked away with the best reviews. 'Tony Curtis, in a performance exactly opposite Peck's, is a knockout,' said the *Hollywood Reporter*.

The *Daily Herald* said, 'If there had not been Tony Curtis, I might have needed one of those paper bags they provide on aircraft. Curtis as the fast-talking Corporal Laibowitz is the very, very good bit of the film.'

Curtis next made a guest appearance, in heavy disguise as an Italian organ-grinder, in *The List of Adrian Messenger*, along with Burt Lancaster, Frank Sinatra and Robert Mitchum, also in heavy disguises. The main stars of the movie were Kirk Douglas as a killer and George C. Scott as the policeman after him. At the end of the picture, after the case has been solved, the guest stars remove their make-up to reveal their identities, a unique novelty that helped the film to success.

Christine Kaufmann was in Germany again to appear in Carl Foreman's excellent anti-war movie *The Victors*. Tony missed her desperately. 'He spent thousands of dollars telephoning me every day until I agreed to go to California,' said Christine. She convinced Foreman to release her so she could return to Los Angeles.

She turned eighteen on 11 January 1963, and Tony – aged thirty-seven – married her on 8 February in a simple five-minute ceremony in Las Vegas with just a few close friends present. Kirk Douglas was his best man and Kirk's wife Anne the matron of honour. Marriage was important to Christine. 'Marriage and babies went together to me, always,' she said.

Tony would later admit that he married her for the wrong reason. He had never been an ordinary teenager and marrying Christine gave him a second chance at experiencing those missed teen years. But it came with a price. He recalled, 'When I broke up with my first wife, there were headlines. "Tony Curtis Leaves Wife For A Teenager." "Tony Curtis Abandons His Girls." It was awful.'

Lew Wasserman at Universal believed the furore would die down if Tony and Christine did another movie, so they made *Monsieur Cognac*, a fast-paced farce about a spoiled and precious French poodle who befriends an American gambler, played by Tony, but becomes jealous when Tony falls for the dog's owner, played by Christine.

Universal retitled the picture *Wild and Wonderful*, a title Tony hated, but he loved the dog so much that he bought one just like it.

While filming in Paris, Christine was hounded by the European press, demanding that she and her mother pose for pictures to quash rumours that mother and daughter were feuding. She refused, insisting, 'We are not feuding, and I don't have to pose for pictures to prove it. It's quite enough if I say so.'

Tony told the reporters, 'If Christine doesn't want to give interviews, that's her business, and if you don't want to talk to me, that's OK by me.' He had lost all patience with the press after years of cooperating with them.

After *Wild and Wonderful* it seemed an appropriate time for Christine to retire from the movies. She said, 'You cannot be an actress and a wife. Anyway, I was never a very good actress.' Her mother was furious that her daughter should forsake the screen stardom they had worked so hard to achieve. Tony had not known Christine had intended to abandon her career, but he didn't object to her quitting movies and becoming a full-time wife. He thought this time he had a wife who would devote her time to him and not to her career, which pleased his sense of chauvinism.

He made *Goodbye Charlie* purely for the money, determined to live up to his financial obligations as a father. If he couldn't be with his children, they were never to go without because he had failed to provide financially for them.

Goodbye Charlie was based on a successful stage production that had starred Lauren Bacall as a guy, Charlie, who dies and comes back as a woman. Twentieth Century-Fox had bought the screen rights for Marilyn Monroe, but she had become difficult and unpredictable so they cast Debbie Reynolds in the part. Tony took top billing as Charlie's best buddy. Walter Matthau co-starred as Charlie's friend who shoots him for messing around with his wife. That's when Charlie dies and comes back as a woman.

The movie was among the year's top ten biggest moneymakers, proving Tony's box-office power was still there, and it kept him in demand.

He decided a change in his image was long overdue. He fired his PR man and hired a new one, Richard Carter, giving him brief and concise instructions. 'I want a new image. The old Tony Curtis is no more, and it's time the public realised it.'

He would have nothing more to do with the fan magazines, and he was through with being a pin-up. He wanted to stay out of the Hollywood limelight, having lived in it throughout his first marriage. The main task of his new PR man was to keep his name *out* of the press. There was an embargo on details about his personal life, and he didn't want to find his name in the gossip columns ever again. From now on, he would only do interviews with very important journalists.

He gave no big Hollywood parties and only a few good friends – including Cary Grant, Kirk and Anne Douglas, the Gregory Pecks and the Billy Wilders – were invited into the home where he and Christine lived in a quiet side street off Coldwater Canyon.

Evenings were usually spent in their own company, with the lights kept low. When they did go out it was often for long leisurely walks. They worked hard at keeping the romance alive. Every night Christine prepared his dinner herself, put on long evening dresses, and they dined by candlelight surrounded by vases of flowers. He insisted the age gap made no difference. 'The only way for a guy to stay young is to marry a girl much younger than he is.'

Jamie and Kelly were able to come and spend time with Tony now, and Christine befriended the girls when they came to stay in the attic room that had been enlarged to accommodate them. Tony and Christine also began a family of their own when Alexandra Theodora Didi Curtis was born on 19 July 1964.

Tony still wanted to be taken seriously as a dramatic actor, and had achieved great things with *Sweet Smell of Success*, *The Defiant Ones* and *The Outsider*, but now he was being offered only comedies. The next one to come along was *Sex and the Single Girl*, a very funny spoof on Helen Gurley Brown's bestseller of that title. The film really had nothing to do with the book. Natalie Wood played, with consummate comedic skill, Helen Brown, a sex analyst who writes a book called *Sex and the Single Girl*, and Tony played a dirty-minded double-dealing writer for a trashy scandal magazine out to expose Miss Brown as a fraud and a virgin.

Henry Fonda played Curtis' best friend and Lauren Bacall was Fonda's wife, tired of her husband's obsession with his work – women's hosiery. Tony masquerades as Fonda and seeks help from Miss Brown just to get the dirt on her but ends up falling in love with her. Their scenes, in which she uses physical tactility as form of therapy thus arousing his love and lust, are among the best in all his, or her, comedy movies.

'Natalie and I always had chemistry on screen,' he told me. 'We had a synchronicity when we worked. The script was good, and my friend Dick Quine was directing it, but we hardly needed them for our scenes, when it was just the two of us. I could say a line or a word not in the script and she could respond, and give me something that came from the moment that made our scenes fresh and funny and romantic.'

For the climactic car chase scene in which everyone chases everyone else in no particular order, Tony drove his own 1937 Bentley. His friend Larry Storch appears as the beleaguered traffic cop whose motorbike isn't fast enough to keep up with everyone else.

Lew Wasserman was now just too busy at Universal to be anyone's agent and, distressed to lose his mentor, Tony reluctantly switched agents, signing with Irving 'Swifty' Lazar, who landed him a first-rate deal for *The Great Race*, earning him $125,000 upfront plus a handsome slice of the profits. The picture was an epic-sized comedy about a fictional car race from New York to Paris in the early 1900s. It parodied the early silent pictures and was dedicated to 'Mr Laurel and Mr Hardy'. Tony played the heroic Great Leslie, Jack Lemmon was dastardly Professor Fate, and Natalie Wood the feminist and feminine reporter Miss Maggie Dubois. Peter Falk and his one eye were hilarious as the professor's often incompetent but never less than loyal accomplice Max.

Blake Edwards directed, but the friendship that had once been there between Edwards and Tony had faded. Tony had asked Edwards for the leading role in *Breakfast at Tiffany's* and felt Edwards had strung him along before giving the part to George Peppard. He admitted he was deeply affected by rejection and found it difficult to handle. 'I used to get so emotional about things. When I wouldn't get a part I wanted, or go to a party, and they treat me like shit, these tears would well up in me.'

Blake Edwards told me, 'There are a lot of reasons why one actor doesn't get a part and another does. It had nothing to do with Tony's talent, but he wasn't the kind of actor I felt the part needed. And Tony felt slighted when he didn't get the part, and that affected our friendship. Listen, I spend my life trying to keep actors happy while working very hard, making sometimes difficult films. It's hard for a director to have real friends who are actors. A director doesn't have the *time* to be friends always. So when I was getting ready to do *The Great Race* I didn't really want Tony Curtis who was still sulking over *Breakfast at Tiffany's*, so I tried to find another actor to play the part.'

Edwards' more obvious preferences for the role of the Great Leslie were Robert Wagner and George Peppard, and among his least obvious were Burt Lancaster and Charlton Heston, who both turned it down. But Jack Warner only wanted Tony Curtis in the role, and Edwards had to concede defeat. It's impossible to think of another actor in the role of the Great Leslie, a character who was always dressed in white and whose smile literally sparkled.

The film's most famous sequence is the incredible custard pie fight, which took eight days to shoot during which more than two thousand colourful custard pies were hurled at Natalie Wood, Jack Lemmon and Peter Falk. Tony remained relatively untouched, walking through the pitched battle unscathed until the very end when one solitary pie gets him in the face.

The one person, however, who ended up covered from head to foot in more pie than anyone else was Blake Edwards. Jack Lemmon hatched a plan so that on the final day of shooting that sequence, when Edwards called one last 'Cut!' two hundred custard pies were hurled at him.

Another of the film's highlights, and one almost out of character with the rest of the movie, is the sword fight between Tony Curtis and Ross Martin as Baron von Stuppe. 'A beautiful sequence,' said Tony. 'That was really good sabre fencing. Joseph Vince, that fine fencing master of California, staged all of that.'

Tony didn't care for *The Great Race*, and neither did many critics – it had quite a savaging in the press – but none of that mattered because the public loved it. And it still does. Warner Brothers successfully reissued it numerous times – it *had* to, to make back the estimated $12 million it cost to make. In 1965 it earned just under $12 million domestic, and around $24 million worldwide. To date it has earned more than $25 million in America alone, and around the same amount in other territories. Tony earned over $200,000 in royalties over the years from that one movie.

When I discussed with him the critical failure of the film, he said, 'In very rare instances you'll find critics were really impressed with it. But it's the audience that makes it successful. They're the ones that make films what you call masterpieces or whatever you call them.' He knew that, despite what he thought of the movie, the public enjoyed it. 'What's a critic? Just another person who gets an opportunity to write a review. Give *anybody* a chance to have that opportunity. Everybody's got two professions – what they make their living at and movie reviews. Ask anybody, "What do you think of the picture?" They'll say, "Well, I thought so-and-so was good. I don't think the story was very good. The direction was a little shoddy." I mean, these people talk of films like they've been reviewing them for years, and they've every right to. They've put down two pounds or two dollars – they're entitled to say anything they like about it.'

Natalie Wood was unhappy making the film, feeling left out of the camaraderie displayed between the male stars and the director. Despite all that, she and Tony found themselves increasingly attracted to each other. Since her divorce from Robert Wagner, Natalie had had a string of Hollywood lovers. She was a very warm, affectionate person, and Tony, already feeling the strain in his marriage to Christine tugging him in all directions, found himself falling in love with her.

'I wasn't in love with Tony *ever*,' she told me, 'but I liked him enormously, and when I was feeling lonely and in need of some affection, and Tony seemed unhappy although I never talked to him about it, we let things take their course.'

They didn't so much have an affair as a one-time romantic encounter in her dressing-room trailer, something Tony described in his book as 'a highlight not just of working on that picture but of my entire life'.

He liked to say that he could never have had a full-time relationship with Natalie because she wasn't voluptuous, but I think he loved her but never pursued her because she was a big star, and he had already had a movie-star wife, and he didn't want another one. He knew it could never work between them. 'Only one man was right for Natalie, and that was Robert Wagner,' he told me, 'and I'm so delighted they finally got back together.'

Tony made a number of public appearances to promote *The Great Race*, and Christine was often at his side. One writer noted, 'You only have to watch the two of them together, as I did, holding hands under the table at the banquet given by Colonel Warner, to celebrate the first showing of *The Great Race*, to realise just how much the parents of Alexandra care for each other.'

Because he was no longer available to the press, the Hollywood Women's Press Club awarded him their 'Sour Apple' award in 1965, a trophy given to the least cooperative movie star. He received news of the award with good nature.

He now wanted to produce more of his own movie projects. Curtis Productions rented space in virtually every major studio in Hollywood, and when he finished working at one studio and needed to move on to the next, he simply took his drawing-room desk and chair with him.

But the projects he wanted to develop never progressed very far because studios wanted him to headline their comedies. He felt Irving Lazar just didn't have the power that Wasserman had and was unable to secure for him the kind of movies he really wanted to do and just made the easy deals. Tony accepted the films because he needed the money and he simply wanted to work. Some of his comedies were good, some not so good, and before long some would be downright bad. His next comedy, though, was good. *Boeing Boeing* was based on a French play about an architect, played by Tony, living in Paris who is happily engaged to three air hostesses, one American, another German and the other French. It's all a question of keeping track of the schedules. An old buddy, played by Jerry Lewis, arrives and decides there are enough girls to go round. Schedules get changed, flights get faster, the three fiancées start turning up at the apartment when they shouldn't, and Curtis and Lewis have to prevent them from meeting each other, resulting in chaos, mayhem and a lot of going in and out of doors.

Most of it was shot at Paramount's studios in California, but some scenes were shot on location in Paris in April 1965. Tony had come to dislike Paris, perhaps because it brought back memories of Janet. Or it may have been that he was just in a lousy mood when he told a reporter, 'I just want to get out of Paris and get home for Easter. You hear all those romantic songs about Paris and all written by Americans. "April in Paris", I ask you! It's a rotten time to be here. It rains most of the time. Talk about April showers.'

Making *Boeing Boeing* proved to be one of Tony's unhappiest experiences on a film set because Jerry Lewis, once one of his best friends, pulled childish pranks to aggravate him. Tony told me:

Jerry Lewis used to drop ashes on me from his cigarette. He used to stand on my feet when we'd do a scene. He'd unzip my fly when we did a medium shot. A number of people on the set said, 'Tony, how can you take it?'

I said, 'What's to take? You think that idiot is upsetting me one way or the other, stepping on my shoes, or dropping ashes on the suit?' The shoes don't belong to me. They're the company's. If they're willing to allow him to burn the suit, then they'll have to get another suit and delay making the movie. But it's not disturbing me. My concentration is as good in every shot.

I don't personalise it. Whatever his problem was, he thought it was funny. So let him think it's funny. Let him have a good time doing it. I didn't think it was funny, but why should I take umbrage at it? It would only have an effect on our work. I didn't want that, so I let him.

That picture was finished, and one of these days you're gonna look at it and compare performances. *That's* when the meaning will come. The meaning comes *after* the work, not with the indignation you have to put up with on the set.

Both stars fared well. The *Times* thought they made 'an astonishingly effective comedy team', and *Variety* noted, 'First rate performances and direction make the most of a very good script.'

After *Boeing Boeing* Tony spent time in New York with an art-dealer friend of his who introduced him to artist Joseph Cornell, who decorated little wooden boxes with pieces of broken mirrors, pins and thimbles to create beautiful patterns. That inspired Tony to create his own boxes. He told me, 'I used to keep things in cigar boxes, like chewing gum, skate keys and marbles, photographs. And I ran across Joseph Cornell's work. He was an odd, interesting man. He *lived* in his boxes. I don't live in mine, but I love them.'

He turned the cigar boxes into deep frames into which he placed all kinds of objects that meant something to him. He described his boxes, and the way he designed them, as 'creating order out of chaos', which is probably what he was hoping to do with his life. He never intended that this order he created should make sense to anyone but himself. 'I make these boxes for myself, not for anyone to see,' he insisted, and yet he let me see some of them. 'They mean nothing to you, right?' he asked. They didn't, and that satisfied him.

The problems between Tony and Christine didn't prevent their family from growing, and on 12 June 1966, Allegra Curtis was born. Tony wanted a bigger house, so on the advice of his attorney, he bought a huge estate belonging to the Keck family that sat on four acres of land in Los Angeles, purchasing it through a scheme whereby the govern-ment allowed him to pay only the interest of $15,000 for the first five years. Tony moved his family into the house and, he said, 'for the next few years we lived like royalty'.

He was hugely successful, was making a lot of money, and he and Christine were trying to make the marriage work. But marital bliss somehow eluded him. Christine recalled, 'Our first baby was born, and I felt very happy, giddy and fulfilled. But there was something wrong with the marriage right from the start, and even after our second child, Allegra, was born two years later. We were becoming very hostile, both of us. Shouting and screaming was all it was; back and forth – "You did this", and "You did this". There wasn't much we had in common beyond sex and the children.'

By the mid-1960s, Tony was at the peak of his profession, but not as a dramatic actor, which is how he would have preferred it. Nevertheless, he continued to be extremely popular in comedy. In *Not with My Wife, You Don't!* he played an air-force officer vying for the attention of the beautiful Julie with his buddy, played by George C. Scott. Virna Lisi, an Italian blonde bombshell, who played Julie, had already appeared opposite Jack Lemmon in *How to Murder Your Wife* and then Frank Sinatra in *Assault on a Queen*. Tony was easily attracted to her, but she kept her distance from him which, he said, made it easier to get the picture made. The film was popular and pleased most critics. 'Tony Curtis has rarely been better,' said the *Sunday Express*, while *The Times* observed, 'While the film has its downs there are corresponding ups, mainly when Mr Curtis is centre screen.'

He accepted a fleeting guest role, uncredited, in a weak horror film, *Chamber of Horrors*. All Tony recalled of that film was that the cheque cleared.

He was in England for his next comedy; it began as *You Just Kill Me*, was released in the States as *Arrivederci, Baby!* but was called *Drop Dead Darling* in the UK. It was a British production, written and produced by Ken Hughes.

Tony played a money-hungry gigolo marrying wealthy women and then disposing of them until he meets his match in a beautiful Italian woman, played by another Italian star, Rosanna Schiaffino. Off the set, Tony met his match in Rosanna's sister, who told Tony to stay away from Rosanna. Among the other ladies falling foul of Tony's despicable plot on screen were Zsa Zsa Gabor, Nancy Kwan, Fenella Fielding and Anna Quayle. Gabor once recalled for me, 'He's a most handsome man and has an eye for the ladies, and it seemed to me he had trouble keeping his hands off them all. He was very sweet, like a boy in a candy shop.'

For all its moments of black comedy and lovely ladies, the film flopped. It was Tony's first outright financial failure since *Sweet Smell of Success* nine years earlier. He was desperate to find a role that offered him a challenge, and said at the time, 'I am asked in my profession to do primarily comedy. But I have not really explored the side of me that did *The Defiant Ones* and *Sweet Smell of Success*. I want to do very deep and mystical roles, like Tyrone Power in *The Razor's Edge*. That was an examination of a man trying to find himself, showing the dark areas as well as the light and airy ones. I've found both of these in my own life and I'm very anxious to do them professionally.'

He next did another comedy, with another Italian star. The movie was *Don't Make Waves* and his leading lady Claudia Cardinale, the only Italian actress who ever came close to achieving the kind of popularity in English-speaking movies that Sophia Loren did. She starred with John Wayne in *Circus World*, Burt Lancaster in *The Professionals* and David Niven in *The Pink Panther*.

Tony played a college professor, fired from his position when caught in a police raid on a student party, who arrives in California to meet Cardinale. She manages to wreck his car, set his trousers on fire and then leaves him with nothing in the world. He reinvents himself as a swimming-pool salesman living in a house perched on a cliff destined to topple over the edge in a downpour. There really wasn't a lot of plot, but it had lots of muscle-bound guys, beautiful girls in bikinis (including Sharon Tate), the gorgeous Claudia Cardinale and Tony giving another good comedy performance that was, by now, no stretch for him at all.

To direct the film, Tony recommended Alexander Mackendrick, who had directed little since *Sweet Smell of Success*, to the producer Martin Ransohoff. Said Tony, 'I felt he had created something so incredible with *Sweet Smell of Success*, I felt if he had the chance to get his career back on track, [then] maybe he would do a really great dramatic film and I could be in it.'

It didn't happen. The film didn't perform well when released in 1967, and Mackendrick all but retired from directing. With another flop on his hands, Tony felt that his career had plummeted to an all-time low. But every actor has rough spots, and Tony just needed to keep his nerve. Contrary to popular belief, he was not a faded movie star in the 1960s. His problem was the same as many other movie actors at that time. Trends were changing. *Bonnie and Clyde* and *Easy Rider* were attracting the young audience. Kids were dropping out and tripping out, and the summer of '67 became known as the Summer of Love. If it wasn't flower power, it was a new degree of screen violence blowing minds. Fewer comedies were being made, and those that were being written were not very good. Even Jack Lemmon and Walter Matthau, two of the biggest comedy stars of the 1960s, were finding it hard, and they both turned their hand to dramatic roles with varying degrees of success. 'A lot of us were struggling to make good movies in the sixties,' said Robert

Wagner. 'That's why I went to Europe, and so did a lot of other American actors. British actors too, like David Niven.'

So did Tony Curtis. Still clutching at the first movie to come his way for the sake of the money, Tony panicked and accepted an offer from director Pasquale Festa Campanile to make a costume comedy, *The Chastity Belt*, in Italy. It turned out to be a miserable experience for him, and for the audience.

His leading lady, Monica Vitti, was involved with the cameraman, so all her scenes were being photographed in her favour and to Tony's detriment, and in the process the film was taking longer to shoot. He complained to the producer and warned him that Warner Brothers, who was backing the movie, would close it down if they found out what was going on – in other words, he would let them know – and consequently Pasquale Festa Campanile began to cut Vitti's scenes down.

Like most European films, it was shot silent and the dialogue dubbed in later, which prevented Tony from injecting his usual spontaneity. When he dubbed his dialogue, he was unable to recreate many moments that happened in front of the camera, and he must have given up at some point because some of his lines were dubbed in by another actor. The film remains one of the worst films of his career, and another box-office failure.

When he returned home, an unhappy actor, to discover Christine had been out and about with Dean Martin's son, Rick, Tony raged at her. 'I felt the most horrible, violent impulses,' he admitted. Despite his philandering, he couldn't bear the thought of his wife doing it. 'I would get insanely jealous. It would drive me crazy. I felt like I was going mad.'

Tony's use of the words 'insanely', 'crazy' and 'mad' in one short phrase is very telling; he lived in fear that his mother's illness, schizophrenia, would overwhelm and overtake him as it did to brother Bobby. He told me, 'When I get angry and jealous, I get these pictures in my head of whatever is troubling me – of my wife with another man – and I hear sounds – maybe laughter sometimes, but not my own laughter – I'm being laughed at – and I really think I am going nuts.'

He justified his extramarital activities by saying, 'With me, it's a one-night thing or just until the film is finished, but [the wives] didn't do that. They were having affairs.' That made the difference to him. He also said, 'I didn't find sleeping around was a detriment [to my marriages]. I found it necessary for me because I wasn't fulfilling myself. For a long time I tried to examine that very point, and it was very hard for me to think of it as a negative experience. I'd meet a woman, and there was a look between our eyes that was most appealing, that we'd understand as a way of attracting each other, and all of a sudden you find you're reaching out a little bit further. And then I felt I reached a plateau. So two strangers that were meeting would erupt, separate and then, like a lady and a gentleman, I'd kiss her hand and say goodbye. I never found that bad.'

Christine was aware that he was often unfaithful. She said, 'There were always women throwing themselves at him, but whenever Tony did anything, I just didn't notice. Still, we were both very jealous of each other.' The intimacy that had been the foundation of their relationship had gone. They no longer enjoyed the same interests, and Christine was becoming bored being the wife of a movie star. 'At first I tried to be with him when he went on location. But I couldn't just sit in a chair and watch him making love to someone else. I'd walk off and go shopping with my secretary, or something.'

She had one particular hobby she loved. 'The thing I enjoyed most was to decorate our house.' She had plenty of opportunity to practise it when married to Tony. 'We started in a house in Beverly Hills, then we got another and another. We had to change houses for show, or status, or for opportunity. Sometimes we just needed the space. So we kept moving. I was spending my whole life decorating other people's houses. The last house we had was a real horror. It was so big I was really lost in it and I was alone a lot.'

She had come to realise she wanted to break out of the mould she had cast herself in as Mrs Tony Curtis, and decided she wanted to resume her career. Tony was dismayed. Allegra said, 'My dad's old-school mentality is a sort of machismo patriarchal sort of approach of "I'm the man, you're the woman".' Her mother had been an actress since she was seven, and she reached the point where she 'didn't want to be a Hollywood martyr', as Allegra put it. 'She didn't want to be "the wife".'

Tony was teetering on depression, seeing no end in sight to his marital problems, nor to what he perceived as his decline as a movie star. *Variety* made him feel worse by describing him as one of those highly paid actors not worth the money he was getting. With three failed films after a very long run of successes, he was convinced his career was at rock bottom.

On top of all that, he had his brother Bobby to worry about. As Bobby moved in and out of mental hospitals over the years, he also slipped in and out of his psychotic state. Tony felt helpless but had him stay over at his house for short periods when Tony had the time to spend with him. It was one moderate schizophrenic trying to help a severe schizophrenic. On one occasion Bobby attacked Tony, trying to punch him. Tony didn't retaliate but blocked the punches until Bobby calmed down.

In 1967 doctors gave a revised estimate of Bobby's condition. He was sinking further into schizophrenia and his mother seemed to be a part of the problem, so Tony had to write to her, trying to make her understand that for Bobby's sake she needed to stay away from him for several weeks while he was treated in a state institution. He knew, he told her, that it was difficult for her to stay away from him. He warned her that she had the power to save or destroy Bobby, and that if she destroyed him, it would destroy his love for her. It was a desperate plea that went unheeded, and she continued to visit Bobby. Whatever spell it was she had over him, it sent him over the edge and he became a full-time ward of the State and he was confined in the mental facility at Camarillo.

Tony would visit Bobby, who sometimes enjoyed periods of lucidity but always slid back into his own lost world for longer periods and became completely unaware who Tony was, until, finally, Tony stopped visiting him altogether.

Depressed over his brother, his marriage and his career, he desperately sought for something that would lift him out of despair and put him back on top.

CHAPTER SEVENTEEN

The Power of A Killer

ate in 1967, Curtis heard that Twentieth Century-Fox was going to make *The Boston Strangler*, based on the horrifying case of Albert De Salvo, who was thought to have killed at least eighteen women. Tony wanted the part, but knowing that he would never be considered for the role, he perched on a stool in his Beverly Hills home, gazed at his good looks in the mirror, and then began to meticulously change his appearance by applying putty wax to his nose, moulding it into a frightening hook, pasting up his eyebrows to thicken and blacken them, rubbing oil-based make-up into his healthy, boyish cheeks to give his face a sallow look, and brushing his hair into a 'frizzy parched scrub' as he described it.

He looked at himself in the mirror and no longer saw Tony Curtis but someone who might be 'some kind of a human monster', he said. He went outside into the twilight and photographed himself with his camera held in his outstretched hand. The next day twenty-four prints of his portraits landed on the desk of the film's director, Richard Fleischer. He took them to Dick Zanuck, the head of Fox, and said, 'Take a look at these.'

'Who is this guy?' asked Zanuck.

'Tony Curtis.'

'Stop kidding me.'

Within a week Tony had been signed to play Albert De Salvo. Suddenly, he had the break he so desperately sought. And he knew he couldn't screw it up. He spent the next few months studying De Salvo's medical reports, and traipsed around Boston to explore where the crimes happened. He completely immersed himself in De Salvo's life and crimes. He told me, 'I read everything available on Albert and in some ways these experiences that I learned had a way of manifesting themselves later. For example, I found out that Albert and his brother used to take starving cats and dogs and put them under crates and let them tear each other apart. It was a sport – very cruel, very primitive. That struck a responsive chord in my head. I thought, how would you dramatise something like that without showing it? And I found a couple of places in the movie. Like when he grabs a woman around the neck, when he came into her bathroom. That young lady let him in, and he grabbed her. It was like a cat. Grrrrrrr! I imagined what a cat would be like trying to defend itself in the box. No one knows about it except you and me, and if I never mentioned it to anybody, nobody would ever know about it, but it's unimportant. But, ya see, it gave me a clue. It made me think of a cat – just a glimmer of a cat – so in an abstract way it dissolves down in a mathematical equation to just a little piece of business.'

He arrived for the first day of work at the Twentieth Century-Fox studio, driving his Rolls convertible and wearing a tartan jacket pinched at the waist which had been specifically designed and fitted for him by Angela of Rome, whose other clients included Prince Rainier of Monaco. He was a man with expensive tastes and an eye for fashion. He never denied that he loved being a movie star, and he lived the life of one.

He was installed in brand-new permanent dressing quarters, a compact complex of rooms, one of which was for his own secretary. He decorated the lounge with etchings and lithographs, and a framed Bronx street map to remind him where he came from. The walls were lined with shelves filled with leather-bound scripts of his past films. He smoked a straight grained pipe – he didn't smoke cigarettes, but he had taken to a pipe – and when friends arrived he offered them cigars of a blend that was prepared and rolled for him in New York.

He had a trailer dressing room on the studio lot to relax in between takes, or study lines. On the mirror he had written with a red grease pencil the titles of books which were all potential film properties he was interested in. He had read that if someone wrote down what they are interested in and referred to those things each day, the chances are that one day those things would be realised. He still had dreams and ambitions, and wanted to produce more films, and also to write.

He was serious about the work at hand. As well as adding putty to his nose, he wore dark contact lenses to hide his blue eyes. He used all his newly acquired knowledge to play Albert De Salvo, as well as digging deeper than he had ever done before into his well of skills. I suspect that at the beginning of production even he wasn't exactly sure how deep that well went, and he tried to overcome his insecurity and lack of self-confidence in bizarre ways. He took to wearing a dazzling array of medals, including, of all things, the Iron Cross. He explained, 'They awarded that for valour. A guy had to be heroic to get that. That's why I wear it. It makes me feel like a hero. You can face up to anything with a medal pinned to your chest.'

A stagehand, seeing the medals, asked an assistant director, 'What's he doing? Sending it up or something?'

'No, he means it.'

'Nutty as a fruitcake.'

Nutty or not, while many around him scoffed, the magic was working. He had the confidence to produce a spine-chilling portrayal of a man living with multiple personalities who, at home, is a loving father hugging his small daughter on his lap, watching the funeral of President Kennedy, while outside he is overcome by perverse and horrific sexual urges that lead him to kill. There were a number of times throughout Tony's life when he found something in life that helped him, for brief periods of time, to work through his anger, and to bear his guilt about Julie, and deal with his paranoia, such as therapy and hypnotism. In an extraordinary way, playing De Salvo did the same thing. It made sense to him, but some people working on the film thought he was quite mad.

He said, 'Playing De Salvo was a sort of purging for me. For years I have wanted to assess what might have happened to me if I hadn't been taken to Hollywood when I didn't have a syllable to rub against another. I might have been on the wrong side of the law myself. By doing this film I knew myself. I lost my anger. I became tolerant. It isn't so much that I became sympathetic with De Salvo. But I got empathy with him. Here was a man whose life became a cul-de-sac. I count myself lucky that I found the open road in time.'

He felt he had certain characteristics that made him ideal to play De Salvo. 'I thought I knew a little about things that go adrift in a man's mind,' he said.

He was now fighting to save his career, and investing every ounce of his talent, mental capacity and emotional stamina into this single role that could make or break him as an actor. George Kennedy, who played one of the investigating detectives, recalled, 'I was sitting next to him on the set, and he was sitting there, his eyes closed, running his lines. Suddenly he just reached over and grabbed my wrist, and he squeezed hard. I knew that he wasn't actually sitting there next to me and it wasn't my wrist he was squeezing, but I don't know what it was to him because I didn't ask him. After a minute and a half, maybe two minutes, he let go, and I had his finger marks on my wrist for another two or three minutes. I don't think he was aware that he had done that.'

Tony suffered emotionally playing De Salvo. 'When I looked into the mirror, I didn't see me any more. I saw an odd-looking stranger, and that had a profound effect on me and made me very insular and quiet. I became full of rage and anger that I had to wear this cover in order to show my feelings, in order to feel that strangling a woman was not such a terrible thing.'

Richard Fleischer recalled, 'He lost himself completely in the role, so much so that he became another character. I was just amazed.'

George Kennedy said, 'He made the change from being an ordinary guy at home with a family and all the things that seem normal to the monster of Boston, and whatever process he was able to use was something that was with him twenty-four hours a day. I don't see how he could have done it any other way.'

When I asked Tony if he could detach himself from the intense method – or methods – he used to play De Salvo, he said:

Suppose you went today to an army base and you say, 'For a couple of hours I'd like to see what it's like to be a recruit.' You step in the door and the first thing that happens is some bully screams at you, they strip you down, then march you into a chair and they cut off all your hair. You're saying, 'Now hold on a minute, this is more than I bargained for.' Before you can get out of that chair, you're lined up with fifteen other guys and you've got your kit in front of you and the next thing you know, you're running on some field and some guy's poking you with his finger and you're taking some tests, and the next thing is you're standing there on guard duty.

Two hours later, they let you go, less a few ounces of hair. But you've had a harrowing experience, because you've existed in that era. You know you're not in the army and you know you're gonna get out in two hours, but you're still part of it. You smell it, you feel it. It's around you.

It's the same for an actor. Any part you play, any environment you're in, you can't keep detached. It's impossible to knock at the door and whisper, 'I've come to fix your pipes,' and the girl says, 'Well, I didn't order anybody to fix them,' and you say, 'The guy told me to come over, but if you don't want me,' and she says, 'No, it's all right, come in,' without feeling the power of being a killer. And for that moment you believe it.

His biggest challenge as an actor came in the final scene, where, under questioning by the detective played by Henry Fonda, De Salvo suddenly slips into his murderous personality and, in an empty white room, acts out one of the killings, complete with dialogue, actions, and even the memory of the orgasm he had in committing the murder. Tony spent two weeks rehearsing the scene so that he would know every move, every nuance, every horrific thought and act.

During a short break in filming, he went to New York where he was introduced by a stockbroker friend to a twenty-three-year-old British model, Leslie Penny Allen. Her mother lived in Boston, so Tony suggested she visit her mother and come and spend time with him. They very quickly became lovers. In retrospect, Tony believed he made a mistake in rushing into a love affair, but he did it because he felt he needed to break out of his marriage and thought the best way was to find someone new. When he returned to Los Angeles, he continued to see Leslie in secret, and went back to work on the darkest movie of his career.

His performance as Albert De Salvo in *The Boston Strangler* is the crowning achievement of his career. After playing in a string of comedies for several years, Tony Curtis had suddenly come back from the brink of professional death to prove that the earlier promise seen in *Sweet Smell of Success* and *The Defiant Ones* was not a fluke but the result of an actor who knew his craft, was prepared to find ways to improve his craft, and was one of the finest screen actors of his generation.

His performance as De Salvo is, to my mind, the finest any actor ever put on screen. It is the most absolute example of what screen acting is all about. What he accomplished, particularly in the scene where he loses himself and almost chokes his wife in front of his daughter, and then comes back into the world again, and then in the final climactic scene where he lives through one of the murders as he is remembering it, is the quintessential embodiment of screen acting.

The critics recognised the quality of his work. The *Sun* said, 'Tony Curtis managed to move me to feelings of great pity in the final scenes of self-awareness.'

TIME said, 'Under orders from some burning sector of his mind he hysterically re-enacts one killing by wrapping his hands around an imaginary windpipe. Hovering between pathos and terror, Curtis suddenly makes the viewer's breath stop in his own throat.'

The picture was a great success when released in October 1968, earning more than $17 million just in America, and many pundits predicted he would at last get a second Oscar nomination. But the studio failed to put his name forward, and nobody else thought to nominate him. He had given a performance that was worthy of an Oscar nomination, but the Academy ignored him. Richard Fleischer told me, 'To my mind, Tony Curtis's performance as Albert De Salvo is the quintessential Academy Award performance, and to not even get nominated was an appalling oversight by the Academy, and I would say even a miscarriage of justice that he didn't get nominated.'

It no longer seemed just a case of paranoia when, after he had proven what he was capable of, and after going through some kind of emotional and mental hell to do it, he felt he had been rejected by his peers and all of Hollywood. He never understood what he had done to merit such treatment. And nobody I ever spoke to about it could explain it either. Natalie Wood said, 'I was astounded by his performance in *The Boston Strangler*. I have always known he is a very good actor, but in that movie he proved he was a *great* actor, and I don't know why he didn't get nominated.'

George Kennedy said, 'I can't explain why he didn't get nominated. It baffled me.'

Frank Sinatra had a theory. 'They were never gonna nominate him for an Academy Award because he dumped Janet Leigh who *everybody* in Hollywood loves. Hollywood is unforgiving.'

Rejection drove Tony deeper into his insecurities, his paranoia, and his schizophrenic side. 'There were a few times when I thought I had almost lost myself during [*The Boston Strangler*], and then when I realised that Hollywood musta hated me, I sank into the depths and thought I'd never come back up. I was smoking a lot of marijuana, and maybe that contributed to the visions and sounds. It was like my little brother Julie was telling me to get back up, and someone sounding like my mother telling me I didn't deserve better. I'll tell ya, it's hard just to come back from all that. I made it, and I have to keep on making it. What else you gonna do?'

Life at home had become intolerable for both Tony and Christine, especially now that the rumours were flying about Tony and Leslie. Christine finally came to a decision, based, she said, on a German saying – 'That which does not kill you makes you strong.'

'One morning I told Tony, "I want a divorce." That was that. We weren't even discussing things at that point. I moved out.'

She got a quick divorce in Juarez, Mexico, on 16 April 1968, without even fighting for all she was entitled to under American law in the way of maintenance. That puzzled Tony, but she didn't want their children suffering the trauma of being caught in the crossfire of a potentially bitter divorce. Christine won custody of the children, and her freedom to pursue her career – she continues to work in movies in Germany – and in doing so she gave him his freedom.

She seemed to display no acrimony, even five years later when she said, 'Tony isn't a bad man. I don't hate him, even though I've been furious with him.'

He announced he would not oppose the divorce. 'I care too much for Christine for that,' he said at the time. 'Our separation is a complicated thing, but we have had beautiful moments together.'

He continued living in the mansion, and had no intention of moving out. 'It's a little lonely around here now, but I've worked all my life to have a home like this, and I'm not about to give it up.'

But being alone in that big house and trying to grapple with reality brought out the demons. There were moments when he heard voices, and other unidentifiable sounds, and he saw shadows and shapes that alarmed him. He felt he was in danger, and was sure he was being followed, especially when he walked alone through his mansion late at night. 'I could sense it,' he told me. 'I could *hear* it.' He knew there was no one there, and he began to fear schizophrenia was developing. 'There are times when it comes through, like a light through the slightest crack in the wall,' he said.

He kept a loaded .22 calibre Beretta and a .38 calibre Smith and Wesson automatic in his home, which wasn't really unusual in America, especially among the rich. Tony joked, 'Every movie actor thinks they're out to get them. And, Jesus, there are some fucking lunatics out there who really are. Look what happened to John Lennon.'

His sense of being in danger seemed to magnify only when he was at home. At all other times, and even after John Lennon was murdered, Tony went everywhere without bodyguards. 'Frank [Sinatra] doesn't go anywhere without his bodyguards, but maybe there are a lot of people who'd like to bump him off, but I'm not in that way of life that he has. The only people who get mad at me are husbands of girls I'm sleeping with.'

I asked him if he was afraid he would become severely schizophrenic. 'Well, yes, ya know, I can't think of anything in life that terrifies me more. Look what it did to my brother. I lost him to it.' Mention of either of his brothers often brought tears to his eyes.

'I'm no good on my own, maybe that's why I *have* to get married, I *have* to be in a relationship,' he told me. 'Maybe that's behind some of my madnesses. I never figured it out. Maybe that's why I took drugs. I've always needed calming. If I'm allowed to be on my own inside my head . . . a bad place! Voices! Visions! Am I just thinking louder than everybody else?'

Perhaps that's why he decided he wanted to marry Leslie – he was afraid of being alone and being inside his own head for too long – so he brought her to see his mansion and asked her to marry him. It was three months since they had met. She told him, 'If this place has an elevator I might marry you. It's got too many stairs.'

Two days later he brought her back to the house. 'I've got something to show you,' he said, and led her to a door which had not been there before. He threw it open, and there was an elevator. 'I had it installed just for you,' he told her.

'Well, how could I refuse someone like that?' she reasoned. 'I loved the flamboyant streak. All our friends were on at us to wait until we'd known each other longer before getting married. In fact, we fell out with one couple over it.'

With his divorce from Christine barely out of the way, Tony married Leslie in Las Vegas on 20 April 1968 at 2am in the morning,.

Tony finished *The Boston Strangler* knowing he had done extraordinary work, but he couldn't wait for it to be released before accepting work coming his way. It is assumed incorrectly that the work dried up following *The Boston Strangler*, but in fact he made three movies in quick succession. Four, if you count *Rosemary's Baby*, in which he was the voice of an actor on the telephone speaking to Mia Farrow. Director Roman Polanksi asked Tony to do it uncredited. He agreed, and it's a remarkable little scene. Tony should have insisted on a credit because they didn't know it was him and so nobody recognised what a very fine job he did with just his voice.

Then he was back in comedies. The first of them seemed like a sure-fire hit. *Those Daring Young Men in Their Jaunty Jalopies* was an attempt by director Ken Annakin and writer Jack Davies to repeat the enormous success they'd had with *Those Magnificent Men in Their Flying Machines*. That film had featured an all-star cast and a race from London to Paris in aeroplanes in the year 1910. The new film would follow the same formula, only it was about the Monte Carlo Rally during the Roaring Twenties (and in some countries was called *Monte Carlo or Bust*).

Paramount hoped *Jaunty Jalopies* would be a mixture of *The Great Race* and *Flying Machines*, and to help them do that they needed Tony Curtis, demonstration that he was still in demand. Filmed in the Dino De Laurentiis studios in Rome, as well as in Monte Carlo, Stockholm and the island of Gotland in the Baltic Sea, the picture was littered with stunts and expensive props. Tony performed the Harold Lloyd-type stunts himself, and for one scene he hung from the front axle of a car perched precariously over a frozen waterfall, dangling 20 feet or more above the ground.

'He was not shy of doing any stunt that many other movie actors would leave to professional stuntmen,' said Ken Annakin. 'I had to admire him for that, and it allowed us to get a lot of incredible shots.' But Annakin wasn't impressed with Tony's seemingly erratic behaviour. 'He was rude to Susan Hampshire.'

Susan Hampshire didn't say he had been rude to her when I inter-viewed her in 1981. 'He was very funny and very energetic,' she told me, 'always on the move. He never seemed to stand still.'

Ken Annakin said Curtis was smoking pot every day and was often bad-tempered. Tony was repentant about his behaviour when I told him what Annakin had said. 'I guess I was feeling let down after *Boston Strangler*. I was on a roller coaster because I had only just begun my relationship with Leslie, which was wonderful in the beginning, but I was depressed – *oh! deeply* depressed – when things didn't happen for me after *Boston Strangler*. I was smoking a lot of dope. I had given up cigarettes and, ya know, when you stop abusing one substance, it's easy to start abusing another.

'So I can relate to what Ken Annakin says about me being up and down, or whatever he said, but as for being rude to Susan, that's not how I remember it. I remember she and I being very close and there might have been something happening between us, although she was married.' In his second autobiography he claimed that Susan Hampshire and he had a sexual fling, but I have some doubt about his recollection which, he admitted to me, was, as he put it, 'lost in a haze of cannabis, which a lot of my life was around that time'. I think when he said 'there *might* have been something happening', he meant he really couldn't be sure in 1985. He obviously remembered it differently by 2008 when he seemed sure he and Susan Hampshire had had an affair. (Susan has always maintained a dignified silence.)

He admitted that he lost his temper on the set during rehearsal for a crash scene when the brakes on his car failed. Annakin assured him the brakes would be fixed, but when they came to actually shoot the scene, the brakes failed again. Tony swerved to avoid the stanchion holding a huge arc light which, had he hit it, could have seriously injured him and Susan, who was in the car also. Tony leaped out of the car, stormed over to Annakin and complained. Annakin told him, 'It's probably gremlins.' Tony replied, 'Fuck you and your gremlins! We could've been killed.'

Terry-Thomas played the arch villain, as he had in *Flying Machines*. He recalled, 'I worked with Tony Curtis twice, in *Monte Carlo or Bust* and *The Persuaders*, and I always found him to be packed with boundless energy and enthusiasm.' This seemed to be a common observation. He added, 'There were a few times when something seemed to be worrying him and he could be moody, and sometimes he lost his temper and yelled at someone, which I thought was a bit much.'

Eric Sykes played Terry-Thomas's assistant, just as he had done in *Flying Machines*. He told me, 'I thought we were in a sequel, playing the same characters, which we were more or less except that Terry-Thomas was playing the son of the character he had played in *Those Magnificent Men in Their Flying Machines*, so I must have been playing my own son. Most of my scenes were with Terry-Thomas so I didn't really work much with Tony Curtis but I remember him as a little odd.'

Those Daring Young Men in Their Jaunty Jalopies – or *Monte Carlo or Bust* – was not as big a success as *Flying Machines* or *The Great Race*, although it did well during the school holidays. And it's a much funnier film than *Flying Machines*.

Tony didn't stop working. He next made one of his least-known films, *Suppose They Gave a War and Nobody Came*, playing a sex-mad con artist soldier trying to improve civilian–soldier relationships in a racist town. The movie featured a hilarious climactic scene as two soldiers drive a tank through the town and into the jail to free Curtis.

It was more a case of 'Suppose They Made a Movie and Nobody Came', because few people went to see it. It was marketed wrongly as 'A Peacetime M.A.S.H.' Robert Altman's groundbreaking *M.A.S.H.* had changed all the rules about comedy, and although *Suppose They Gave a War and Nobody Came* was a pleasing service comedy, it was suddenly unfashionable.

In an effort to avoid making another comedy, he accepted an offer in 1969 from Columbia to make an adventure action movie, *The Dubious Patriots*, produced in Turkey by Gene Corman and co-starring Charles Bronson. Tony, accompanied by Leslie, stopped off in London en route to Turkey and was asked by a reporter about the secret of his youth. He replied, 'A great deal of loving, stroking and kissing. Any way you like it, but do it. Then your sleep improves and your diet. That is the secret of my youth.'

He seemed settled and very happy with his new wife, and said, 'I was a bit of a tearaway before I met Leslie. Now I feel I never want to cheat. And no one can possibly say I am rude or disloyal. Leslie is a very gentle, kind person. I have never known a woman who cares for me so much.'

When asked why she was going to Turkey, Leslie answered, 'I go everywhere with him. At the studios I sit and sew. I'm not following a career of my own because I don't like the separation involved.' Tony had found the kind of wife he felt he needed – one who wasn't an actress and had no ambition to pursue a career.

The Dubious Patriots was set in the days of the Ottoman Empire in 1920. It had a budget of just $2 million, not a huge amount for the kind of big-set action the film called for, but costs in Turkey were relatively low, and it was hoped that with such a modest budget the pairing of Curtis and Bronson – named the world's biggest box-office draw because his films made more money in Europe than those of any other star at the time – the picture would produce enormous profits.

It turned out to be one of the toughest movies Tony ever made. 'Tough! Oh, *tough!*' he said. 'I'd never known anything like it. We were staying in a hotel, Charlie Bronson too, and this place was falling apart. We had no electricity or water. Every time a door slammed, the plaster fell off the ceiling. A lot of people got hurt making that movie. And a couple of kids got killed by a unit car.'

The children were killed when they ran out from behind a school bus and were knocked down by one of the film unit's cars carrying one of the movie's actors, John Acheson. He maintained that his driver was only doing ten miles an hour and couldn't avoid hitting the children. The driver was arrested and put in jail for three months to await trial, then convicted and sentenced to eighteen months in prison.

A week after the accident, a catering assistant fell in a trailer and died the next day. Anything that could go wrong did go wrong. Dozens of stuntmen were injured every day in falls involving horses. Following a disastrous accident in which stuntmen and horses piled into each other, one horse had to be shot.

A fight broke out one evening in a port-side club between members of the unit and local villagers. It was like a scene from a movie as chairs and tables were thrown across the room while police swarmed into the place to make arrests. Six of the film crew ended up in court.

Drug smuggling was big business in that part of the world, and all the cast and crew came under suspicion when the local police turned up to investigate. 'We believe that members of the unit are involved in drugs,' the police chief told them. 'If proof is forthcoming, the maximum penalty under Turkish law will be enforced.'

Tony pleaded ignorance. 'I don't know of anybody taking the stuff,' he said. 'But I'm told this whole area is one of the world's centres for getting it.'

Some members of the unit became very concerned by the presence of the police. 'Everyone on that movie was smoking hashish except Bronson,' one of the cast told me. 'Tony Curtis was smoking hashish but not cigarettes while the rest of us were smoking dope *and* cigarettes. It was no big deal, although it would have been if we'd been rounded up and put in prison.'

Tony said he got on well with the usually reclusive and elusive Charlie Bronson. 'We were like brothers in arms – both up to our necks, fighting to survive.'

Bronson recalled, 'We both had to put up with a lot – it was a lousy script and an inept production. I was in a bad mood, Tony Curtis was in a bad mood. So we complained together, and tried to make the best of what we had. We rewrote most of our lines, and we didn't do *that* particularly well, but it had to be better than what we had.'

The slam-bang action adventure movie was poorly directed by Peter Collinson, and it was uninspiringly retitled *You Can't Win 'Em All*. As *Variety* rightly noted, '*You Can't Win 'Em All* is both a title and a kind of dismissal to this Gene Corman potboiler.'

The *Hollywood Reporter* complained that Curtis and Bronson 'are forced to engage in some of the lamest repartee that can ever have passed for wit in an American movie'. But it did well throughout Europe and Japan, where Charles Bronson was a huge star.

Tony had no movies offered to him to step into after *You Can't Win 'Em All*, so an agent he knew, Freddie Fields of CMA, asked him to emcee some shows in Las Vegas. Fields put together various acts for a show in a hotel, and for two weeks Tony not only introduced the acts but also performed magic tricks.

Back in Los Angeles, Tony hawked his ideas for dramatic movies from studio to studio, and was turned down by every one of them. He almost produced *The Night They Raided Minsky's* about a burlesque house, and he would have played the lead role, but after a while he gave up on it and producer Norman Lear took it over and produced it. What Tony really wanted to produce was a movie about the Jewish gangster Bugsy Siegel, and for several more years hoped some studio would make it.

In his frustration, he accepted an unusual offer to do a television series in England. Sir Lew Grade and his ITC company, responsible for the long-running series *The Saint*, were going to make a multimillion-dollar TV series that would be the costliest, most glamorous adventure series ever made.

CHAPTER EIGHTEEN

Through With Movies

oger Moore (now Sir Roger Moore) had just spent what he called 'seven years in slavery' making *The Saint* for Grade's ITC television production company, and in 1969 wanted to be free to make movies. He had been approached to play James Bond a number of times but was always under contract to Lew Grade and hoped this would be his chance to finally play the role.

Lew Grade called him and said, 'I'm in Hollywood, and you're going to do another series for me. It's called *The Friendly Persuaders*.'

'The answer is *no*,' Moore told him.

'It's already sold with you in it.'

'That's immoral.'

'Think of your Queen. Your country needs you.'

Moore stuck to his guns, but so did Grade, who called him every hour, on the hour, for a weekend. Eventually Grade said, 'Listen, if you do the series, you can have any co-star you want.'

Moore thought of the person least likely to do a TV series, and said, 'OK, get Tony Curtis and I'll do it.'

So Grade got Tony Curtis and called Roger Moore. 'You recall that you said you'd do the series if you had Tony Curtis? Well, you've got him.'

That's the funny story Sir Roger Moore told me, and it's more or less the way it was, except that he would write in his autobiography that Grade had already lined up three possible American stars –Glenn Ford, Rock Hudson and Tony Curtis – before calling him. He had worked with Ford before and didn't want to again, and he felt he and Hudson were too alike physically. So he approved Tony Curtis. Moore didn't want to do another TV series, and probably hoped that Curtis would turn it down. But he didn't turn it down, no doubt to Moore's surprise and dismay, and so Moore found himself back in slavery but this time with Tony Curtis.

Tony said that when Lew Grade asked him to do the series, he had asked Grade, 'There's just one question. Do I call you Sir Lewis or Sir Louie?'

Sir Lew said, 'Call me what you like as long as you do the series.'

Tony replied, 'OK, you're Sir Louie!'

The movie offers coming at Tony might have been fewer than ten years earlier, but he was not yet on the scrapheap. It wasn't as though there were suddenly no offers, but Tony was sick of Hollywood because of the way he felt he had been treated, and when he got the offer to make *The Persuaders* (The *Friendly* in the title was dropped because there had been a film called *Friendly Persuasion*) in Britain, he decided it was a chance to escape Hollywood for a while.

He even put up with ridicule from some in Hollywood at a time when it was still considered a kind of betrayal for a movie star to do a television series. He told me, 'I got a lot of criticism from some quarters for doing the TV series, but the people who criticised me were the ones that, number one, wished they were doing those roles and, number two, were not my agents when I did it. Freddy Fields was head of CMA and used to be my agent, and he said that people like James Garner and myself were whores for taking those television jobs and to take the money. I only assume Freddy said that because I wasn't signed with CMA when I went ahead and did that series, which would have given a commission to the agent who was handling it of over a hundred thousand dollars. So you can see what prompts people to say certain things.'

Sir Roger Moore recalled the first time he met Tony:

I flew out to California with [the producer] Bob Baker and [script editor] Terry Nation, and we went to Tony's house, and that's the first time I discovered that he was an ardent anti-smoker. We talked, and I didn't have a cigarette, and the longer we talked, the more I felt I needed one, and finally I took one out and said to him, 'Do you mind?' and he said, 'No, not really,' and he started to look for an ashtray and asked his wife, 'Darling, where's that ashtray we used to have?' He found the one and only ashtray in the house, and then he opened all the windows and started the electric fans until there was a gale blowing through the house to clear the smoke.

With each draw on my cigarette, Tony said, 'That's another minute outta your life, pal.' I finally gave up cigarettes because of Tony. Now I only smoke cigars. Well, I have to smoke *something*. And I do have expensive tastes.

Tony had to smoke something too, but it wasn't legal. He had completely given up cigarettes, cigars and his pipe, and had become the president of an anti-smoking lobby in America, appearing on TV shows and in ads in an attempt to persuade people to give up smoking.

He flew into London's Heathrow Airport on 26 April 1970 to start work on *The Persuaders*. Robert Baker had told Tony on the telephone not to bring any illegal substance into the country and assured him he could get Tony whatever he needed. He was met by the series' production manager Johnny Goodman and as they passed through customs about a dozen customs men suddenly swooped upon them and found a hand gun and an ounce of marijuana in Tony's luggage. Somehow, Tony managed to pass a small amount of pills wrapped in cotton wool to Goodman to hide. Goodman never knew what they were but assumed they were pep pills.

Tony Curtis was taken straight to West Drayton police station and charged with possession of drugs, but not for possessing a gun, which puzzled him. He came to the conclusion that someone had tipped off British customs. He told me in 1985, 'Why else would they have taken such a special interest in me? They didn't search everyone else's baggage. And they didn't care about the gun, just the drugs. Someone had told them to look for drugs, so that's what they looked for. They accepted my explanation about the gun but all they wanted was to find drugs. I coulda been an assassin come to England to shoot the Queen or the Prime Minister or Roger Moore, but they didn't care. They only wanted the drugs. I've often wondered about that. It was a tip-off but I never knew who. Someone had it in for me, I tell ya.' It might have been paranoia, but he had been singled out by customs officers.

He spent a night in a cell at the police station. 'Everyone was very nice to me and I was treated very well,' he said. The next morning he was brought before the magistrate at Uxbridge and pleaded guilty to possession of cannabis. He left his defence squarely in the hands of

Queen's Counsellor Mr Geoffrey Leach, who urged the court to fine Mr Curtis rather than deport him. 'He does not smoke cannabis,' said Mr Leach. 'A friend seeing him off from New York on Sunday gave him this to relieve the tension he might face here. He noticed the accused was looking strained and worried. He is staying for at least a year to make a television series with Roger Moore.'

Leach made sure the court was aware that Curtis took an interest in cancer, which his father had died from. 'Mr Curtis joined the anti-smoking campaign, making films, appearances and speeches without a fee, and is now their president. He is also cognisant of the danger of hard drugs.'

A murmur went up from the court when Leach said that Curtis would need time to pay any fine because he was not a rich man. 'There is no country in the world where actors of his standing can land in an aeroplane or ship and relax without being recognised. They are always wondering if next year's work will pay last year's income tax. The accused is not a man of considerable wealth.'

Newspapers didn't fail to report that Tony had been handed a reputed (though unverified) $12 million contract to make *The Persuaders*, although that wasn't confirmed. What they didn't report was that much of his money went on taking care of his mother and brother, and also on heavy maintenance bills for two wives and four daughters.

The magistrate fined Tony a mere fifty pounds. Fans in the gallery raced outside to catch a glimpse of him leaving court, as did the horde of press photographers and reporters, but he left by the back door.

A few hours later he emerged at the Grosvenor Hotel where he gave a brief press conference. He said, 'Everyone has been truly wonderful to me. I discharged my responsibility at the court, and that is that. Let the past be the past.'

He was informed that three American television networks had cancelled his anti-smoking commercials. He commented, 'I'm not disappointed or even surprised at the cancellation,' and he went on to assert that cigarettes have no relation whatsoever to marijuana. He added, 'I've been subjected to a great deal of strain over the past months. I have a lot of alimony to pay and I have to make sure that my four children are well looked after. The case is over and forgotten. Now I've got a great TV series to work on with Roger Moore. We'll be here about a year, and my wife Leslie and I plan to make England our home.'

And they did, moving into a sumptuous house in Chester Square in the elegant part of London called Belgravia. Lew Grade made arrangements with a bank for Tony to be able to buy the house, although the way that Roger Moore put it, Lew Grade actually bought him the house.

Tony played Danny Wilde, a self-made millionaire from the streets of New York, and Moore was Lord Brett Sinclair, born with a silver spoon in his mouth and all he ever did was lick the jam from it. The two are brought together – for reasons never entirely explained – by a retired judge to fight injustice. The series was so much fun to watch that nobody ever questioned the premise. Both actors played exaggerated versions of their real-life personalities.

The first few months of filming were spent in the south of France, which doubled for various parts of Europe, giving the scenes a glossy Mediterranean look. Then the unit returned to England in the autumn to shoot interiors at Pinewood Studios and on the back lot there.

When filming began at Cap Ferrat on the French Riviera, Tony celebrated his forty-fifth birthday by relaxing on a powerboat that swayed gently at its mooring by a large villa, and being told by Leslie that she was pregnant. The baby would be born around January 1971, by which time they would all be back in London. 'Hey, I'm gonna have an English kid,' he said. 'How about that for a Hungarian Jew from the Bronx?'

The TV series had reinvented Tony Curtis even before it had been aired. There was a wealth of publicity being fed to the media, and the fact that someone considered to be a major Hollywood star was in a British TV series certainly did no harm. The British media were already celebrating him while the British public took him to their hearts. They already loved Roger Moore as *The Saint*, and now stories and photographs of the two of them laughing and enjoying each other's company were being seen in British magazines and newspapers.

Tony enjoyed being big news once more, and didn't mind giving interviews. 'I have good firm hands on the reins of my life – at last,' he said. 'I don't need anything or anybody as a crutch any more. I have no hang-ups at all. I don't need any gimmicks to sustain me – certainly not booze, cigarettes or drugs. OK, they found an ounce of cannabis on me when I arrived in England. I'm not prepared to qualify that situation in any way, but here's what bugs me. The government takes tax off you for using cigarettes that kill you. I got fined fifty pounds for having an ounce of cannabis that isn't lethal. Until I can solve that enigma, I'm going to be as puzzled as hell.'

Here was proof that Tony was still unprepared *not* to speak his mind, and, of course, he still wasn't being honest about his use of marijuana.

Most people working on *The Persuaders* knew he smoked it. Years later, when nobody cared any longer whether Tony had smoked dope or not, Roger Moore revealed that Tony had smoked it on the steps of 10 Downing Street. One of the regular directors, Val Guest, said in an interview in 2005 for the British Film Institute, 'Tony was on pot at the time, and I used to have to say, "Oh, go and have a smoke," because he always had some gripe of some kind.'

Stories began appearing in the columns that Curtis and Moore were feuding. Tony denied them. 'There were rumours that Roger and I were beefing and fighting. Not true at all,' Tony told me. 'But for some inexplicable reason people thought that. These newspaper people who picked up on it thought that they had some value of some kind. It just created a tension which is unnecessary.'

The tension he spoke of wasn't between the two stars, but rather between Tony and some of the directors as well as members of the production team, some of whom seemed to loathe him. Claude Hitchcock, the sound recordist on the series, told me, 'Tony Curtis is not the easiest of people to work with, and he thinks purely of himself. If you want any help from him, you might as well forget it. Sound recording is easy if you can just put a microphone in the middle of a room but if you want quality you have to put the microphone in a good position all the time. Tony Curtis will not do anything the same way twice. He'll rehearse in one part of the room, and when they come to shoot it he'll be over there instead. Now, if you don't know these things [you] can't get a mike there, and no way would he play ball and say, "Well, right, I'll do it in that direction to help."

'On one occasion there were four mikes out trying to catch him because we had to literally put them all round him because he wouldn't say which way he was going to go. He got out of it – he didn't say anything at all!"'

Roy Ward Baker directed an episode called 'The Gold Napoleon' in which Danny Wilde had to climb up a drainpipe, over rooftops, leap on to a moving lorry and grab hold of a bar to hoist him on to another building. 'Tony Curtis wanted to do it himself,' said Baker, 'but I told him we couldn't have him getting injured and to let the stuntman do it. The next thing is, he's at the foot of the drainpipe and I realised he was about to start climbing up it, so I told the cameraman to start filming him because otherwise he would have done the whole stunt and if we didn't have it on film he would have exploded.'

Baker's point was valid; had Tony injured himself the series would have been held up indefinitely. But so was Tony's point: if it was good enough for Billy Wilder . . .!

Val Guest told of an incident in Croisette, in Cannes, where Curtis arrived on the set and began complaining to the wardrobe person, saying, 'In Hollywood you would have been fired.' Roger Moore came over, took him by the lapels, looked him in the eye and said, 'And to think those lips once kissed Piper Laurie.' Everyone,* even Tony, collapsed with hysterical laughter. It was invariably Roger Moore who smoothed over any problems and calmed Tony down.

Not all the directors disliked Tony. Basil Dearden directed the pilot, 'Overture', and some other early episodes (before being killed in a car crash), including 'To the Death, Baby', which guest starred actor/dancer Lionel Blair who told me, 'We had this one scene together, and it was really a nothing scene. So Tony got me in the corner and he said, "Now let's work out what we can do. Why don't I walk around you and say this and that." We got in front of the cameras and did the scene in one take. The director Basil Dearden said, "Why can't all actors do that?" Tony is a very inventive actor. He made that one nothing scene work. He really was marvellous.'

When Curtis and Moore shot a simple scene in a car – just getting in and driving off – they invented dialogue to bring it alive, and Tony was able to make an unrelated reference to *Some Like It Hot*. Wilde says, 'Let me be navigator. Give me the map.'

'Thank you, Daniel, I remember the last time we went to Berlin?'

'So?'

'We were supposed to be going to Madrid.'

'Nobody's perfect!'

Brett replies, 'Certainly not you!'

When *The Persuaders* was finished and it was suggested they do a second series, Roger Moore, according to Val Guest, said, 'With Tony Curtis? Not on your life.' In later years Roger acknowledged that he had a good time making *The Persuaders*, and that he enjoyed working with Tony. No expense was ever spared. 'When we drank champagne,' said Moore, 'it really was champagne. Not prop stuff.'

The two actors enjoyed friendly banter off camera, and even when they weren't in scenes together they were asked to remain on set because their joking kept the spirit of the series going. They often called each other rude names, and this was fodder for the gossip columnists, who reported that they were arguing. Tony still had considerable contempt for Hollywood columnists like Rona Barrett and Rex Reed. He told me, 'You may or may not be friendly with someone you work with. But who cares? Sure, Rona Barrett and Rex Reed care. But what's the difference anyway whether or not you get on with someone? That's got nothing to do with the exercise of it all. That's just cheap publicity – so-and-so is having a beef with so-and-so. Who cares?'

Joan Collins claimed in her 1996 memoir *Second Act* that Curtis's bad temper created tension on the set when she appeared in the episode 'Five Miles to Midnight'. He counteracted in his 2008 autobiography, saying that she held up filming on a crucial scene to redo her make-up, and subsequently he famously called her 'a cunt'. He apologised by sending her flowers, but he was as unforgiving as she.

Joan Collins might have loathed Tony, but Catherine Schell, who guest-starred in the episode 'The Morning After', said, 'I had a great time making *The Persuaders* with Tony. We'd swear at each other in Hungarian the whole time.'

Tony complained about the quality of some of the scripts. 'There was a line like, "Give me the gat." Nobody says "gat". So I changed it to "gun", pure and simple.' On the set, he was, said Roger Moore, 'very free with the script', ad-libbing frequently.

Sir Roger said, 'Tony is a first-class comic and brilliant at ad-libbing. I never knew what he was going to say but it was important that I thought of *something* to say because it kept the scenes we were in fresh and spontaneous, and people believed in that friendship between Lord Sinclair and Danny Wilde.'

Said Curtis, 'There isn't one episode that doesn't have at least one solid piece of business. In every one Roger and I tried to find something.' He was referring to moments where the two stars could elaborate on something and make it better that it was on paper, or simply invent new dialogue, which was what Curtis often did. 'There's one I remember,' he said, 'where he was going to the House of Lords and he had his cape on, and the judge says, "What do you want to do?" and I grabbed Roger's arm and said, "We wanna get married!" Roger and I still think of that. It was fun.'

Clearly it was fun for the best part, but stories of Tony's temperamental outbursts during this period of his life, such as when he was making *Monte Carlo or Bust* just two years before, suggest something had changed about him. There had been a time when he made every effort to be pleasant with the people he worked with. It couldn't just be that he was making a British TV series and finding that things weren't always quite up to the standards he had been used to in Hollywood. He might have been justified in expecting things to run a lot smoother than they did, but he was prone to outbursts that simply alienated some of the people he was working with. He had always been a volatile character, but where he had once been able to contain it, he now seemed unable to control his temper.

His behaviour was sometimes bordering on the bizarre. As is now known, cannabis increases schizophrenia in people with a predisposition for psychosis and paranoia. According to studies looking at the relationship between cannabis users and schizophrenia, cannabis abuse is common among people with schizophrenia as an attempt to cope with psychotic symptoms or irritability or hallucinations. When the feeling of wellbeing which cannabis produces wears off, the user can become disoriented and start to hallucinate, becoming angry, depressed and anxious.

Tony's use of cannabis had increased considerably in the late 1960s. Schizophrenia, depression, paranoia and anxiety were all a part of Tony's genetic make-up, and something he couldn't have helped without having it diagnosed and treated. It isn't difficult to see that his behaviour, which Roger Moore kindly described as 'eccentric', was possibly due to the correlation between his underlying psychosis and a regular use of cannabis.

On top of all that he was incredibly insecure as the only American among a family of Brits who had all worked together on *The Saint* for years, and the crew all loved Roger Moore. My impression is that they all let Tony know that, and I don't think he was really very happy making *The Persuaders*. Except for when the cameras were turning, which for him was where it all happened. Over the years his memories of making the series mellowed.

Even those who disliked working with him conceded that his contribution to the series was invaluable, and certainly fans of the series considered him to be the perfect foil for Roger Moore.

Tony had no regrets about making *The Persuaders*. 'I tell ya, one of the best things that ever happened in my career was to do those *Persuaders*, and to do them with Roger. We were so nice together. I just liked that combination of those two men.'

When *The Persuaders* hit British TV screens on Friday evenings in

TONY CURTIS

1971, it was an instant hit. It became such a huge success in Europe that episodes were linked together to make feature-length movies and released in cinemas..

Its success in America was rather more muted. It is usually reported that it was a flop Stateside and that this failure prevented a second series being made. That isn't the case. It was popular with American audiences, but it didn't capture the largest proportion of the American market. 'It just took a little while to get successful in America,' said Tony. 'We were on the ABC network, which had seventy-two outlets, whereas NBC and CBS had hundreds of outlets between them, so you see that just in outlets alone we were in trouble. And then they put it on at about ten o'clock on Saturday night. They were showing it to the wrong audience.'

The reason there wasn't a second season may or may not have been because Roger Moore wouldn't work with Tony again, but the fact was he had finally signed to play James Bond, and that left them short of one persuader. Producers considered giving the role of Lord Sinclair to Noel Harrison, but everyone knew that the combination of Curtis and Moore had been the foundation of the show's success; all further ideas of replacing Moore were dropped and *The Persuaders* was axed.

Tony always considered *The Persuaders* to be twenty-four 50-minute films, or put together they made twelve feature films. 'There is no difference between those *Persuaders* and movies,' he said. 'It's the same process. The acting doesn't call for anything more or less. And I got to play a range of emotions and actions throughout that made it really interesting for me as an actor.'

When reminded (by me) of an episode called 'Angie! Angie!' he recalled, 'That was easy for me to play because I was a kid from the streets, right out of my own background, and my good friend Larry Storch played my friend from childhood, and that made our friendship on screen easy because it was real, and we were both out of that kind of background. That episode had some humour and some real pathos. I'd say that episode for me, in acting terms, was more like a movie than any other. I liked that episode. Danny mourns for his friend when he sees him shot. It's got genuine pathos, and I really liked that.'

Before Tony had finished filming *The Persuaders* his first son, Nicholas, was born in London on 31 December 1970. Tony was forty-five but said he felt younger than ever, and reiterated his philosophy that a man should marry a woman much younger. 'It's the secret of staying young, really it is, being married to someone younger than yourself.' Or, as he said to me, 'You're only as young as the woman you feel!'

He had, however, allowed himself to age a little more gracefully as he hit his mid-forties, and he stopped dying his hair, allowing it to turn grey even while he was filming *The Persuaders*. But he still had tremendous vanity, and because his hair was beginning to thin at the crown, he grew his hair long and lacquered it down to hide it. (He didn't wear a toupee in *The Persuaders* as is sometimes reported.)

In 1972, Tony decided he and his family should move back to Los Angeles, where he hoped to find offers of movies waiting for him. He estimated that he must have paid the American government about $10 million in taxes during his career, which he figured meant he had earned for himself about $20 million, and so had managed to keep $10 million for himself, much of which he had blown. He said that he had become wiser. 'Right now my wife, our son and myself require about ten thousand dollars a year to live OK. But that's a lot less than I pay for child support. Then there are taxes and money I invest, education for my four daughters and physical comforts for them, and other expenses connected with previous marriages, and my own personal expenses. All of a sudden that ten grand I live on has to grow to $250,000 just for me to break even. Now if anybody can figure out why it has to be that way, I'd gladly split the difference with him.'

He had made some good investments over the years. He had bought three hundred acres of land in Perris Valley, California, for just $800 early in his career, and by 1972 it was worth $1,000 an acre because of a new dam development there.

He had bought another two hundred and fifty acres of land in Perris Valley that he leased to vegetable farmers. Over the years the land had grown in value, and he was able to sell ten acres of it for $100,000. He had other pieces of land which all made him handsome profits. He wasn't in danger of starving.

His family suddenly grew when he won full custody of daughters Alexandra and Allegra from Christine Kaufmann in a brief hearing in Santa Monica Superior Court. Tony and Christine had reached an amicable settlement whereby she could apply at any time for future custody. He later wrote that his girls were not well cared for by their mother; Christine remained silent on the matter.

Allegra recalled, 'They took us to see a psychiatrist and I remember telling them that my dad had remarried and we had a more stable life with him, which was the reality of it.'

Now Tony's family at home consisted of three children.

There were no movie offers so he returned with his family to London, where he still had his Belgravia house. He had little to do in 1972 but tour Europe with Roger Moore promoting *The Persuaders*. The local children in Belgravia missed him because he often went out to play football with them – or any other game, except cricket, which he hated. They would knock on his door and ask Leslie, 'Can Tony come out to play?' and she would tell them he was away at the moment.

They returned again to Bel Air in 1973, and his family swelled again when he gained custody of sixteen-year-old Kelly and fourteen-year-old Jamie. 'It's unusual for a man to get custody like that,' he said at the time, 'particularly since I had been busted in London over a drug offence. But the judge overlooked that. He said what really counted was the kind of home I was offering the girls. Since it appeared to be a happy one I got them. I was very lucky.'

The family grew bigger still when, on 2 May 1973, Leslie gave birth to another son, Benjamin, in Los Angeles. With no feature movies being offered him, Tony guest-starred in the TV series *Shaft*, and was then in a TV film, *The Third Girl from the Left*, with Kim Novak. 'I liked working with Tony,' she told me. 'We both came out of the fifties and worked hard for years, so we both understood what we were about. And we've been friends for years.'

Now that he had all of his children with him, he relished being an active father again. Allegra recalled, 'I remember being in the back of the Rolls-Royce and my dad would be in his underwear driving us to school.'

It quickly became apparent that he had a problem with Jamie. They spent a seemingly happy summer together in 1973, but each knew that something was lacking in their relationship. She looked upon her father more like a happy-go-lucky uncle and finally decided she wanted to live with her mother. He didn't want to play any tug-of-love games with his children, and he reluctantly allowed her to return to live with Janet. The father–daughter relationship between Jamie and Tony would never be quite right.

At least his marriage seemed on track, but still there were no movie offers, so he decided to accept a play, *The First Offenders*. It should have run on Broadway, but it failed to materialise. Meanwhile, he worked on a novel which he called *Julie Sparrow*. He hadn't known quite how to go about writing a novel so had gone to a friend in the Writers Guild and asked, 'How many words make a book?'

His friend looked surprised but answered, 'About fifty thousand.'

Tony began to narrate his novel into a tape recorder and passed it on to his secretary to type out. When he reached 50,000 words he stopped. The book was based on his own experiences in New York during the 1920s and 30s, and he based his characters on people he could remember, especially his brother Julie. The rest he made up.

After living in Bel Air through the first half of 1973, he decided he'd had enough of Hollywood for a while, and the family returned to their London house. There he made a startling announcement. 'What the hell! I'm finished with show business. I'm through with movies. From now on, I'm my own man.'

He was ranting against a Hollywood which had perhaps turned its back on him. He backtracked a bit, telling the *Times*, 'I am going to take no more crap from anyone. I have spent twenty-five years in the clink. I won't make a feature film for anyone except myself.'

He returned to New York in the summer of 1973 to appear in a new play by Bruce Friedman and presented by David Merrick, called *Turtlenecks*, partly financed by Tony's close friend Hugh Hefner. Tony played a middle-aged man who writes shows that air on American TV during half-time breaks in football games. It was to play the provinces before hitting Broadway, and then was due to come to London's West End the following year.

He began rehearsals with enthusiasm, and was in a pugnacious state of mind, determined to prove that he could do without movies and Hollywood. 'Everyone keeps telling me about the risks but the theatre is right for me now. Everything else is so automated. In the theatre you have got live people and that is what counts. I'd sooner be starting on stage now than twenty years ago. If I'm going to be a flop at least I'll be a better flop now. But who cares? I don't need any critic to tell me if I'm good or not. My insides will tell me.

'I don't need a 400-year-run. If it does only five performances that are good, that's fine. It's not a numbers game any more. I'd be up the creek without a paddle if I thought that.' He even reasoned that the money he was getting was better money than he would get making movies. 'For eight performances a week – twenty-four hours' work – I'll get between 7,000 and 9,000 bucks. How many film players are earning that kind of money?'

He regarded his film career with a surprising amount of acrimony. 'I've been making pictures for twenty-five years and I've bull-shitted myself and people round me long enough. I can't exactly look back and say they were the good old years. It never came easy to me. If I had my way I'd load all those Hollywood producers into a van and drive them into the middle of the Pacific.'

That wasn't the kind of talk that was going to build bridges with Hollywood, but he was a disenchanted man, disillusioned not only with Hollywood but with America. 'In America, unless you have a good education, you are through. These are hard-nosed times we live in. The age of innocence has gone. That's why I'm doing this play. At least it's relevant to man's problems today and you don't find much material like that around these days.'

But the experience of being back on stage proved to be a disaster. 'It was very disappointing,' he said. 'Everything turned out to be wrong with it. I went into it with all the vitality, drive and energy at my command. Then you find you have made a mistake, another mistake, and you get your head handed back to you on a plate, again.

'I felt very alone, despondent and in the middle of a vortex at that time. I had an option to get out at Philadelphia, so I did. I had to nurse my wounds after that play. It was a very tough time. I was a basket case by the end but there is nothing you can do. It is the nature of the profession.'

He nursed his wounds by announcing that he planned to turn *Julie Sparrow* into a screenplay, even though it had not yet found a publisher. Then, in 1973, he was offered two films, and suddenly his career looked like it was about to make a recovery. He had also quickly forgotten that he had quit movies.

CHAPTER NINETEEN

Comeback

The first of Tony Curtis's comeback movies was *Lepke* from Warner Brothers, about Jewish mobster Louis Lepke Buchalter. He was following it with *The Count of Monte Cristo* from ITC in which he was cast as Mondego, arch-enemy of the story's hero, Edmund Dantes, played by Richard Chamberlain.

When I interviewed him in 1975, he denied having said that he had quit movies and Hollywood. 'I'm just not gonna work in films now unless I work on my terms,' he said. 'I'm not just gonna put on funny noses and someone else's jacket and come in and read someone else's lines unless I can find a reason for that character's existence.

'In *The Count of Monte Cristo* I play the villain, and I liked the role because it gave me an opportunity to play a series of emotions that I hadn't had the chance to play. And *Lepke* was that kind of a part. Like Albert De Salvo was – a man unto himself, a man motivated and driven by himself and not by factors surrounding him.'

He went on to explain what motivated him to accept film roles at that time in his life – or rather what he *wanted* to be the motivation behind his choices.

Usually parts are motivated and written with the outside incidents provoking the character. I'm trying to find *people* to play, not *situations* to play, if you know what I mean. I find everybody's got a story. *The Six Million Dollar Man*, or situations where you come in and find your wife in bed with another guy, or your child comes in and says, 'I've got two cavities.' Or you wake up one day and find you're a woman – *everybody's* got a story. Everybody's got a book. Everybody's got his own operation, if you know what I mean. Everybody says, 'You think you had a terrible time in hospital? Let me show you *my* operation.'

All that doesn't interest me as much any more as an actor. Writers used to sell stories like that. They'd say, 'Let me tell you this incredible story. This guy finds out in the middle of the story that his mother's brother's father is his sister's cousin.' And it's just one variation on another. No one really examines the man or the woman.

Look at *Wuthering Heights* – the idea of that motivating drive of a man who just won't give up. It was unique. That was a great role for an actor, to bring a mystery to it, to bring those unknown factors that makes us all have those irresponsible and indefinable responses we have once in a while to ordinary situations. It's those things that interest me.

I like roles now that don't give you all the details. That used to be a Hollywood concept of film making. Show it, say it, then show it again and let another character come in and repeat it again just in case you were in the toilet while they were on. It's *moving* pictures, after all. A look, a gesture, a move easily suffices. One doesn't need too much dialogue and over-emphasis on areas that really the simplest of mentalities can grasp what the meaning of it was.

Look how Olivier was motivated in *Wuthering Heights*, how he was driven by that girl. How he felt from the time he met her, that she was *his*. So of course he came back. Maybe he murdered fifty girls to get all that money. The point was he's gonna come back for some kind of revenge, and when those people were together, you had the sense that they were a boy and girl again as they were sitting on that rock. That every-thing else was unimportant. They were back to that square one again in their relationship.

And I think that where an actor can really help a film is he's allowed that personal ability to create. That to me is what acting is. Not when you have to come in and you have to go out and make sure you say that line because that line is a clue or a cue for someone else's line just because some writer has figured out what he thinks is cute or charming. I've made enough of *those* movies.

Lepke was a chance for him to explore what it was that drove a man to become a crime lord. He said, 'Lepke was a victim of his environment and establishment of the period. No other mobster ever went to the chair except him. Why Lepke? Why not Capone or the others? Sure, some of them were bumped off, but how come none of the rest ever went to the chair, ya know? Was it because he was a Jew? It's possible. But look what he created. A murder force of two hundred men. So they had to bump him off, any way they could to get him. When he pushed people out of the window, stuck 'em full of ice picks, did ya see the cops running up and taking him? No way. They were on the payroll. That's how Lepke took care of business. "Put 'em on my payroll or bump 'em off." He was a brilliant man, powerful, who had to take all of his genius and turn it into something foul and degrading, for he had to take a life in order to make his point. He had to kill to survive.'

Tony had to survive too, and he found filming *Lepke* particularly gruelling. He was working very long hours, and he was tired. A woman from wardrobe offered him some cocaine, telling him it would help revive him. She also handed him a little straw to sniff the powder into his nose.

Almost immediately he felt more aware, more awake and full of energy, and he was able to continue working until four in the morning. He continued to get a regular fix to keep his energy levels up and get him through the rest of the film. He believed, at that time, cocaine was not addictive. He was sure he could stop whenever he wanted. He was aware that a lot of people in the movies were using cocaine, and that the cost of it on many films was being paid for in the budget and lost with creative bookkeeping.

He immersed himself in the role, first by doing historical research. 'Every part that I play that has a life basis to it, and even the ones that don't, I do a great amount of research for myself.' He never believed in the method school of acting, but broke it down into something much simpler and, for him, far more effective. He told me:

Katharine Hepburn once asked Spencer Tracy, after she'd seen *Bad Day at Black Rock*, where he had learned to karate Ernest Borgnine. And he said, 'I didn't learn it. I just thought about it.'

And I thought that was a very concise, very astute statement about the art – or artlessness – of acting. I thought, there was a man that really encapsulates it for me by that one phrase: I thought about it a lot.

You *have* to think about it a lot. You have to fantasise. How would this character respond to this? And you get these little bits and pieces in your head and lo and behold you're on the set and the director says, 'It would be nice if you had a little bit of business that you could do,' and right away you remember that little bit of information that you've read about how Lepke liked to open his cigarettes with his right hand, and he'd light from a book of matches which he'd take out in one hand, and he'd take out the match and close the book and be able to strike the match – just a little piece of business, but one that is pertaining, not gratuitous, not just doing it to keep yourself occupied. It's got a life to it, it's got a reason for it. It's the character doing it, not you. That's what I like, and research is the only way to find it.

Research is ninety-five per cent of the job. The other five per cent is turning up on time, getting along with the director, and watching your diet so you don't get sick. And only one per cent of that has got to do with talent or intellect or anything else. You just have to be so well prepared with that role that they could ask you to do it a hundred times and every time you can always improve, add, polish, clean.

One of the film's most startling scenes is Lepke's electrocution. It is bleak and disturbing, the result of Tony's dedication to detail and an ability to put himself into the situation. 'I got to do the electrocution scene by knowing of five different accounts of it and by talking to a guy who had a friend who used to make a point of seeing these electrocutions. He told me his friend said that one of the things that stuck in his mind about Lepke's electrocution – and this made me feel that what I had been researching was true – was that when Lepke came into the room and looked around the room, he almost defiantly put himself in the chair. He didn't leap into the chair – he just put himself in the chair – go on, take it, ya know?'

Every little bit of information Curtis could find about the process of electrocution, and what happened in the hours and minutes before the execution, became integral to how he would play the scene. 'The thing that really stupefied me was the fact that the guys who went to the chair took baths before they went. They were taken into a bathroom, they sat in the tub, took the soap and washed before going to the chair.' During the washing scene, Curtis displayed that sense of bewilderment which he carries into the execution room. 'Normally I go and look at all the sets that are being made so that they don't come as a surprise to me. Seeing the set gives me ideas for bits of business. Lepke's office became *my* office. His bedroom is *my* bedroom. But I avoided that green electro-cution room like the plague. I wanted my first response to be the response that Lepke had when he walked into the room.'

Tony wore no stage make-up at all throughout filming, and used only hair dye for the early scenes playing Lepke as a young man. He had gone through a similar process in *Six Bridges to Cross*, playing a young man who becomes a crime lord in later years – only in that he was then a young actor having to grey his dark hair as he aged throughout the film. I asked Tony if making that earlier film had in some way prepared him to play Lepke. He said, 'Every film you do early in your career prepares you for what you do later, and in some sense I could say that playing that part in *Six Bridges to Cross* was a precursor of playing Lepke. Maybe I couldn't have done it so well if I hadn't played that earlier part. But I like to think I would have done because of what I have come to understand about acting and what it is that works for me in getting under the skin of a part.

'Clothes make a big difference to a part. Laurence Olivier said to me once that expression about clothes makes the man, and as an actor he likes to work from the clothes outside and work his way in. Makes a lot of sense. Those boots, big collars and capes like he wore in *Wuthering Heights* and *Spartacus* all add to the ambience of a performance. It's all integral and important. So that had a big response in me.'

Tony had become very upbeat with his career back on track, and his anger at Hollywood subsided. He was happy in work, marriage and life, and looked very fit and younger than his real age – he was almost forty-eight when *Lepke* was premiered at Cannes in May 1974, where he happily agreed to interviews. 'Keeping in shape is part of my profession,' he said. 'I exercise all day long and often make up exercises. For example, I tense my muscles on the steering wheel of the car. Of course, being married to a good-looking woman helps. Sex is very important to keep a man of my age fit.'

Leslie was with him in Cannes, and he spoke glowingly of her. 'My wife and I are good friends. I love her body and I love her mind. I have a good time with her.'

And Leslie had wonderful things to say about him. 'Tony is a very moral person. If he starts an affair with a girl he's got to marry her. Since we married we have only been apart two nights. It was terrible. We must have phoned each other about ten times.'

Lepke opened to rapturous applause in Cannes, and after the screening Tony threw a party on the Carlton Hotel's terrace where he was besieged by photographers, radio interviewers and hysterical guests. He eventually had to retreat and head back to his suite. 'The response at Cannes was so stimulating,' he said. 'You spend years searching for a way to express yourself in films and there are not many that you find. When you do, it is very exciting.'

Basking in the glow of Cannes, he began working on *The Count of Monte Cristo* in Rome in September 1974. He had only a few scenes, which took just a week to film. The film was not particularly good, neither was he, but he was in the film's only real highlight – a sword fight with Richard Chamberlain; Tony staged the fight himself. 'It was quite a thing to be taught to use a sword by Tony Curtis,' said Richard Chamberlain, 'and he staged the sword fight really well – as well as any stunt arranger.'

Before filming was over, Tony signed to do *The Man in the Iron Mask*, to be made in Rome by the same producers as *Monte Cristo* and again starring Richard Chamberlain. It was ironic that he seemed to be making costume swashbucklers as part of his comeback, and he remarked, 'I seem to be interested in period films, but am I back where I started? Yeah, perhaps I am. I had thought about it. But please God I don't have to go through it *all* over again. I don't think so.' He didn't have to do it all over again. *The Man in the Iron Mask* was made in 1976 without him.

In October 1974 he was back in London, full of optimism and enjoying being father to his four children who lived with him. London had become his home. He said, 'When I first arrived in London four years ago the square was full of Americans. Now, because of the threatened tax changes, they've all gone back. But not me, pal. I am here because I love it, not to save money. I have been offered three times what I paid for my house but always said *no*. When I bought it there was a thirty-eight-year lease. There are thirty-four years left and I plan to use up all of them. I see no point in earning money so you can live the way you want and then letting the money determine where you've got to go. Anyway, I'm crazy about London.'

In early spring 1975, Tony was still living in London with his family. He was a lot more sanguine about his life and career than he had been a couple of years before when he had ranted about Hollywood and his career. 'Only in retrospect do I feel that I got what I felt I wanted to do,' he told me. 'It's a little early to start reminiscing about those things because I still hope I can get opportunities. But that's being cut down all the time. You see, there are less and less movies being made, and there are parts that I can do, but I just don't want to do those parts unless I can have something in it that I'd like to do like a fencing sequence such as in *The Count of Monte Cristo* – a really good one that I was able to stage myself. It gave me a chance to expose myself and extend myself in that area.'

He had become sanguine to the point of actually seeming not to care any longer too much whether he worked in movies or not – a front, I think, because he had been desperate to get back into movies, and now that he was, he felt he could afford to show that he didn't care too much.

'Movies are not that important to me any more,' he told me. 'They are important in the way they let me live my life and the people I'm connected with, but by and large I find that the most important thing for me now is gathering my energies and my strength, preparing myself for the rest of my life as an author.'

This new career, then, was his future, as he saw it. 'I've written a book about Hollywood and Las Vegas and New York.' This was the book that began as *Julie Sparrow*. 'I haven't done an autobiography yet. I'll do that one day. I'm recalling and retaining memories on everything I do, and maybe perhaps one day I'll compile all the fabulous stills that I just stuck away somewhere.' He would blow hot and cold over an autobiography for the next two decades and would, at times, insist that he never would write his autobiography. His big ambition in 1975 was to write novels.

Believing that he would be home a lot more as a writer, he decided to concentrate on his family. 'Right now I'm dedicating a lot of my time to my children. I've got a lot of young children around me – a couple of little boys and a couple of girls, so I'm trying to make as much of a life for them as possible – that is, my wife and I are.'

He had dreams of a happy family life, and he seemed to have a plan as to how his life would go from that moment on. 'In just a few years my little boys will be in school and then my days really will be quiet, and then my wife and I will be able to attend to our own needs. Right now I feel like a camp counsellor that has dedicated himself to running a camp, and that's what I'm doing. You have to do that. I enjoy it. Then along with my book writing, I paint a lot now. [Painting is] not a profession in that sense, but not amateur either. It's not a hobby. It's a way of life and an attitude that I have. I don't sell the paintings because they weren't made to be sold. They were made for me.'

Lepke opened in London to good business – it was out-grossing *The Towering Inferno* for a while – and some good reviews. '*Lepke*, by the strength and sincerity of the central performance by Tony Curtis, is compelling,' reported *Films Illustrated*. 'Curtis convinces us utterly of his ruthlessness, and while we don't exactly share his conviction of his immortality, the savage realism of the electric chair climax is quite horrifying.'

Films and Filming said, 'Brooklyn mob leader Louis Lepke Buchalter is endowed by Tony Curtis with a nice line in compulsive viciousness.'

The Count of Monte Cristo played on American TV and went out on general release in European cinemas to reasonable business but poor reviews. 'Richard Chamberlain looks as though he could give a good account of the title role if only the director would help a bit,' said *Films and Filming*, adding, 'Tony Curtis is appalling as Mondego.'

The *Observer* said, 'Tony Curtis shouldn't be asked to do this kind of thing any more; his disbelief has been too much suspended already.'

In 1975, Tony turned fifty. He hadn't made a movie since *The Count of Monte Cristo* in 1973, and there was nothing on the horizon. It began to dawn on him that his comeback had not been quite as assured as he had thought.

A lot of stars from the 1950s were struggling into the 1970s – such as Rock Hudson, Robert Wagner, Natalie Wood, James Garner, Elizabeth Taylor, Richard Burton, Burt Lancaster and Kirk Douglas – as newer trendier stars came along like Clint Eastwood, Robert Redford, Robert De Niro and Al Pacino. Studios and producers went where the money was to be made. Tony Curtis was probably no more ignored by Hollywood than others of his generation. Occasionally the older stars managed to find minor and even major screen triumphs, and Tony was no exception.

Some, like Garner, Wagner and Hudson, retreated into television series. In fact, Tony Curtis had made it acceptable for movie stars to do regular TV. The important thing for any actor was to keep working. Tony did, but he yearned for his movie career to take him to the top again. He would have his minor triumphs, but as he moved through middle age into old age, he went fighting and kicking all the way, never less than determined to remain a leading man, never cut out to be a character actor. And yet, his best roles to come were in character roles.

He moved his family back to Los Angeles yet again in the hope of being noticed once more by Hollywood. In the summer of 1975 he did a magic show in Las Vegas for four weeks, but decided that wasn't his thing. From time to time he picked up the telephone and called producers, asking if they had anything for him. He was finding Irving Lazar no help and felt desperate and embarrassed to have to go asking for roles. He was making more money from real-estate deals than from movies.

In 1975, he got an offer from his old studio, Universal, but not for a movie. Universal had done very well with TV, producing series with feature-length episodes such as *McMillan and Wife* with Rock Hudson, and *Columbo* giving Peter Falk long-deserved stardom.

Universal offered Tony the starring role in such a series, *McCoy*, as a con man setting stings to catch the villains. It owed a lot to the success of the movie *The Sting*, although Tony preferred to liken it to *The Great Imposter*. He never considered it a TV show but a series of movies made for TV, shot quickly and cheaply.

He really felt it was a comedown but put on a brave face. 'It's perfect casting for me,' he said. 'I mean, anybody who survives for twenty-five years in Hollywood must be a con man.'

His first day of filming took place on the same sound stage where he danced with Yvonne de Carlo in *Criss Cross* in 1948. 'Rock Hudson and I are about the only ones left on the lot from those days,' he said on the set. 'We only made theatrical films then, but nowadays most of the activity comes from television.'

He emphasised that making *McCoy* was no different to making his early Universal movies. 'When I was a kid here, we turned those pictures off the assembly line much more rapidly than they do television shows. I used to make pictures that were seven- and nine-day wonders. Eighty-five to ninety-five per cent of my old movies were made in half the time, or even a quarter of the time, it takes us to film one *McCoy* episode.

'It takes around twenty days to film each episode. The TV stars who talk about the good old days when films were made on much more relaxed schedules just don't know what they're talking about. Universal developed a stock company of young actors back in the forties and fifties. They just kept tossing us from one movie to the next. Everything seems much better organised now.'

He seemed resigned to making his living on TV, although he still hoped he could do it also on the big screen. 'It's all entertainment. People keep trying to make a distinction between the two [cinema and TV] but there is none. I'll do either, as long as they pay me the money I ask.'

He talked as if *McCoy* was another comeback – he seemed to be making a career out of comebacks. 'It was inevitable. Show business is the toughest rat race there is. It's the ultimate challenge. I grew up in a tough Brooklyn slum, but I got my real education in Hollywood. It's the cruellest, most heartless town I've ever lived in.'

He insisted that this was just the first step in his comeback. 'I've never been one to look back. I am very fortunate that I can view my professional past in the third person. To me, the past is like stepping off a kerb. Once you have done it, there is no reason to go back, because across the street there are new things to do and see, and another step up. Right now the only thing I'm concerned about is making *McCoy* a damn good series.' Only five *McCoy* films were made.

But what he really wanted was a movie, and he waited for the call. The phone did ring, but not always for the reason he hoped. 'Last year Mike Nichols rang up and I thought he was going to offer me a part. Instead he really wanted to rent my [London] house.'

Then he got a call from producer Sam Spiegel. 'He rang me at my home in Hollywood and asked me to come down to his office. I thought he wanted to rent my house. Instead, he offered me a part in *The Last Tycoon*.'

He had a real movie at last. It was based on Scott Fitzgerald's unfinished book about the movie business in the 1930s. Spiegel had it in mind to cast Tony as Rodriguez, a dashing and handsome movie star desperate to maintain his image despite having become impotent. Spiegel asked Tony to come to his office to meet with him and film's director Elia Kazan.

Tony recalled, 'I said, "Do you guys mean it or are you kidding? If you are going to give me the part, tell me now. Don't call me when you've thought about it. Kazan embraced me and said, "You *are* Rodriguez."'

Tony had said he would never play a cameo, but he needed the work, and he admired Kazan. He said, 'I figured if it was good enough for Jack Nicholson, it was certainly good enough for me.'

Nicholson was one of a number of major players in the movie, although Robert De Niro had the plum role of the movie producer trying to run a studio, deal with everybody else's problems and insecurities, and maintain his seat of power. Robert Mitchum, Ray Milland, Dana Andrews and Jeanne Moreau were among the cameo stars.

'Acting with some of those guys is like stepping into the ring with [Muhammad] Ali,' said Tony. 'Robert De Niro is a brilliant actor. We were pleasant with each other, but everyone is competing. You must have that sense of competition to give an edge to the performance. You can have a good time with each other on those closed sets, but in the final analysis you are on your own.'

He didn't shy away from the root of his character's problem, that of impotency. 'We've all had that problem somewhere along the line. You are with someone you really desire but find yourself incapable of making love to her. What is this mental block? Are you thinking of an ex-wife? Your mother? Or what? It takes a lot of delicacy to overcome the problem, and that is the dilemma of this man.'

He wasn't shy to admit to me in 1983 that he'd had his own problems with sexual dysfunction. 'My problem used to be getting overexcited and dealing with that. Premature ejaculation!'

A key scene, in which Rodriguez attends a sneak preview of his latest film, was shot at a movie theatre in Los Angeles where hundreds of extras were at Kazan's command. To get them to respond to Rodriguez's entrance, Kazan stood before the huge crowd and announced, 'Tony Curtis is a god!' Tony made his entrance and the crowd went wild. They were cheering for Rodriguez, but more than that, they cheered for Tony Curtis.

'I enjoyed working with Kazan. He's the greatest swordsman of them all, in a manner of speaking. He once said he'd never work with an actor who wasn't a hungry actor. I asked him what he meant by that remark and he replied, "There's a lot of ways to be hungry." He meant actors must have the desire and the need to express themselves. I'm always hungry in this respect. Insatiable. It drives me. Perhaps it's also my New York background.'

Kazan became Tony's new mentor. 'I talked quite a lot with Kazan. He suggested I should become a director because that's where the power is, on the floor. I would certainly like to write my own screenplay. In fact,

I've just begun one and have written eighteen pages,' he said in a 1976 interview. 'It is about six beautiful women who come to California to try to get into the movies. I've thought of situations rather than solutions. For example, is the quality of love-making affected by whether you are a success or failure in Hollywood? The screenplay will be about their one-to-one relationships with each other. The most valuable thing we have is our own responses and reactions to other people. We have it all when we are young and it is beaten out of us by adults.'

Scot Fitzgerald never finished *The Last Tycoon* so playwright Harold Pinter, who wrote the screenplay, had to fill in all the gaps. Tony was impressed. 'It wasn't a good book. Pinter's script is much superior. He makes it real where Fitzgerald made it nebulous. I must say I don't understand the Fitzgerald legend.'

Filming began in October 1975 and was finished before Christmas. After the first private screening for its stars, Jack Nicholson put an arm around Tony and said, 'Tony, you scored big.' Tony always felt, right to the end, that he had never received the recognition from his peers he rightly deserved, and so when the younger members of the cast of *The Last Tycoon* paid him compliments, he was genuinely touched. He recalled other younger stars praising him. 'Ryan O'Neal was equally flattering. I was touched. To them, I'm the older generation, of course. They grew up with me the way I grew up with Cary Grant and Gary Cooper. Those two men were always solicitous to me. So I try to be the same. Not that Jack or Ryan need my help. But I do give them advice. I tell Jack to lose weight, Ryan to concentrate on comedy. *Me!* The *older* generation! It's hard to believe.'

Kazan told him, 'You're going to win an award for this.' Tony liked the compliment, but was as pugnacious as ever when he said in an interview, 'You won't find me in any audience, baby, sitting with five other guys waiting to hear, "And the winner is . . ." They can take their awards and shove them.

'I've been in this business – what? – twenty-nine years. This is my hundredth movie.' (It was actually his sixty-third, which was a considerable achievement, but he counted *The Persuaders* as twelve movies, and *McCoy* as another five, and a few TV movies, but it still didn't come to a hundred.) 'I've made a lot of good films and never won a thing. They don't give awards to encourage talent the way they should. They give them out like they give gold watches to railwaymen – when it's all over.

'Look at Cary Grant. Who's better than Cary Grant? But they waited until he retired to give him an Oscar. [It was a Lifetime Achievement Award.] And he was so gracious about it. Me, I'd have told them to shove it. I don't speak out of rancour. Really I don't.'

It was not the kind of statement to endear him to the Academy. He never forgave them for not nominating him for *Sweet Smell of Success* or *The Boston Strangler*, and for denying him the award for *The Defiant Ones*.

He continued to criticise the Academy for years to come prompting Gregory Peck in 1985 to admonish Tony for sounding off about how disillusioned he had become with Hollywood, and with the Oscars which had never rewarded him, and about his publishers. 'Tony, stop knocking Hollywood, the Academy and everything else,' Peck told him.

Tony gave his most angelic smile and replied, 'I'll never do it again.'

Peck found his response, 'typically charming, the way Tony is'.

It's questionable whether he would have accepted a Lifetime Achievement Oscar – I think he might have when the time was right, probably during the 1990s when his work was being reappraised, largely due to the publication of his first autobiography. He was doing a lot of interviews on TV, and people were suddenly remembering that he had been outstanding in a number of films. But no such award was offered, despite a lifetime of dedicated work and some really great movies.

Critics didn't care for *The Last Tycoon* but did like his performance. 'Tony Curtis, whose own screen career has shown how to climb hand-over-hand from pretty boy to middle-aged character actor, turns in a concentrated highly self-critical portrait of an Errol Flynn superstar with hardening arteries,' wrote the *Sunday Times*. The *New Statesman* said, 'Tony Curtis, let it be said, also has his moments of relishable interest as the star-stud gone twitchily impotent.'

His personal success in *The Last Tycoon* lifted his spirits, and he was optimistic and positive about all things Cinema. 'I find now I love movies more than ever,' he said. 'There is something about getting involved with a camera, an impersonal machine. You have to pit yourself against that machine and beat it. I'm intrigued by working in films because it is such an abstract profession yet so devastatingly personal.'

He had been such a youthful man for so long, but as he left his fifth decade behind him, he decided he wouldn't keep on pretending he was still young. 'I'm fifty now. I suppose it's nothing really. I know I must surround myself with interesting people and young people. In a funny way your life can be similar or dissimilar to other people. I have a young man drive me when I'm here and when the car goes along a street market near here he always points out, "That's where I had my street barrow." I know that if we were going along together in a certain street in New York, I could say, "That's where I had my street barrow."'

He knew he had come a long way. And he wasn't ever going back.

CHAPTER TWENTY

Give A Struggling Actor A Break

He was back in London in January 1976. 'I like coming to London. One has to change emotionally when you come here. Life doesn't go the same way as California. I find it easier to think about London in geographical terms rather than cultural terms. This is an island and you feel the vibrations of that. You can't cop out. Critical assessments are sharper, films tend to be the view of a single person, critical acclaim here is more pertinent. And on top of that you can't find a programme like *Top of the Pops* in America.'

When Roderick Mann interviewed him, he reminded Tony that he had said he'd quit films a few years earlier. 'I did say that,' Tony conceded (having told me the year before he hadn't said it). 'But now I'm getting all these offers. It's always the same. When you get to the stage you don't care and tell them to shove it, they come running after you.'

But few were running after him, except those making cheap movies who wanted a star name, which can be the only explanation why his next movie was *Casanova and Co*, a sex comedy made in Italy. He headed for Venice in 1976, unaware that it was going to be turned into a soft-porn film and retitled *The Rise and Rise of Casanova*. Certainly the film's leading ladies, Marisa Berenson, Britt Ekland and Marisa Mell, couldn't have known that there would be beautiful young starlets cavorting naked in soft-porn scenes.

Tony played a dual role, the great lover Casanova and Giacomino, a thief who happens to be his double. He put on another of his brave faces and said, 'This film is fun. I'm enjoying it. We even got permission to film in Casanova's prison cell. It's solid rock, and the bars on the windows are intertwined – not the sort that Charlie Bronson cuts his way through in movies.'

After Casanova and Giacomino escape from jail at the same time, the thief ends up with all of Casanova's women. 'A lot of it is me acting opposite myself. Fortunately, I'm wonderful to work with.'

By coincidence, Federico Fellini was making *Casanova* with Donald Sutherland in the title role. When asked if he was concerned about clashing with the Fellini version, Tony replied, 'Fellini–Bellini. There's no comparison.' That was true. He seemed to be under the illusion that he was making a good movie, and said, 'I was determined not to do any more crap. No more *Earthquake Revisited* with me playing the elevator boy, and no more *Son of Ali Baba's Mother*. I was sick of it all. I'd get to the stage where I couldn't stomach the idea of starring any more in bad films with actresses with bad breath.'

Could he really have believed *The Rise and Rise of Casanova* was a superior film? Perhaps being paid $300,000 motivated him to stay upbeat about a film he must have known was going to be awful. In some countries, distributors changed the film's title to *Some Like it Cool*, because in one scene Tony had to disguise himself as a woman. He had even suggested an additional line: 'Nobody's perfect.' But nobody was fooled. 'As if to underline how far Tony Curtis's career has declined from the heyday of *Some Like It Hot*, he is requested not only to parade in unconvincing drag but even to repeat the "nobody's perfect" punch line,' complained the *Monthly Film Bulletin* with justification.

He had some good news, though. In the winter of 1976 New York publisher Doubleday & Co liked his novel enough to give him a contract for two books. It's estimated that he was paid more than a quarter of a million dollars in advance.

The novel was now called *Kid Andrew Cody and Julie Sparrow*. After originally starting out as *Julie Sparrow* he had written a second story about Kid Cody and integrated them into one book – he probably found out that 50,000 words were not enough for a book after all, and he had to double the wordage. He said, 'After I completed the stories I shuffled them together like a deck of cards and wrote some additional stuff and combined them into one novel. I tried to tell a narrative and envisage the characters without embellishment. And I chose a period that didn't take any research – from 1922 to 1960. I could call on my own experiences.'

All his life he was caught somewhere between being Bernie Schwartz and Tony Curtis, and as much as he tried to lose Bernie and his background, it never left him. 'I know about street life and how and why a guy climbs out of that environment. I research life, I remember textures, recall eras, and I have a sense of what people are like. Look at all the people I've played, all those environments I've been in, all the stories I've heard. It's a tremendous background for writing fiction. I can now take little pieces of all those experiences and tell my own stories. It isn't all that different from acting. It's like playing a lot of parts all at once. But in acting you're at the mercy of a lot of other people. That's not the case with writing. Maybe that's my motivating factor, to tell a story and express myself, but I also wanted the leverage some writers have, so I went on a quest.'

The final draft was completed with the help of Doubleday editor Larry Jordan following a series of meeting between him and Curtis in New York. Convinced he was setting out on a new career as a writer, Tony admitted he was nervous about having his first novel published. 'Kazan told me, "You've got a lot of courage, exposing yourself as a writer." I know it. After what the critics did to me as an actor, can you imagine what they'll do to me as a writer? But I'm ready for it. And the truth is, they just can't hurt me any more.'

But they could. And they did. The critics didn't care for the book. Tony remained typically pugnacious. The first print run was 25,000. Those copies sold and another 15,000 were printed. He was due to do the rounds to publicise the novel, but he was overconfident and thought its success guaranteed, so he cancelled the tour.

Sales dropped off. Hopes that the paperback edition, due the following year, would do well were optimistically high.

'They just didn't take my book seriously,' he complained. 'They treated it as they would if someone like Jayne Mansfield had written it.'

He was advised sales could be a lot better if he spent some of his own money. 'I was given the chance of buying myself on to the bestseller lists,' he told Roderick Mann. 'It would have cost me about £8,000. When they told me this I was shocked. But it seems to be a regular practice. My agent Irving Lazar told me there's one writer here in Hollywood who does it regularly. They select certain key spots for you, and you buy in your own books. It was disillusioning for me because I've always criticised unfair practices in my own industry and I felt sure the writing game must be different.'

Impressed by an eight-page outline for his next novel, *Starstruck*, adapted from the screenplay he had been working on, Doubleday agreed to renegotiate the contract for his second novel on 7 September 1977. He would receive $100,000 as an advance, the first half to be paid upon signing the contract, and the balance due on 'acceptance of complete satisfactory manuscript' by no later than 1 October 1978.

Doubleday had a reprint agreement with New American Library which would pay $200,000 to Doubleday – half of which would go to Tony – for the rights to publish *Starstruck* in paperback providing it was published in hardback by Doubleday before 31 December 1980.

Movie offers were few but still coming. Demonic horror films were all the rage, so he accepted *The Manitou* in 1977, one of the many descendants of *The Exorcist*. It was the creepy tale of an Indian spirit which is reincarnated by implanting itself in the neck of the film's leading lady, Susan Strasberg, and possessing her. Tony played her psychic boyfriend who, with the help of a Native American, played by Michael Ansara, tries to exorcise the Manitou.

William Girdler produced and directed, hoping to get as much as he could for his modest budget by hiring many of the special-effects technicians who worked on *The Exorcist* and *Star Wars* to create an earthquake, an eight-foot lizard, flying comets, torrential rain, a hurricane that rips through a mansion, and apparitions rising from tables. In one incredible scene, a hospital ward is transformed into a crystalline ice palace with driving snow and sub-zero temperatures.

Between scenes, Tony dictated *Starstruck* in his dressing room. 'The beautiful girl wore a light-green silk dress. The seams of her long silk stockings were straight on her shapely and slender legs,' a reporter from *Photoplay* found him saying into his tape recorder. His technique was to dictate only the narrative, but type out all the dialogue. Then he scribbled additional material on a pad, and handed it all to his secretary. That way he was able to write thirty pages a day for four or five days, and then he always took a break. 'That's as far as I can think ahead,' he said. 'I don't know how my characters are going to end. They don't know their destinies any more than I do. Their lives must be as unpredictable as mine or anyone else's. As an author I want to have the same surprises as the reader does.'

While Tony was making *The Manitou*, Leslie was in hospital recovering from an appendectomy, and he called her four or five times a day. 'She's a remarkable girl,' he told *Photoplay*. 'The finest woman I've ever known. The smartest move I ever made was marrying Leslie. We're truly happy.' Everything seemed idyllic.

He had taken the advice of Elia Kazan and decided he might become a director, because there was a possible deal to turn *Kid Andrew Cody and Julie Sparrow* into a movie. 'There's no part I could play, but I'd help write the script and maybe direct it. If I can write and act in movies, why not direct? And if I direct, maybe I could produce and make the kind of pictures I'd like to do.'

He had no intention to just enjoy being an actor. 'I got ideas for a lot more books. I can't rest. I don't feel like I've done anything. I feel like it's all just starting.'

He suddenly saw whole new professional horizons before him. 'I suppose one reason why I can work so hard at two careers and keep my cool is the fact that my home life is so great. I'm relaxed, at ease and enjoying myself more than I ever have before. And at the age of fifty-two, that's not bad.'

When *Kid Andrew Cody and Julie Sparrow* was published in paperback in 1978 he went on tour to promote it, and even starred in a commercial for it, saying, 'Why don't you give a struggling actor a break?'

But the paperback didn't do well, the movie deal came to nothing, and Tony didn't direct. He failed to deliver *Starstruck* by the scheduled deadline, but he didn't give up on it and Doubleday waited patiently.

He realised that having tried to buck the Hollywood system, he now had to make a permanent return to Los Angeles and sold his London house for £250,000. 'It was a wrench because my wife Leslie and I love London,' he said. 'But we hardly used it.'

Part of the profits from the London house went to buy Leslie a 15-carat canary-yellow diamond which he presented to her in a Beverly Hills restaurant on their tenth wedding anniversary. Producer Robert Evans saw them celebrating and sent over a bottle of champagne with a note, 'Congratulations. Your marriage has lasted longer than my four.'

But like his writing career, and like his movie comeback, not all was as rosy as it seemed. He couldn't put his finger on what was wrong, but the romance had gone, and he and Leslie were arguing. He suspected her of being unfaithful, but he seemed to have no foundation for that belief. What he did have was a growing problem with cocaine. When he was depressed, he took cocaine, and when its effect wore off, he became more depressed. Then his demons came, and the paranoia grew, and the sliver of schizophrenia slipped through the cracks in the marriage.

He was still working, and had an occasional supporting role in the TV series *Vega$*, about a private eye starring Robert Urich, which ran until 1981. Then he starred in a good TV movie, *The Users*, based on a book by ex-gossip columnist Joyce Haber, which looked at the seedy and cruel side of Hollywood. In a way, making the movie was a warning. He said in 1980, 'I've seen what Hollywood can do to young people. They have to know it. For any kid it was a tough place, not just for a girl but for a boy too. A young attractive girl could have a career because God endowed her with a beautiful pair of tits, so she goes to see a producer, a director, and she knows if she does a number on this guy, she's gonna get the job. And you don't have to do that a lot. And a boy too just has to get that number done to him by some guy just one time maybe.'

He was bitter when I interviewed him in 1980, and it showed. 'I'm just telling you what the facts are. Sure, Hollywood made me. But look what I had to go through. They gave me away as a prize in a "Win Tony Curtis for the Weekend" competition. And the studio would pay a crowd of girls to chase me down the street and rip my clothes off. I'm telling you, it was all put up, all part of the old Hollywood.'

When he made *The Users* in 1978, he was still relatively unaffected by cocaine – on the surface – and he still looked amazingly handsome and was able to demonstrate that he had the ability to deliver a powerful performance, playing an ageing film star who goes through a personal and professional crisis and finds refuge in the bed of a handsome young man. Considering Tony's screen image of the macho, heterosexual screen lover, it was a courageous and touching performance.

Then came his most bizarre movie, *Sextette*, the last hurrah from eight-five-year-old legend Mae West. Tony was one of a number of leading men who should have avoided this terrible movie, but Tony said he wanted to do it because Cary Grant had made some movies with Mae West. He demanded and got a fee of $150,000, and was paid the same amount that year, 1978, to star in *The Bad News Bears Go to Japan*.

It was the third in a series of films about a kids' baseball team that had begun with a smash hit, *The Bad News Bears*, just two years earlier with Walter Matthau coaching the kids. Bill Lancaster, Burt's son, had written the original movie, and was invited back by producer Michael Ritchie to write this third instalment, which, going in, looked like a good thing, giving Tony a starring role in a movie that was part of what Paramount hoped would be an ongoing franchise.

Ritchie was happy to get Curtis, who had, after all, been a star longer than Matthau. 'It's strange, but Curtis has retained his star status through public fads and internal shake-ups at the major studios,' Ritchie remarked.

Tony enjoyed working with the team of kids, but despite what the title promised, none of the cast set foot in Japan as the whole thing was filmed, on a tight budget, at Paramount in Hollywood. The script was not up to the standard of the first two films, but it did very well for a low-budget movie, earning $14 million in America.

He was in Canada for the summer of 1978 filming *Title Shot*, playing a crooked boxing promoter. He later said he accepted the movie because 'the separation might give Leslie and I some breathing space in which to rebuild our fractured relationship'. The movie premiered at the Toronto Festival of Festivals in 1979 and then went straight to video.

When he got back from Canada, the problems at home were still there. 'We had hardly been separated since we married eleven years ago, and suddenly here I was away all the time, and exhausted and bad-tempered when I did come home. So I moved out of the house for a while.'

He spent time at the Playboy mansion, a place not conducive to solving his marital problems, on top of which he was struggling with his drug addiction.

Despite his need for money, and his desire to be a writer, he was turning down offers to write his autobiography. 'You wouldn't believe the money they've offered me to write my memoirs,' he said in May 1979. 'A fortune! But I told them, "Not a chance!" My agent Irving Lazar said, "Don't make that a final *no*." "Why not?" I said. "It *is* the final *no*." How could I do it? How could I betray all those confidences I've enjoyed over the years. If I did I'd never be able to look at myself in the mirror again.'

One publisher sent a representative from New York to show him a long list of all the people he had worked with. When he spotted the name of Jack Benny he said, 'I never worked with Jack Benny.' She said, 'Oh yes, you did. You did a radio show with him years ago.' He had forgotten, even though he had a pair of gold cufflinks Benny had given to him. 'They had certainly done their research,' he said. 'I could have made over three-quarters of a million dollars. They would sit me down with four writers and a lot of tape recorders and the whole thing would be wrapped up in six days.'

He said he wasn't going to tell about what happened at the Sands

Hotel in Las Vegas with Frank Sinatra, or about his relationship with Marilyn Monroe, 'who was one of the first people I met when I arrived out here in 1948'. Or about Cary Grant, or about his marriage to Janet Leigh, 'and how the studio told me not to go through with it because it would ruin my career. To write about them in a book – that's something I would never do.'

He said he would never do it, but eventually he did. But at that time that he didn't want to join the list of stars who were telling all, 'even if it would make me a fortune', and he was also still convinced he was going to be a serious writer.

Now his third marriage was in deep trouble. 'We had this widening communication gap,' he explained in 1982. 'But every time I asked her what was wrong, or tried to talk it through, she would shrug it off. "Wrong? Nothing's wrong," she would say. "You're imagining things." But I knew I wasn't.'

He roamed the house at night, talking to himself in the dark, asking himself, over and over, 'What's gone wrong?' He said he knew their sex life had come to an end when she started wearing tights in bed. He took to sleeping in the back of his car, unable to face the reality of his disintegrating marriage.

'I came to the conclusion that my wife was deliberately forcing me out of our relationship. With the mounting problems between us, I was driven into the arms of other women. Convinced that Leslie was seeing other men, I started running wild.' He was jealous whenever she just spoke to men. 'I accused her of flirting all the time, which was denied. She also told me that my jealousy was unnatural, although I still cannot accept this. Surely jealousy is entirely natural.'

Feeling rejected and cuckolded, even though he had no evidence that she was being unfaithful, he became convinced he was losing his looks and that Leslie no longer found him attractive, so he wanted to prove that other women did. 'I got no solace from my extramarital relationships,' he said.

But if anything had become unattractive about him, it was his drug addiction. He was in denial about some of the root causes of his problems, and said in 1982, 'People were saying that I had become a drunk and drug addict. That I was wasting away, just a shadow of my former self. Those stories were completely untrue. I did not turn to drink or drugs for comfort, although it might have been understandable if I had.'

He *was* drinking and using drugs heavily, but maintained the denials.

'My emotional breakdown which followed was a nightmare. And it was made worse by the terrible rumours about me which were flying around.'

He said in 1982, 'Let me put the record straight once and for all. I've never had a drugs problem and I've never had a drink problem. I've never been addicted to either in my life.'

And yet two years earlier, he made a surprising confession to David Lewin. 'I used to drink. I took drugs.' But he was still in denial because he added, 'I pulled myself back.' However, after battling with his drug and alcohol addiction in 1984, he became completely open about his use of cocaine and other drugs, and anything else that got him through the nights – and the days. 'I wouldn't say drugs destroyed the marriage, but it didn't help,' he told me in 1985.

In January 1979, he accepted the starring role in *It Rained All Night the Day I Left*, which proved to be one of the most miserable experiences of his entire career. It was shot almost entirely on location in Israel where he, Sally Kellerman, Lou Gossett and John Vernon had to pretend they were involved in gun smuggling in Africa.

The film's director Nicolas Gessner called it an 'action adventure comedy'. Tony called it 'a thoroughly inept operation, and I'm too old to put up with that kind of thing'.

He was in a terrible frame of mind. He hated making the film, and Leslie had remained in Los Angeles. 'We've had our difficulties, but we've always worked it out because we've wanted to,' he said while on location in the Sinai Desert. Astonishingly, he said, 'I am not a promiscuous man. Nor do I encourage affairs. I live a very sexual life with my wife. And I would do nothing to interfere with that relationship.'

He even talked about the possibility of divorce, saying, 'If Leslie and I divorced I would give her everything and let her give me what she didn't want. To me it makes no difference in the world. I've told her that and I've also told my attorney. In my past marriages, I never gave division of property any thought until the time came. But I was always more than fair – until they became most adverse, and then I fought back.'

His thoughts and feelings about both Janet Leigh and Christine Kaufmann had turned bitter. 'I never liked those women as much as I like my present wife.'

That wasn't true. He had thought the world of Janet Leigh when times were good, and also of Christine. In time he would seem to hate Leslie more than his other wives, and in his first autobiography would write that he could never forgive her after he read her quote in the Andy Warhol diaries that she couldn't imagine how she could ever have married an actor and a Jew.

The only thing that really kept him going through the miserable experience of making the film in Israel was working on *Starstruck*, although he found it virtually impossible to utter anything intelligible into his tape recorder. He used cocaine, he used uppers and downers, and he tried to get by.

While he was in Israel, Leslie and the two boys moved for the summer holidays to the cooler climate of Cape Cod, Massachusetts. Tony phoned them several times every week, 'and it seemed to me that things were getting better'. The boys told him stories of the fun they were having, and Tony was convinced that Leslie was 'more like her old self'. He was hoping for a reconciliation. 'I felt better, I worked better.'

He was impatient to get home to Beverly Hills and be back with his family. His two boys were waiting for him; they had flown back from Cape Cod with their nanny. He promised his sons he would spend more time with them and their mother – a promise he had made before and never kept, not for selfish reasons but because he had to work. Often in life, Tony's aspirations were unreal, no doubt spurred by the fact that his childhood aspirations to become a movie star had been fulfilled, and if *that* had been possible, then *anything* was possible. He once said, 'The only thing I ever wanted was to be Tony Curtis. And I am!'

The moment Tony made his promise to the boys, Nicholas said, 'Dad, I've got something to tell you. You won't like it, but it's something you ought to know.' He said that a man had been staying with them all summer; a man who had been 'a father figure'.

In an instant, Tony dropped from the heights of elation into the depths of despair. He stumbled into his bedroom, locked the door and cried. 'I was heartbroken,' he said. 'I felt humiliated.' When Leslie returned home a few weeks later, he told her that he knew about the other man and said he would do whatever he could to salvage their marriage.

He went to work on a remake of *Little Miss Marker*, which was closer to the Damon Runyon story than *40 Pounds of Trouble* had been, but not as entertaining. Walter Matthau played Sorrowful Jones, a bookie who finds himself landed with a kid after her father offers her as a guarantee against his bet. Tony was in a major supporting role, as the gangster Blackie. The role Shirley Temple had played in the first film version in 1934 and then by Claire Wilcox in Tony's 1963 production was now played by Sara Stimson, and adding a touch of class was Julie Andrews as Blackie's moll.

Working with old friend Walter Matthau proved to be an enjoyable experience. They hadn't seen each other for many years, and when they met on the set for the first time in decades, Tony said, 'Walter, friend of my youth,' and hugged him. Matthau said it was a remarkable moment that stayed with him.

The film was disappointing. *Variety* noted, 'Writer-director Walter Bernstein blows his directorial debut completely. It's a shame, because seemingly if ever there was an actor who should play "Sorrowful Jones" it's Walter Matthau . . . and Tony Curtis could have been a respectable antagonist. But they are all flat in their parts and that has to be Bernstein's fault.' The film raked in a meagre $6.3 million domestic.

Tony went from the joy of making *Little Miss Marker* to the trauma of doing a Neil Simon play, *I Ought To Be In Pictures*, which was to open in Los Angeles and then move to Broadway. He had been invited to do it by its director Herb Ross, and since Tony considered Neil Simon a friend, he decided to take it on. But in rehearsals Tony clashed with Ross, who didn't like the way Tony was playing the part. Tony felt he understood the character, who had come from New York and was driven in a way 'that only comes from a New York background', he said. He knew this guy, he said, because 'he was like me: angry, aggressive, and fighting to get out of the mess he was in.'

At the end of each day, Tony couldn't bear to go home to Leslie, so he slept in the back of his Trans Am. He felt he had no friends, and was lost in a state of never-ending depression.

After the play opened in Los Angeles, he discovered that Ross and Simon were planning to replace him with Ron Leibman before hitting New York. He went out on stage and played his opening scene, and after delivering the scripted tirade, he ad-libbed, 'Fuck you!' and walked off stage before the scene was over. He picked up his things in his dressing room, walked out to his car, got in, drove away from the theatre and never came back.

He complained about 'the rumours spread about my departure [from the play]. People began saying that I was on drugs. That's criminal, man, saying a thing like that.'

Hugh Hefner later recalled going to see the play, and expecting Curtis to be still in the play when it went to Broadway. Said Hefner, 'He was not in it because of his lack of reliability because of the drugs.'

Tony picked himself up and played producer David O. Selznick in *The Scarlett O'Hara War*, an entertaining TV movie about the search for an actress to play Scarlett O'Hara in *Gone with the Wind* (it was one of three TV movies from Garson Kanin's novel *Movieola*). Tony was nominated for an Emmy for his performance.

He went back to real life and sank into another depression. He was in the throes of a complete emotional breakdown. 'I was living in an unreal world with my irrational moods, my obsessive worries, and my desperate fears about my future and that of my childhood.' He said he was troubled by 'fantasies, illusions and delusions'.

In 1985 he told me, 'I had visions I couldn't control. I saw her [Leslie] with other men. Those are the moments I go from being paranoid and insanely jealous and unbelievably insecure because I think I'm not attractive enough, to becoming terrified that I'm turning into a complete basket case because my mother's illness is there, and I'm sick with it when my life is as bad as it can get. Visions and voices! I'm getting old and ugly, and I look in the mirror and where I once saw a handsome boy I see a tired old man losing his looks not to age but to drugs and alcohol. You got to know when it's time to stop all that, but if anyone was saying that to me, I wasn't listening.'

Allegra and Alexandra moved back to live with their mother, Christine Kaufmann, because of their father's heavy drinking and drug-taking. Jamie Lee Curtis recalled, 'When I look at my half-siblings I get sad because we were all denied a life with our dad ultimately.'

In April 1980 Tony delivered an incomplete first draft of *Starstruck*. Doubleday overlooked the October 1978 deadline, and New American Library said it was willing to extend its own deadline to Doubleday by one year, to 31 December 1981.

That same April, Tony suffered a complete nervous breakdown and was admitted into a psychiatric hospital, where he was said to have looked like a 'hunted and haunted shambling wreck' upon his arrival.

He said that his doctors diagnosed 'severe melancholia', and he was given medication to calm him down. He talked at length and with great anguish to a psychiatrist. 'Until then, I'd kept my thoughts and feelings to myself. Not even my closest friends knew how my mind was being tortured by the loss of the family I loved so dearly.' It's possible that he was diagnosed with schizophrenia, but if he was, he never admitted it.

Leslie came to visit him, and on one occasion, as he remembered it, when the doctors asked her if it was wise for him to return home when he was better, she replied, 'Certainly he can come home. We have no problems at all.'

He recalled, 'I looked at her in amazement when she calmly said that.'

While he was in hospital the rumours began to spread that he was an alcoholic and a drug addict. He continued to deny it all and said the rumours only made his condition worse. But his condition had been largely caused by drugs that had increased his schizophrenia, which was the root cause of his condition in the first place. It was a devastating spiral of destruction which he was powerless to escape without help.

Leslie and the boys moved out of the house to live in Cape Cod and Tony moved into a condominium he owned. He maintained his position of being the wronged party, and never shifted from that. The ensuing divorce battle became very bitter. Leslie claimed he had tried to throw her down the stairs and kept guns. Her attorney described her as being in 'a constant state of fear that he would molest, attack, strike and batter or kill' her. The Los Angeles Superior Court dismissed Leslie's claims on legal technicalities.

Tony would state in 1982, 'My ex-wife has claimed that I threatened to kill her. That is rubbish. I have never been violent, even in my most aggressive moods.'

But he was in denial about the worst aspects of his life and continued to deny the rumours that he was taking drugs. He had descended into the worst period of his entire life when he was, by his own admission, 'living in an unreal world with my irrational moods, my obsessive worries'. He admitted he had been through 'a period of deep depression', during the last year of the marriage 'in which my petty tantrums and my uncontrollable jealousy had made life very difficult for those around me'.

If his temper, stimulated by drugs and schizophrenia, *had* got the better of him, he may not have been entirely aware of everything he did – or else he was in complete denial. Or Leslie's accusations were entirely false. Whatever the truth, he was a man suffering several serious illnesses – alcoholism, drug abuse and schizophrenia.

Suddenly the phone had stopped ringing. 'It was as if I had died, only someone forgot to tell me about it,' he recalled.

His use of cocaine increased. He had been told it was good for sex. It acted as an aphrodisiac, but it also made men less sensitive, allowing them to last longer during intercourse. Tony had suffered with premature ejaculation since he was a teenager, and he hoped using cocaine would solve his problem. 'Cocaine helped me to overcome a certain lack of, shall we say, performance. It really worked for me. When you find that you are letting the side down, so to speak, and you find that drugs solve your problem, you're gonna take advantage of cocaine. Therein lies the danger of such a drug. It does for you what you think you can't do for yourself, and then it's got you.'

Some cocaine dealers were gun-toting gangsters, and some down-and outs peddling for criminal organisations. He remembered one dealer working from an apartment who kept a .45-calibre handgun at his side, cocked and ready to use. Leaving the apartment, Tony saw a girl appear from another apartment, offering him oral sex in return for half a gram of coke. He accepted the deal.

'I didn't think I could sink any lower,' he told me in 1985. 'I'd been with a lot of girls before, and it was always nice, ya know. But when I was using . . . it was the fucking pits. Soon all my so-called friends – they were just drug users like me – they were all getting high and that's all they wanted to do, and girls who were addicted were throwing themselves at you in return for a gram or two, and I couldn't say no to them or to drugs.'

He was now regularly freebasing – smoking cocaine through a pipe. 'That was something else again,' he said. 'After two or three pipefuls of cocaine you didn't care about anything. What career? What wife? You just got happy.

'I did acid three times. I heard some people had bad experiences with it, but I had good ones. I felt it freed me up in an abstract way. Lucy in the sky with diamonds! That's what's so bad about it because it can feel so good and then you don't want it to stop.'

He had a reprieve from his troubles when he was offered a good cameo role in *The Mirror Crack'd*. This Agatha Christie thriller was filmed at London's Twickenham Studios and on location in the quaint English village of Smarden in Kent during the summer of 1980. In this whodunit Tony played the producer of a film about Mary, Queen of Scots. Rock Hudson played the movie's director, and Elizabeth Taylor and Kim Novak had great fun playing acid-tongued actresses. Geraldine Chaplin played the producer's secretary.

The murder victim meets her doom at a party thrown by the Liz Taylor character at her rented mansion, and it is left to the redoubtable Miss Marple, played by Angela Lansbury, to solve the crime, aided by her detective nephew played by Edward Fox.

It's an engaging movie due more to its stars than story. As the

Financial Times noted, 'What you buy your tickets for, the makers undoubtedly hope, is the gaudy galaxy of stars, all encouraged to "Do Their Own Thing" to the point of parody – Hudson strong-jawed and immovable as Mount Rushmore, Curtis mercurial and Brooklynite.' It cost $5 million to make and earned a respectable $11 million domestic (and probably as much again outside America).

While filming at Smarden, Tony was met with great adulation by the British public who had taken him to their hearts as one of *The Persuaders*. He was well aware that he and the rest of the Hollywood contingent were past their prime, and he joked, 'If nothing else will bring people to see this film, it will be to see how well we've all aged.' I visited the set, on location and at the studio, and Tony had aged more than I expected since seeing him five years earlier. Where he had looked ten years younger, he now looked his age, fifty-five.

He still suffered from severe bouts of depression, and he was still taking cocaine. He went dancing at fashionable London discos with young women who were shop girls, secretaries and receptionists but never actresses. He continued to find solace in painting, and he set up his easel in his London flat off Belgrave Square, painting every day and often through the night.

During an interview with journalist David Lewin, he broke down and cried, admitting, 'I am not a happy man. I have rushes of happiness. But basically I am very moody and the black clouds of melancholy come across my horizon like the four seasons all in one day. I'll be sitting somewhere enjoying myself with people and suddenly I'll start to sob and weep and don't know why.'

Hearing that Tony was suffering moments of deep despair, Suzanna Leigh, one of his co-stars from *Boeing Boeing*, spent time with him at his flat. 'Right now, Tony needs friends,' she said. 'For me, Tony is a really special friend. Most of the time he's fine. But I've told him that when he needs a friend, he can call me, and I'll go straight out to Los Angeles to help him.'

After returning to Los Angeles, Tony embarked on a string of affairs. One was with the glamorous Soraya Khashoggi, estranged wife of Saudi millionaire Adnan Khashoggi, but that affair, like the others, lasted just a few months. 'I take the responsibility of ending them because I was emotionally unstable at the time,' he said. 'I fell for each of them very deeply and I was sorry that my unreasonable behaviour had to bring each relationship to an end.'

He was very aware that, having already walked away from two sets of children, he was now doing the same to a third set. 'I am never going to be the perfect father,' he admitted to me in 1983. 'But I needed to figure out how I was going to maintain my relationship with my boys, Nicholas and Benjamin. It was really important to me that they were not turned against me, especially as I had no regular access to them.' He was always convinced that Janet Leigh had tried to turn Kelly and Jamie Lee against him, and that Leslie was doing the same with their sons.

Tony wrote that he wasn't getting any work at this time. In fact, he was working a good deal. He just wasn't getting starring roles in major movies, and he resented it. Towards the end of 1980 he played a small role in a TV movie, *Inmates; A Love Story*. He was still in *Vega$* – appearing in sixteen episodes– and did a TV movie, *The Million Dollar Face*, which premiered in America in March 1981.

CHAPTER TWENTY-ONE

Freebasing

n August 1980, the incomplete first draft of *Starstruck*, which had passed through various hands at Doubleday, had landed on the desk of editor Adrian Zackheim, who spent the next four months reading and analysing it. He composed a seven-page letter to Curtis outlining numerous inconsistencies and suggestions to tighten the plot, but also praising him for his story-telling ability and emphasising that he was 'charmed' with the 'wonderful possibilities' of *Starstruck*.

Zackheim tried to work with Tony to produce a satisfactory and complete draft of *Starstruck*, but with all his problems Tony gave Zackheim little time. In August 1981, he delivered his final draft. Zackheim was reportedly appalled by it and concluded it was unpublishable. His supervisor, Elizabeth Drew, thought it 'junk, pure and simple'. Desperate to salvage the book and the agreement with New American Library, Zackheim suggested to Irving Lazar that Curtis submit the manuscript to a 'novel doctor', but Lazar demurred, and consequently Doubleday cancelled its deal with New American Library and terminated its agreement with Curtis, demanding repayment of the $50,000 advance. Tony refused, and Doubleday began investigating its legal options.

Over Christmas 1981, Tony met actress and dancer Andria (sometimes spelt Andrea) Savio, who was thirty-eight years younger than he. They embarked on a long affair, and he insisted he was in love again.

His divorce from Leslie became final in February 1982. He kept his mansion, and Leslie got the house in Cape Cod. With more maintenance bills to meet, Tony accepted any film he was offered. In the spring of 1982 he was in *Brainwaves*, playing a scientist performing experimental treatment that brings a patient out of a coma with severe side effects leading to horrific consequences. When filming in the Pettis Veterans Administration Hospital in Redlands, Tony posed for photographs with patients and signed autographs.

He was looking gaunt and his hair had thinned considerably. He struggled through his twelve days on the movie because he was using drugs more heavily than usual, and he didn't understand exactly what his role was all about. 'I just got there on time and said my lines,' he told me. 'I'd get on to the set and I never forgot to remember *I want the tip*. I was able to work, and go home and smoke cocaine and any shit I could get hold of. And I looked terrible. *Oh! That's* when I started to realise I was in trouble.'

Immediately after he finished *Brainwaves*, he played Iago in *Othello, the Black Commando* for which he was paid $300,000 by the film's producer Max Boulois, who also starred as Othello. Filming took place in late spring 1982 in New York, Martinique and Spain. Shakespeare's play had been turned into an action film in which Othello is an American mercenary in Africa who falls for a Boston senator's daughter, played by Joanna Pettet.

Boulois ran out of money before the film was completed and asked Tony to give back half his fee in return for fifty per cent of the profits. Tony declined. Boulois ended up with a film which, said *Variety*, 'has a fatal lack of continuity'. It had a limited release and never went into profit.

Tony had his house completely redecorated and refurbished. 'There is not a trace of my ex-wife left,' he said. He grew oranges, lemons, plums, avocados and guavas in the two acres surrounding the property. When his boys visited, he buried things in the garden so they could have treasure hunts, and they built a tree house. He stopped going out and stayed home painting and writing poetry, and it seemed as if he had become more emotionally stable.

He was in a terrible movie, *Balboa*, playing a tycoon steeped in corruption who owns a large slice of Southern California. What slim plot there is amounts to nothing, and at the end a narrator announces, 'The saga will continue.' Thankfully it didn't, and it went straight to video with soft-porn scenes added to no effect whatsoever.

Even without the soft-porn scenes, the film featured a bevy of beautiful girls, and Tony had fun chasing them. His son Nicholas came to stay with him and proved to be a chip off the old block by also chasing the girls in the movie. Nicholas was only eleven years old.

By 1982 Tony was battling drug addiction with physical assertion. He could do twenty press-ups in just thirteen seconds, took fencing lessons, and admitted his age of fifty-six. 'I never lie about my age,' he said. 'I remember when I made *Trapeze* with Burt Lancaster and Gina Lollobrigida, I was thirty and she was thirty-three. When I reached forty, I read some place she was twenty-seven. When I was forty-three she was thirty-three. I come right out and say it.'

He was neglecting his daughters by Christine Kaufmann, so she published nude photographs of Alexandra, then sixteen, claiming, 'I want to make Tony Curtis mad at me because of these photographs. I want to show him how beautiful his daughter has become.' She revealed publicly for the first time that her girls had left their father because of his drug use. He replied that he was well aware of how beautiful his daughter had become and dismissed her claims that he was using drugs.

On 3 April 1983, Doubleday sued Curtis in the United States District Court for the Southern District of New York for breach of contract and recovery of its $50,000. Tony counterclaimed for breach of agreement alleging, as both a counterclaim and affirmative defence, that Doubleday failed to provide adequate editorial services, preventing him from completing a satisfactory manuscript. A non-jury trial was set for 4 October 1984.

In June 1983, while holidaying in the south of France, he announced he and Andria Savio were to wed, but remained vague about the exact details.

In autumn 1983 he made *Where Is Parsifal?* in England. Much of it was filmed at Hampden House, a wonderful Tudor mansion in Buckinghamshire where a number of gothic horror films were made. The house represented a castle where Parsifal, played by Curtis, holds a dinner party for potential investors for his latest invention, a laser sky-writer. Playing one of the guests was his long-time friend Peter Lawford, also on a self-destructive path through drug abuse, and Orson Welles also appeared as a magician. 'Tony is a gifted actor and able to perform with tremendous spontaneity,' Welles told me. 'I gave him a few hints that the director didn't think of, encouraging him to ad-lib and make more of what he was doing funnier, and he loved it and said, "You are Awesome Welles."'

I interviewed Tony on the set and thought he was now looking older than his fifty-eight years. I didn't know he was taking drugs, and found him as engaging as ever, but just a little erratic, seeming louder and more loose-lipped than usual, freely telling me how Marilyn Monroe had tried to trap him into marrying her (two years later he was unable to remember telling me any of it).

He returned to Los Angeles, continued freebasing, and guest-starred in the TV series *The Fall Guy*. In June 1984, he signed to make two movies. The first was *Club Life* (also known as *King of the City*), playing the owner of a Los Angeles club and getting murdered by gangsters. The film was released in 1986, but was little seen.

The other movie was *Insignificance* for director Nicolas Roeg. Tony was thrilled to be asked by Roeg to play The Senator in this acclaimed fictional account about Marilyn Monroe, Joe DiMaggio, Albert Einstein and Senator Joseph McCarthy all staying in the same New York hotel in 1953. For legal reasons none of the characters were named, but it was clear who they all were, with Teresa Russell as The Actress, Michael Emil as The Professor, and Gary Busey as The Ballplayer. Tony gave one of his finest and most acclaimed performances, and although the movie was not a major commercial hit, it was an art-house smash, and stands as one of the triumphs of his career.

Time Out said, 'As usual with Roeg, the firmament is streaming with large ideas and awkward emotions, which grow larger and larger in significance, and most of which come together in a delightful scene when Marilyn (Russell) explains relativity to Einstein (Emil) with the aid of clockwork trains and balloons. Curtis is Senator McCarthy, still witch-hunting phantoms of his mind; Busey is the washed-up ballplayer, aching for Marilyn's return. It may be a chamber piece, but its circumference is vast.'

'Those on the lookout for philosophical reflections will find plenty to think about in the pic's meditations upon relativity and the coming together of time,' said *Variety*. '*Insignificance* also works on a simpler level as a depiction of four people struggling against despair.'

Tony always felt that other directors should have given him greater consideration because he knew he had become a better actor with age, and denied that drug addiction was holding him back. In 1994 he said, 'At that time a lotta people working in movies were using cocaine, so, no, I don't think that had anything to do with it. I think I had just reached an age where producers and directors saw me as someone who had represented youth and vitality, and there I was turning sixty and there just weren't the parts for me.'

When he made *Insignificance* he knew he was working in a quality movie, and he described it as 'a good moment' at a time when he was slowly killing himself with drugs. 'I knew it,' he said. 'But I kept right on going.'

When I interviewed him in 1985, I was impressed by his complete honesty about his drug addiction. 'I was an alcoholic and a drug abuser. I wanted to be a hero all my life. I didn't want to end up as the enemy.' He leaned forward, gripped my hand, his eyes filled with tears and, choking, he said, 'I'm so sorry, Mike. I'm so sorry I did that to you.' The apology was personal, to me and all his fans.

In 1994 he was very happy and very proud to tell me, 'I'm a recovering alcoholic and a drug abuser. I'm now ten years straight and sober and that means everything to me because it is a disease, and being so far into my recovery isn't something we should feel negative about or ashamed of.'

He said that the darkest period of his life when he was using intensely was about eighteen months. 'It was a very powerful eighteen months.' During that time his schizophrenia was at its most potent. He told me, 'When I was freebasing, I found that there was a little section of me that was kind of left alone, like there was an angry kid, no more than eight, watching it all from some level in my consciousness. And this little kid was telling me straight that he wasn't going to be a part of it all, and he told me what it was doing to me. It shook me every time, I can tell you.'

He related the same experience to Dr Pamela Connolly in *Shrink Wrap*; she was of the opinion that the little boy was Bernie at the age of eight. But when he told me about it, in 1985, he believed the little boy was Julie, who was eight years old when he was killed. He said he often heard Julie's voice among other voices during the darkest periods of his life, and no period was darker than the time he was freebasing. He told me:

I was totally schizophrenic [then], and that shook me more than anything. Julie tried to save me. There he was, on another level of my subconscious – not a ghost, not from the other side or wherever it is the dead go – but like a little piece of my subconscious, and I found myself reaching out to him but he was beyond my reach, or I beyond his, and he said it was because of what I had become and what I was doing to myself that he was trying to connect.

And then there were others, from another corner of the same place – with their thoughts or their mouths, I couldn't tell because it exists only in my head with all the other madnesses – but they wanted me to keep on what I was doing because I wasn't worth preserving. I had my brother one side trying to save me, and others trying to destroy me. Maybe the other voices were all me. During the moments they came, when I was freebasing, it all had clarity somehow, and then after, when they've gone and I'm down again, it's all a dream and I can't recall it.

But I heard my brother the loudest. My little brother saved me. After I let him down when he got killed, my little brother still saved me.

Somebody else who saved him was his attorney, Eli Blumenfeld, who got Tony to sign an agreement so that he couldn't dispose of any of his assets without Blumenfeld's signature, otherwise he would have sold everything to feed his drug habit and be left with nothing. Said Blumenfeld, 'Tony is extremely charming. He could charm any-body out of anything so he was able to get whatever he needed without money, and that became very difficult for me and for everybody else.'

On 4 October 1984, Judge Sweet presided over a six-day non-jury trial in the case of Doubleday versus Tony Curtis. Tony testified that Adrian Zackheim was apathetic and incompetent, and that he had received no indication from Doubleday that *Starstruck* would not be suitable for publication until informed by Irving Lazar of the publisher's irreversible decision to reject it.

Zackheim asserted that Curtis had all but ignored his carefully considered suggestions, and that the second half of the manuscript was abysmal. He and Elizabeth Drew testified that they both considered the manuscript irreparable in light of Curtis' refusal to hand it to a 'novel doctor', and that their termination of the contract with New American Library was based on ethical and artistic considerations.

Judge Sweet concluded that the decision by Doubleday to reject the manuscript was based on a genuine belief that it was unpublishable, and he also dismissed Curtis' counterclaims. The court dismissed Doubleday's claim to seek recovery of $50,000 because it had waived the 'time of essence' clause by accepting the manuscript almost eighteen months after the deadline, and had led Curtis to believe *Starstruck* would be published.

On 1 May 1985 the Second Circuit of Appeals heard arguments from Doubleday and Tony Curtis, and on 22 May the court reversed the dismissal of Doubleday's claim, agreeing that Curtis had refused editorial assistance and the suggestion to consult a 'novel doctor'. It also held that Doubleday had not waived its rights in allowing the delivery date to pass and that the editors, 'who were forced to harmonise an inferior manuscript, a lucrative reprint agreement and a recalcitrant author', had acted in good faith and Curtis was ordered to return the $50,000 advance. He appealed to the United States Supreme Court, but the appeal was refused. The matter was settled, and Tony's dream of writing more novels was at an end.

One night in the summer of 1984 Tony collapsed at his Bel Air mansion and was rushed to the emergency room at Cedars-Sinai medical centre in Los Angeles. He had severe cirrhosis of the liver and internal bleeding, and he almost died. When he recovered, he checked himself into the Betty Ford Clinic, came out four weeks later and went right back to using drugs and alcohol.

On 3 May 1984, newspapers reported, 'Last week, Curtis was discharged from the Betty Ford Alcoholic and Drugs Treatment Center,' and announced that he 'proudly presented his fourth bride to the world'. Andria Savio was described as 'Curtis's constant companion for three years'. But clearly she wasn't as there had been a number of other women in and out of his life. A lot of Tony's obituaries counted Andrea (as opposed to Andria) Savio among his wives, and supposedly the marriage lasted until 1992.

However, there is no evidence the marriage ever took place, and no mention of Andria is made in any of Tony's books. An article in the *European Stars and Stripes*, 3 July 1984, reported:

Actor Tony Curtis walked hand in hand with actress Andrea De (sic) Savio to a Los Angeles-bound plane at London airport but snapped at reporters who asked whether they were married. A year ago, Curtis, 59, said the 21-year-old actress would become his fourth wife. But De Savio later said Curtis had asked her to play along with the marriage story while he went into a hospital to try to beat a drinking problem. 'I helped him get over drugs and he turned into a creaky, complaining old man,' she was reported to have said. 'He wanted to resume his career and part of the process was saying that he was married. He thought it gave him an image of stability. He wanted to look good.'

It was a mad ploy, and demonstrated that Tony's state of mind was still unhinged. His friends and family tried to get him to go back to the clinic. He told me, 'My friends said to me, "Tony, I don't know how you can be alive. You won't live another year." These were friends looking me in the face and saying that to me.' One of those friends was Eli Blumenfeld, who didn't think Tony would live another thirty days so talked with some of Tony's children and friends and they agreed they had to convince him to get off drugs and alcohol once and for all. Blumenfeld told Tony that Drew Anderson of the Betty Ford Clinic was waiting in his bedroom to talk to him. He walked in, wearing his now traditional white shorts, and was shocked to see Kelly, Jamie, Allegra, Nicky Blair and Anderson waiting. Blumenfeld locked the door. 'As soon as he saw that this was a planned thing, he was ready to leave,' said Blumenfeld.

Tony became angry. They all began telling him how much they loved him and wanted him to get well, and he calmed down and finally agreed to allow Blumenfeld and Anderson to take him straight to the Betty Ford Clinic for an extended stay.

He lived in a room with two other men, all going to bed at the same time, getting up at the same time, going for breakfast at the same time, and taking part in group therapy sessions, where they were encouraged to talk about themselves. For the first few group sessions, Tony said nothing. Finally, when prompted, he related his childhood and talked about drugs. The group met every day for the first five days. Tony became very frank about the beatings his mother used to give him, and realised that the events in his early life – being beaten by his mother, being beaten for being a Jew, and feeling guilty over the death of Julie – all contributed to the anger and self-loathing that led to his addiction.

He told me in 1985, 'My addiction started long before I took cocaine. I was using all kinds of pills and potions just after I got to Hollywood. I was so insecure. It didn't matter how often anyone said to me, "Tony, you're doing really well," I just felt they were being kind, or maybe cruel, and I felt I was never good enough. With Janet I never felt good enough. She was always watching me, at parties, making sure I used the right knife and fork, and when I lit a cigarette, she told me to light the other person's cigarette first. I felt I was never going to live up to her expectations. Not that I blame Janet. I blame *me*. Or rather, I blame that guy called Bernie Schwartz. He wouldn't leave me alone. So I tried other things. Marijuana. I thought that was OK. When it wasn't enough for me, I drank more – much more – and when that didn't work for me I did drugs – hard drugs.

'I came out of the Betty Ford Clinic feeling like I might just have it under control, and I never want to go back into that place – where I was when I was using drugs – *ever*.'

After twenty-eight days at the clinic, Tony felt less anxious and more confident of the future. He had stopped using drugs and, he said, never used them again.

Hugh Hefner's Playboy mansion became a halfway house for him. 'When I was in recovery Hugh Hefner proved he was a real friend. He let me stay at the mansion. I had a tiny room. I didn't have to deal with anybody. They brought me my meals. I could stay in bed all day long if I wanted. I didn't have to come out of my room. Hef was a true friend. He knew what he was doing for me.

'I tell ya, the recovery was a painful experience, and nobody in Hollywood or in the business made any effort toward me – nobody! Maybe one or two of the children. I did it on my own.'

In July 1984 he was dating twenty-six-year-old actress/model Sylvia Sachs in London. Their first date didn't go well. 'I wasn't impressed,' Sylvia said. 'He didn't take kindly to me asking for wine and wouldn't even allow me to smoke.' After the second date, Sachs turned down his invitation to a third.

By January 1985 he was involved with eighteen-year-old Debee Ashby, an English topless model. After she flew to Palm Springs to spend a week with him, newspapers began offering her four-figure sums to tell her story. She was eventually paid £5,000. Unsurprisingly, the affair was short-lived.

By the time I interviewed him in 1985, he was a new man. He looked fit and well, if a little overweight as his once-flat stomach had become a paunch, and he wore a toupee, grey and with the classic 1950s Tony Curtis quiff. His vanity had kicked in, and he loved his new look.

His hairdresser, Leonard Lewis, who had persuaded Tony to have his hair cut to a very neat and handsome close crop during the 1970s, later revealed that Tony had once stuck his hairpiece down with superglue because he had a girlfriend who tended to pull at his hair while in the throes of lovemaking.

One night she pulled so hard she took the toupee off along with some of his scalp. He called on Leonard for help, and the hairdresser took him to the doctor to have his head treated to prevent it from going septic, and then fixed the toupee.

He no longer looked younger than his years, but he looked incredibly well and handsome for a man of sixty. He credited his new outlook and demeanour on the increased time he devoted to painting.

'The ultimate experience for me is the painting experience where I like colour and shape. It almost has a way of expressing *itself*; it doesn't need me in a way. That sounds a little hokey but I mean that. It's almost as if the painting has a life of its own. I always work in acrylic. I find oil is messy and smells bad.'

He described his paintings as mostly 'abstract and surrealist, expressions of my fantasies, thoughts, and ideas'. He had no idea that in time his paintings would become sought-after works all over the world.

He was able to draw on his memories of Sam Giancana when he played him in *Mafia Princess*. Susan Lucci played Giancana's daughter, the Mafia princess of the title, and the film focused on the troubled father/daughter relationship between 1935 and 1975. Both Lucci and Curtis were excellent in a good telemovie which tended to gloss over the murderous side of Giancana while demonstrating he was a tyrant in his family life. 'I think it was an OK movie,' he told me. 'It was a chance to play someone I had actually met, and I did some research, and all that gave me some insight into a man who was a powerful gangster and a lousy father. If I learned anything from it, it was that I wasn't such a bad father after all. I thought Susan Lucci did a beautiful job playing Antoinette Giancana, and the movie was good, ya know? But movies made for television don't get respect.'

He was engaging in another 1986 telemovie, *Murder in Three Acts*, opposite Peter Ustinov playing Hercule Poirot for the fifth time (he would play it once more). Then he was in *Banter*, filmed in Spain, playing the father of a girl whose alcoholic husband becomes a paranoid maniac when he reads letters that appear to predict to real-life horrors that possess his deranged mind.

In 1987 he was one of a number of stars – including Mel Blanc, Vincent Price, Corale Brown, Nancy Olson and Cloris Leachman – providing his voice talents for the much-liked animated short, *Sparky's Magic Piano*.

In 1988 he demonstrated that, at the age of sixty-three, he was still desirable to young women by dating twenty-four-year-old Cornelia Guest. He was in a curious arty German semi-documentary called *Der Passagier* (its English title was *The Passenger – Welcome to Germany*) with some scenes shot in colour and some in black-and-white. It made little impact.

And then he landed the role that would make him a cult favourite, *Lobster Man from Mars*, which borrowed heavily from Mel Brooks' *The Producers*. He was paid $100,000 to play washed-up one-time TV superhero turned movie producer who is in so much debt to the Internal Revenue Service that he decides to make a film – *The Lobster Man from Mars* – that is so bad it can only flop and its expenses can be written off as a loss. It was filmed during the summer of 1988, and six months later it was premiered at the Sundance Film Festival and went on to become (much like the film within the film) a surprise hit.

Tony continued to work, accepting roles in almost anything that helped him to make his maintenance payments and to live well. In 1989 he had a supporting role in a TV movie, *Charlie*, and played Tarzan's girlfriend's dad in a terrible TV film, *Tarzan in Manhattan*.

He made a surprising appearance in a Danish movie, *Walter & Carlo i Amerika*, and had a major role in *Midnight* in 1989, which starred Lynn Redgrave in the title role as a sultry late-night horror-movie hostess who has the highest rated show on TV. Tony played Mr B, who wants to steal the rights to the show. Their fight turns into a deadly conflict. It was a campy, over-the-top movie and really rather fun if not taken seriously.

He was in a 1990 TV movie, *Thanksgiving Day*, a light comedy in which he appeared with daughter Kelly as members of a dysfunctional family. Apart from her brief appearance as a child in *The Vikings*, Kelly had made her screen debut in a small role in sister Jamie's movie *Trading Places* in 1983 and, while lesser known than Jamie Lee, enjoyed quite an active career as an actress.

In early 1990 Tony was dismayed to learn that Allegra had posed nude for *Playboy*, and it seemed for a while they would become estranged over the matter. In March he was admitted to hospital with suspected prostate cancer. Allegra and Jamie Lee rushed to his side and were relieved to discover he didn't have cancer after all. It proved to be a tearful reunion for Allegra and her father, who forgave her for baring all. He told me in 1994, 'There are worse things you can do than pose naked.'

In 1991 he went to Canada to make a forgettable movie, *Prime Target*, playing a mob informant and was then in the TV movie *Centre of the*

Web. He felt he was still being ignored and forgotten by mainstream Hollywood. But he was still working.

He had long stopped seeing brother Bobby. One day Bobby walked out of the state mental facility at Camarillo and refused to go back. He lived rough until 22 August 1992, when he was beaten to death in a street in Los Angeles. Tony always thereafter mourned the brother he never really knew as well as the young brother he had lost.

By the early 1990s Tony's relationships with his children varied from one child to another. He and Kelly had remained close, perhaps because she was his first-born. In the late 80s, she went with him to Budapest to support a Hungarian association that raised funds for the restoration of synagogues in Hungary. He had been invited because, their spokesman said, he was the most famous Hungarian in America. With Kelly throwing her support to the cause, they established the Emanuel Foundation for Hungarian Culture, in honour of his father. Kelly was very close to her grandparents and considered herself to be the family historian.

Tony's relationship with Jamie was not an easy one. He felt that Jamie blamed him for leaving her mother. She saw him drink a lot and take drugs and, she once said, they both smoked marijuana together.

She had a successful acting career away from her father, although at the beginning her name certainly helped, and she landed a regular role in the 1977 TV series based on *Operation Petticoat* at Universal. But she made it on her own, becoming a star through a string of horror films, and later proved to be a good comedy actor in films like *A Fish Called Wanda* and *Freaky Friday*.

In 1993 she said, 'I now have a wonderful relationship with my father because I don't *need* him.'

When Jamie married actor/director Christopher Guest in 1984, Tony joined all of his children and Janet also – it was their first time together in many years – for a family wedding photo. Jamie noted, 'He's standing there like, "This is my flock." It was the one and only time in my life when all of these people were in the same room.'

Allegra had become a hair and make-up consultant in Florida while her older sister Alexandra ran a theatre company in Tampa, producing and directing shows. Benjamin was going to Marymount College in Palos Verdes. He was particularly proud of his dad's accomplishments, and his favourite of his father's movies was *The Defiant Ones*.

Nicholas was the most troubled of Tony's children. He was, in many ways, more like his dad than any of the others. He drew and painted, and created assemblages and collages. He didn't show any desire to be an actor, although he was in one TV movie, *Crazy from the Heart* in 1991. He was a musician, and he liked to write poems. He was also addicted to heroin, and had become something of a recluse, living in a garage apartment at his mother's house in Cape Cod. Tony saw little of him.

In 1992, Arnold Schwarzenegger asked Tony to be in a TV movie he was cutting his directing teeth on, a remake of *Christmas in Connecticut*. The film relied heavily on its actors to overcome shortcomings in the story and direction. Dyan Cannon was excellent as a TV chef who can't cook, and Kris Kristofferson was also good as the forest ranger hailed as a national hero who is invited to spend Christmas with Cannon's family as a publicity stunt, only to find her family isn't quite what her TV show would suggest. Tony was excellent in a hilarious performance as the show's producer and Cannon's fake husband. Ultimately it's a feel-good movie, and still plays regularly on TV at yuletide.

Tony didn't spend so much time in Los Angeles any more. He loved being in Las Vegas, and he had a home in Hawaii. Mediocre movies, often for TV, continued. *The Mummy Lives* was terrible. He was completely miscast as an Egyptian high priest who comes back from the dead to exact vengeance on those who excavated his tomb. Much better was *Naked in New York* in which he was among a number of other well-known actors appearing briefly in this tale of New York theatre life produced by Martin Scorsese. Whoopi Goldberg played the 'masks of Comedy/Tragedy', Kathleen Turner was 'the Actress', and Timothy Dalton was 'the Actor'. Tony played the off-Broadway producer. It was a good film, although not a commercial success, but Tony was delighted simply to have been asked by Scorsese to do it.

And yet Scorsese never used him again, and major players in Hollywood still didn't come to him. Peter Ustinov, who had known Tony for years, believed, cruelly but probably correctly, 'Tony has become a caricature of himself. He's a gifted actor and a charming man, but he has too much vanity. If he would only remove the hair piece which I think covers virtually all his head by now, and say, "Take me as I am." When we last worked together [in *Murder in Three Acts*] I said to him, "Tony, I'm old and fat and they still give me parts to play. I am sure you're just as good-looking without that hairpiece. Take it off." And he wouldn't. He wanted to look the way he did when he was in his twenties and thirties. That meant more to him than almost anything, I think.'

It was once more a case that he had more vanity than ego. His vanity was fed once again when he began seeing a woman half his age. She was Lisa Deutsch, a law graduate whom he met at the Friars Club on 11 September 1992. Tony was there with Jamie, Benjamin and Kelly to receive an honorary Juris Doctorate.

After dinner he stood and told stories about his life and Hollywood, and then he went around and introduced himself to everyone. He spotted Lisa and was immediately attracted to her. 'She had the most inviting plunging neckline and the most beautiful and inviting breasts I'd ever seen – and I've seen quite a lot,' he told me in 1994.

He asked her to be in a photograph with him. A little later, he sent a friend over to ask for her phone number. A few days later he sent her a dozen roses, and then he called her on the telephone. A week later he sent another dozen, followed by another phone call. He invited her to his house for dinner. She insisted she drive herself to his home but didn't let on it was because she wanted to be sure of a quick getaway if necessary.

When she arrived, he gave her a tour of the house and then, instead of eating in, he drove her to Robata, a Japanese restaurant. After they went for a walk, and then he drove her back to his house, where he showed her his art collection of Picassos, Chagalls, Rouaults and Braques. Then she went home. 'He was the perfect gentleman every step of the way,' she recalled.

He was carried away by the love and attention of this young sexy lady and quickly proposed marriage to her. His vanity was satisfied, but, he later admitted, 'I fell into the trap of going with women who physically looked like what I needed. Big bosoms, a good bottom, great legs, a smile, a kind of vivaciousness.'

She took him home to meet the parents. Her family was Jewish, and her father had been the victim of anti-Semitism and was pleased that Tony was also a Jew. But Lisa's father was also a lawyer and wanted him to sign a prenuptial agreement, guaranteeing half of everything he owned to Lisa in the event of a divorce. Tony refused to sign. They were married on 28 February 1993.

From the outset, Jamie Lee felt that the marriage was a mistake and that her father was attracted to that marriage not as Tony but as Bernie. 'She was from a Jewish family and I think that was very important for him to be married under a *chuppah* held by his sons.'

Lisa did a lot of *pro bono* work as a lawyer, and Tony began to feel that she was more devoted to her clients than she was to him. Her work was particularly stressful and perhaps because of that she might have drunk a little more alcohol than Tony would have liked. He had avoided alcohol since his rehabilitation, and he was intolerant of people who drank too much.

In autumn 1993 he was in London for an exhibition of his paintings at the Cato Gallery, where he sold around thirty out of forty-five of his works on display. He claimed that this marriage 'is different to the other marriages. We're both working at this marriage; I know I am. We all bring with ourselves our own madnesses and our own history. Wouldn't it be wonderful if you could forget your history and come into a relationship pure and simple and straight, but we don't. And with these experiences I would bring to these relationships my own unhappinesses, my frustrations and perhaps mistrusting.' When asked if this marriage was 'special', he replied, 'I find it different to the other marriages.'

In 1994 he had his autobiography published, co-written with Barry Paris. He had decided he would write his life story shortly after coming out of the Betty Ford Clinic. He was determined not to write the kind of autobiography that Shelley Winters had written in which she told about all the famous people she had worked with, and known and loved. So Tony left out everything that the readers really wanted to know about, and it was a disappointing memoir.

When he went to Paris to promote it, Lisa went with him and they enjoyed a romantic time. But back in Los Angeles the romance quickly dissolved when she came home drunk late one night. He told her to get out and not to come back until she sobered up, so she slept in a down-stairs bedroom. At that very moment he knew the marriage was over. He reasoned, 'I could see she didn't care about being with me.' He felt relieved, and he moved swiftly on with his life, divorcing her that year.

Shortly after returning from his publicity tour of Britain, he was working out at Gold's Gym in Los Angeles when he felt ill and needed to lie down until he felt better. He went straight to see his doctor, who diagnosed a heart attack. He was sent immediately to hospital and within twenty-four hours was given a heart bypass to replace a blocked artery. He surprised his doctors by recovering quickly for a man soon to turn seventy.

On 2 July 1994, his son Nicholas died at the age of twenty-three from a seizure, brought on by a drugs overdose. The news devastated Tony, who felt guilty for more reasons than he could count. He wondered if Nicholas had used drugs to fill the void where his father should have been. Or was substance abuse something Nicholas had inherited? He anguished over such thoughts and sank into a depression to the point of feeling suicidal.

His children rallied to support him, all coming together 'as a family', as Jamie Lee Curtis emphasised, to grieve together. 'All of his surviving children went to his house and we lay on his bed and we all connected physically in our own way to this grieving man.'

He pulled himself together enough to be able to attend the funeral, where the minister talked about the terrible loss suffered by Leslie without ever mentioning the loss suffered by Tony. He was angered and saddened.

He was being offered less work now. In 1994 he made a *Perry Mason* TV movie. His only work in 1995 was a straight-to-video movie, *The Immortals*, playing a gangster double-crossed by a nightclub owner played by Eric Roberts. He seemed to play a lot of gangsters in his more mature years, and it bored him. In 1996 he guest-starred in an episode of *The New Adventures of Superman* and then *Roseanne*.

'I had noticed that my career wasn't as intense, and I got angry at my profession and the people in it, and at times like that I felt I could have used the help of the Screen Actors Guild and the Academy,' he said. 'All those organisations that support our profession had thrown us away like tired little toys. It broke my heart.'

The long career that had started in 1948 had begun to wind down. Nevertheless, his career had spanned six decades, from the 1940s to the 90s, and would stretch into a seventh.

CHAPTER TWENTY-TWO

The Armani Cowboy

One night in 1996 Tony Curtis arrived to have dinner alone at Nicky Blair's restaurant. At the table next to his sat a man and a woman. She immediately caught Tony's eye. She was young, blonde and had 'a magnificent body', as he put it; exactly the kind of woman he was attracted to. Wanting to find out more about her, he pretended to know the man and asked, 'How have you been? We haven't talked in ages. How's your family?' Then he smiled at the girl and said, 'Hi, I'm Tony.'

He once said, 'I'm still very nice and pleasant with every woman I meet. I want them to get a little touch of my magic!' His magic was working on her, and she introduced herself as twenty-five-year-old Jill Ann VandenBerg. He told her, 'I'm so happy to meet you, Jill.'

She said she lived in San Diego and drove to Los Angeles at weekends. Tony told her he was often in San Diego. 'I ramped up the charm a notch,' he recalled, and he asked the man if he minded if Jill gave him her number in San Diego. The man, just a friend as it turned out, didn't object, and Tony got her number and then left them alone.

When she returned to San Diego that Sunday, Tony called her. She gave him a hard time because she was a big fan of Marilyn Monroe and had been upset with him for saying kissing her was like kissing Hitler. Tony apologised, and she forgave him. He left his number with her, and when she was next in Los Angeles, she called him. They met up, and the first thing he did was give her a copy of his autobiography so she would know a good deal more than he could tell her on one date.

There was just one acting job in 1997, playing another gangster in a low-budget thriller, *Hardball*, starring low-budget screen hero Michael Dudikoff. It went straight to video. Much better was *The Continuing Adventures of Reptile Man and His Faithful Sidekick Tadpole* in which he played a washed-up actor who is famous for playing a superhero, now trying to come to terms with the modern entertainment world. It was a quirky movie, balancing reality and comic-book enchantment with some really heartfelt moments, especially from Tony. Said Stewart Schill, the film's director, 'Tony really knew Reptile Man as a guy who had experienced a peak and could really identify with that and the tragedy of it.'

In one profoundly serious moment, Tony as Jack Steele, the former Reptile Man, looks at old photos of his once-handsome self, and unexpectedly quotes a scene from Shakespeare's *Richard II* – 'Hath sorrow struck so many blows upon this face of mine . . . How soon my sorrow hath destroyed my face.' It's delivered with tremendous sadness and sheer brilliance. Said Morris Ruskin, the film's producer, 'It's really unexpected in the movie, and it's really surprisingly touching. And you're looking at the guy and you're going, my goodness, you know why this guy is a star. He just has it.'

In 1998 he had top billing in a low-budget sci-fi movie, *Stargames*, directed by Greydon Clark, who had made a long string of low-budget movies popular in the drive-ins since the early 1970s. That same year he was opposite Steve Buscemi in *Louis & Frank*, directed by Alexander Rockwell, who enjoyed considerable success as a maverick independent film maker with acclaimed films such as *Hero* and *In the Soup*. Unhappily for Tony, Rockwell had lost his stride when he made *Louis & Frank* but got back into it with his next film, *13 Moons*. It's too bad Rockwell didn't cast Curtis in that, but the sad truth was, Tony had become too much of an ageing caricature of himself, and the best had now passed.

Also in 1998, he guest-starred in the TV series *Suddenly Susan*, and then appeared very fleetingly playing a ringside fan in the boxing movie *Play It to the Bone* starring Woody Harrelson and Antonio Banderas. Four years would pass before Tony made another movie.

One evening he told Jill, 'We're going to my friend Frank's house for dinner.' She asked if she should wear anything special. He replied, 'It's just my friend, Frank Sinatra.'

Whenever Tony and Jill were in Palm Springs, they visited Frank and his wife Barbara. Tony had painted a picture especially for the Sinatras which they kept at their Palm Springs house. As Frank's health declined through 1998, Tony and Jill often visited him and Barbara. After playing poker and remembering the good times, Tony went with Frank into the bedroom, and Jill and Barbara would hear them laughing and sometimes crying. Tina Sinatra recalled seeing Tony cradling her ailing father during his final months, and kissing him 'as a son would his father'. Jill believed that the day Frank died, 14 May 1998, 'a little piece of Tony died' too.

After Jamie Lee met Jill, she told her father, 'Marry her now.' Jamie was 'genuinely happy for him for his happiness'. On 6 November 1998, Tony and Jill were married in Las Vegas at the MGM Grand, which was owned by Tony's friend Kirk Kerkorian who picked up the tab for the entire event.

Jill, who came from a big family, encouraged Tony to spend time with his children. When reporters asked her about the age difference, she said that she always had to stop and think about it because 'we don't think about it. He acts like he's twenty.'

Tony decided to finally leave Hollywood behind once and for all, and they moved to Las Vegas in 2001, settling in nearby Henderson. Rarely did the careers of leading men in Hollywood survive into their seventies, and although he was looking remarkably well and still dashing, he looked neither young nor old in the quiffed toupee he continued to wear in public. He could only ever be cast playing Tony Curtis, and he was, in the TV series *C.S.I.*, appearing in a single scene with his friend Frank Gorshin in the episode 'Grave Danger', directed by Quentin Tarantino in 2005. In the scene, as the two actors talk over old times, Curtis says to Gorshin, famous for his impression of Kirk Douglas, 'Didn't I make a movie with you?'

He spent his time painting and selling his works, and was barely able to think too much about movies any longer without gnashing his teeth. 'I'm angry with my profession,' he said. 'I spend my life dedicated to it, and these motherfuckers won't even call me. I'm just saying, why is the system so vicious toward age?'

Allegra Curtis understood his strong emotions, saying, 'His gift is his incredible ability to feel things, but I think for a lot of people who are that sensitive it makes life much more difficult because you can't brush things off, you can't ignore things. But he has found that outlet for his sensitivity which is his painting.'

'I paint every day,' said Tony, 'and it's a very important part of my living experience now. It's a very creative way of expressing my emotions. What I like so much is the fact that's it's an unspoken language, a language of feeling and sense and it provokes your thinking process. So towards that end I'm dedicated.'

His studio was packed with his paintings and boxes. 'This is really an intriguing place for me,' he said for TV cameras which he allowed into his studio for the *Hollywood Greats* series. 'I come in here during the day. I either work or don't work, and I just go from box to box. Why would I do that? Am I nuts? Maybe I'm nuts.' Although he joked about being 'nuts', mental illness remained a fear for him. 'I don't want to be in a straitjacket stuck away in a room somewhere, so I act normal, OK?'

He tried to explain what his boxes meant. Or what he *thought* they meant. 'Perhaps it's bringing order to a disorderly life. When I was using drugs [my life] was very untidy, and before that time. And as I improved I found I have become much more orderly, and in my order I find peace and happiness.'

He had hundreds of boxes, all for his own private viewing. 'Nobody's ever seen these boxes. I had them in one show. A guy said, "Won't you sell 'em?" I said, "Why would I sell 'em?"'

He taught box-making classes at the University of Nevada, Las Vegas, and told his students about Joseph Cornell, the shy, eccentric box artist who dedicated much of his life to caring for his cerebral palsy-afflicted brother, Robert. He shared with them the story of how Cornell created a special box for his brother that contained a 'thimble forest' which could only be seen by peering through a small opening.

'He created a whole sense of art out of his love for his brother,' Curtis explained, which was a clue to why Tony created his boxes. His inspired students recreated Cornell's box as a gift for him, and he was greatly moved by their gesture of thanks.

Over the years, Tony had established a style that was all his own. He loved wearing white shorts, one favoured white Stetson and white sweaters – he loved one particular sweater so much he kept having it mended over the years. Most of his clothes were Armani, and Jill and his friends and family called him 'The Armani Cowboy'.

In 2002 he appeared in his penultimate movie, *Reflections of Evil*, not so much a horror film as an assault on American consumerism as well as a satire on Hollywood, directed by underground movie maker Damon Packard. Tony played 'the host' while unknown actors filled the cast playing characters with names like Charlie Hestons (there are references to the Charlton Heston movies *The Omega Man* and *Planet of the Apes*),

Quinn Martin Jr, and Young Steven Spielberg. It even satirised Universal Studios tours by featuring a Schindler's List Ride. I suspect Tony enjoyed a lot of the jokes at the expense of mainstream Hollywood.

He was overwhelmingly delighted when offered the role of Osgood in a musical stage production of *Some Like It Hot* to tour America for a year. He spent months training to tap dance and learning his lines before going to New York to start rehearsals. On 4 June 2002, the day after he turned seventy-seven, he began touring in *Some Like It Hot*. He appeared in 237 performances in thirty-seven cities across America, starting in Houston and ending in Portland on 6 May 2003. His friend Larry Storch was among the cast, playing Beinstock.

Tony took particular delight in delivering the show's final immortal line – 'Nobody's perfect!'

He didn't act again until he guest-starred in the TV series *Hope & Faith* in 2004. His acting career had almost concluded.

He now luxuriated in a contented life in Vegas. On the occasions he and Jill went to New York, they stayed at the St Regis Hotel where he used to stand outside to shine shoes. Whenever they arrived by chauffeured limousine outside the hotel, Tony paused to look at the spot near the sidewalk where he shined shoes. Jill said one of the things she loved about him was 'his appreciation for just how far he has come'.

Jill had no ambitions to be an actress or a model, but she did have one big passion in life – rescuing animals. She recalled, 'When I met Tony, he did not have any animals and his LA home was filled with pristine white carpet.'

She encouraged him to join in with her efforts, and in 2003 they set up the Shiloh Horse Rescue Foundation at their ranch in Sandy Valley, 30 miles outside Las Vegas. In his final years Tony enjoyed spending time with Jill and her mother Sally at the rescue centre where around 200 horses lived, saved from slaughter and abuse.

The ranch was also home to many cats and dogs. He loved one particular scraggy hound that had been abandoned in the desert. He called him Jack, after Jack Lemmon. Jack followed Tony everywhere, and when Jack died, Tony had him cremated and kept the ashes. He had another little dog he loved, called Bronx.

Their house also became filled with injured animals of every kind, including a paralysed chicken called Ernesto. Tony bottle-fed an orphaned baby burro for ten days before it was moved to the ranch.

To celebrate turning eighty, Tony posed nude for *Vanity Fair* by the pool at his home in Henderson. He jokingly held his Yorkshire terriers, Daphne and Josephine, to protect his modesty, while Jill looked fabulous in a bikini.

On 13 March 2006, *Empire* film magazine awarded him the Sony Ericsson Empire Lifetime Achievement Award, doing what the American Academy had failed to do. Tony travelled to London to accept the award, presented to him by Sir Roger Moore. It was an emotional reunion for the two screen sparring partners.

Tony had now become a much-loved celebrity and was in demand to appear on talk shows where he could relate any of the myriad funny stories he had stored in his memory. It didn't matter how accurate they were because he had become a raconteur with a miscellany of risqué tales that had audiences in hysterics. He now literally basked in his fame, enjoying being recognised as a Hollywood legend. Everywhere he went he enjoyed signing autographs and having his photo taken. Alexandra said, 'If [people] don't recognise him, he will introduce himself.'

Jamie Lee Curtis said, 'If he is in a bar or the finest restaurant in the world, and somebody comes up and says, "Mr Curtis, hi, I'm from Dubuque and I'm here with my wife and . . ." he'll say, "Hello, you fine man. Dubuque is a wonderful town."'

Tony felt he had finally discovered 'the joy of living'. 'I just want it to continue,' he said in the 2001 TV documentary *Tony of the Movies*. 'A Margarita once in a while – that's not a girl, that's a drink! A new car once in a while. Some nice Armani clothing, a scarf, my bullfighter hat. Listen, I'm not asking for everything. A little dough in my pocket. And that's what I got.'

Finally, at long last, with Hollywood just a memory, and a whole new way of life that delighted him, he was as close to being at peace as he had ever come. But providence and old age was about to deal an almost fatal blow.

On 9 December 2006, Jill had left home to tend the horses at the ranch. Their housekeeper, Liz, went to the grocery store. Tony's assistant hadn't yet arrived. Tony was home alone, but exactly what happened next nobody ever knew and Tony wasn't able to remember. All they knew for sure was that he dialled 911, and paramedics arrived to find him barely breathing. They put a tube down his throat to help him breathe, and rushed him to the St Rose Hospital in Henderson, Nevada. He was diagnosed with chronic obstructive pulmonary disease (COPD).

The hospital reached Jill, and she raced to St Rose to find Tony on a ventilator. Pneumonia was filling his lungs with fluid. He had to be sedated to prevent him from pulling the tube from his throat, and then he was put into a drug-induced coma. The doctors told Jill that they had done everything they could and that it was up to Tony to fight it.

She remained constantly at his bedside. Christmas came and went, and the New Year was welcomed in with subdued celebration by Jill as he showed no sign of coming out of the coma.

After thirty days in intensive care he regained consciousness and was taken off the ventilator. He was breathing on his own but he had lost all motor skills and couldn't move at all except to blink his eyes. Jill was devastated when the doctors told her that they didn't know if he would improve.

One day she was sitting by his bed, watching a movie on her DVD player, when she heard his 'unmistakable gravelly voice', asking, 'What movie are you watching?' She hugged him and wept for joy.

His recovery was slow as he underwent months of intensive rehabilitative therapy at the HealthSouth clinic in Henderson. He had to learn to write his name, and was confined to a motorised wheelchair.

His vanity finally caved in; not only did he not wear a hairpiece again but he shaved his head completely. He had also grown a beard while in hospital. Not long after he finished rehab, he was given a small role in a movie, *David & Fatima*, bald and bearded, and in a wheelchair. It was the best therapy he could have hoped for, and he was so overwhelmed to have been allowed this new chance at life, he sped past Jill and her mother in between takes in his motorised chair, yelling, 'I'm having the time of my life, girls.' He was adamant that he would walk again, and had been making good progress in therapy and through exercise.

He had to go back into hospital to undergo an ileostomy. This is a major operation whereby the small intestine is separated from the large colon and the end of it passed through the abdomen to be attached to a colostomy bag. This can sometimes be due to cancer, and also ulcerated colitis. No details were ever given publicly and it has to be assumed that thereafter Tony had a colostomy bag and no doubt wished to maintain his personal dignity by not having every detail of his surgery revealed.

He had put on considerable weight, and hired a personal trainer to begin weight training, working one day on the upper body, the next on the lower. He also started doing Pilates, and was put on a special diet as he was unable to eat certain high-fibre foods following the ileostomy.

On 3 June 2007, he celebrated his eighty-second birthday at the Tuscany Grill in Henderson with Jill and some of his family, and wowed diners when he rose from his wheelchair and walked in public for the first time.

He was no longer able to drive but still loved to wear driving gloves – he had decided his character Danny Wilde in *The Persuaders* would *always* wear driving gloves purely as an idiosyncrasy for that character, and he had chosen to carry that over into real life.

He hated not being able to drive and took pleasure in telling everyone, 'Jillie won't let me drive.' She recalled that, before his illness, he had a number of 'minor fender bender' incidents, and whenever she arrived on the scene he was always charming the other drivers involved and signing his name on their damaged hood or bumper. He never gave up trying to convince her that he would be able to drive and was always, she said, 'plotting ways to get his driver's licence back'.

In 2007 he played God – or rather the voice of God – in a very appealing and funny short film, *The Blacksmith and the Carpenter*, in which the blacksmith, Ishmael,'has no idea his carpenter friend, Jesus, is the Messiah until Jesus is sentenced to be crucified.

He worked on his second autobiography, *Tony Curtis: American Prince*, in 2007 with author Peter Goldenbrook, and it proved to be a far more candid and revealing book than his first memoir. He had done what he said he wouldn't do – tell all.

In 2008 he travelled to Britain to launch an exhibition of his paintings at Harrods in London where he had thirty-five canvases for sale, priced up to £20,000. His appearance there, in a wheelchair and with his head completely bald, took everyone by surprise.

He was met by the store's owner Mohamed Al Fayed, whose son Dodi had been a very good friend of Tony's. Tony was able to stand briefly to greet Mr Al Fayed, but seemed relieved to sit down again. Sitting in his wheelchair, and in front of fans and the Harrods staff, Tony painted a picture of a vase of flowers. When he posed for pictures with Mr Al Fayed, the two shook hands, and then Al Fayed patted Tony's bald head, pretended to paint his face and gave him a banana. Tony explained that it was a private running joke between the two of them, saying only, 'He's always given me a banana.'

He happily answered questions from the press and fans, enjoying the whole experience of holding court. When asked what the secret of his enduring vigour was, he replied, 'The saliva of beautiful women!'

He explained that he followed a strict diet. 'I have no sugar in my diet. Eliminate sugar and your body will equalise its weight.' He explained his frail condition. 'I had pneumonia and I lost the use of my legs. In a week or so I will be up and about.' He assured everyone he was still improving, and attributed his renewed health to wife Jill, who was with him at Harrods. 'I keep her young, too,' he said.

Never far from his side, she said, 'He's doing great now. He was very ill. He couldn't even move a finger when he first got ill. Look at him now.'

A few months later, Tony was back in Britain to promote the publication of *Tony Curtis: American Prince*, appearing on television shows and signing books in stores where fans queued to meet him. Jill said, 'Tony absolutely adored his fans and loved it when people would approach him for an autograph or to take a photo.'

He spent a little time with each fan, talking to every one of them rather than just signing his name and having them move on to make way for the next. 'We would watch as fans nervously approached with shaking hands but they always left with a big smile and stars in their eyes,' said Jill.

At just about every stage in his life, Tony had always said he was at his happiest, only to find he still had not found lasting happiness. He said the same about his marriage to Jill and about living in Las Vegas, and I think that this time he really was at his most content. There was much about Jill, physically, that must have reminded him of Marilyn Monroe, his first true love, but Jill had no desire to exploit her fabulous looks and figure for any purpose. She had eyes for no one but Tony, and she became his perfect companion. He said, 'For the first time I've had a companionship, a sharing.'

He admitted in 2008 that he had never completely come to terms with his background, nor with his psychological problems. 'I'm eighty-two-years old, I've had the most wonderful life and I'm still so screwed up I can't stand it. I'm still fighting my demons.' He stopped worrying about if he would ever get another role in a movie. 'Mostly I live in this moment. What I live for is today.'

He savoured the still too-rare moments with his children. His first-born, Kelly, had enjoyed some small success as an actress, and when she married a theatrical producer the couple formed a company. But the marriage didn't last and she gave up acting to work for Jamie Lee.

Jamie and husband Christopher adopted two children, Annie and Thomas. When Christopher inherited the barony of Saling in the county of Essex on the death of his father in 1996, she became Baroness Haden-Guest of Saling. When Tony read about it in a newspaper, he declared, 'How about that? Queen for a day!'

Alexandra quit acting and became a child therapist. Allegra went from being a hair and make-up consultant to designing jewellery for a home-shopping company in Germany. She also has a son, Raphael.

Benjamin shunned show business and went to work as a carpenter. He and his father became estranged after a series of arguments about Ben's son, Nicholas; as of 2008 they were still not talking.

In 2009 Tony had a third memoir published, *Some Like It Hot: Me, Marilyn and the Movie*. In May he made unwanted headlines over a telephone interview he did with Radio Ulster to promote the new book. Unaware it was being aired live, he explained that when he remarked that kissing Marilyn Monroe was like kissing Hitler, 'some bastards go ahead and make them headlines'. The interviewer, William Crawley, immediately apologised to listeners for the bad language.

About his Oscar nomination, Tony said, 'They nominated Sidney and I for the same part in that film, and that was bullshit. I was offended by that.' Crawley apologised to the listeners for 'yet more Hollywood realism'.

Explaining why he was anti-Oscar, Tony said, 'I think it is unfair the way they treat actors in that town. They can fuck off.'

When Crawley told him he couldn't use that kind of language, Tony replied, 'You can always cut those bits out. We are not live, are we?' When the penny dropped, he said, 'I apologise to everybody for what I had said. I didn't want to offend anyone.' Tony always had a colourful vocabulary, and in old age, when he became angry about the way he had been treated by Hollywood, his language knew no bounds. He was as pugnacious as ever, and probably more so. He had nothing to lose. And yet he hoped he still might work again in movies, and as he turned eighty-five in 2010, he announced, 'If you've got a part in a picture, I'm available. I'm looking for some kind of acting job I can do.'

He had come to love Shiloh so much that he and Jill planned to build a house there to live in permanently. He looked forward to a whole new phase of life and told Jill, 'It's going to be fabulous.'

Early in July 2010, he began experiencing breathing problems at home and was rushed to hospital with another serious COPD attack. On 22 July, Jill announced that he was doing well and responding to treatment. She was optimistic that he would be 'his old self in a few weeks'. His condition was serious, especially for an octogenarian, but, she pointed out, 'As Tony always says, "It would have killed an ordinary man."'

He was transferred to a physical rehabilitation hospital in the hope he might regain some strength. It transpired that this was his third attack within the space of a year, and he had almost died in hospital, but, said Jill, 'In true Tony style, he fought his way back.'

He was allowed home but was back in hospital on Wednesday, 25 August, for 'a simple procedure'. With characteristic style he flirted with the nurses, and was home again twenty-four hours later. But he was in a seriously weakened condition. The attacks of COPD had taken its toll on his body which had, after all, survived for eighty-five incredible years despite a long period of drug and alcohol abuse.

He had made the decision to end his life at home rather than in hospital. Jill described this as 'his final gift – time to talk, to love, to kiss and hold hands, to sit together and watch a movie, to hug'. Tony knew he was finally losing the battle to live and he was, in Jill's words, helping his family to 'let go gracefully and to finally accept that his long and full life was coming naturally to an end'.

That end came very quietly and peacefully in the early evening of 29 September 2010, 'on his terms and at just the right time', said Jill. He died from cardiac arrest, asleep in bed next to his perfect wife. His heart, which had survived so much that 'would have killed an ordinary man', had finally stopped beating.

The following morning, on the steps of the home she had shared with Tony, Jill graciously met with reporters to give a statement and emphasised that his illness was due to his heavy smoking in previous years; it was important to her and it had been to Tony for people to know that.

News of his death brought in tributes from friends such as Sir Roger Moore who said, 'I'm shocked. I knew Tony had not been well but you never think that friends are going. I'm very sad. He had a great sense of humour and [made] wonderful ad-libs. He was a hell of a good actor. I shall miss him.'

'This is a personal loss for me,' said Kirk Douglas. 'Tony and I were two Jewish kids from poverty-level families who could not believe our luck in making it as big Hollywood stars. We had a lot in common, and shared a warm friendship and many adventures both on and off the screen for more than half a century. I still have one of Tony's first paintings which he gave me years ago. I did three movies with him, and he was a much better actor than people realise. Look at *Some Like It Hot* or *The Defiant Ones*. It's hard for me to believe he's gone because we had a long phone visit not too long ago. My heart goes out to Jill and all of his children.'

Kim Novak recalled, 'He was such a charming man. He always had an upbeat outlook on life. We got along very well because we both were interested in the visual arts and we had a unique perspective on life.'

From Italy, two of his leading ladies paid tribute. Virna Lisi said, 'I'm really very sad. More than anything else he was a very nice man, always approachable and able to put everyone in a good mood.' Gina Lollobrigida remembered him as 'someone who had a look of eternal youth and was a real fun guy'.

Jill announced that the memorial service would be held on Monday, 4 October, at the Palm Mortuary in Las Vegas, and she opened it up to everyone, family, friends, stars or fans, who wanted to pay their last respects. Tony wanted it that way because he had been one of the mourners at Frank Sinatra's funeral, which was closed to the public and no cameras were allowed, and as he'd sat there listening to the tributes he had thought how devastating it was that those tributes were destined to be heard by no more than fifty people. He believed Frank would not have liked it, and he wanted to be sure that his own funeral would be open to everyone.

More than 400 people gathered for the public funeral, which was led by Rabbi Mel Hecht. Seven of Tony's paintings and three black-and-white drawings stood on easels, while a photo of the young, dark-haired movie star was projected on to a screen. The coffin was draped with an American flag. A montage of his famous film roles opened the service. The crowd laughed when an animated 'Stony Curtis' appeared in a scene from the TV cartoon series *The Flintstones*.

Jamie Lee stood up and described her father who was, she said, 'a little *meshuga*', which is Yiddish for 'crazy but full of life'. 'All of us got something from him. I, of course, got his desperate need for attention!' She related how, the evening before the funeral service, she and siblings met to recount their favourite anecdotes about their father, and to do their best impressions of him.

Arnold Schwarzenegger, then the Governor of California, recalled Curtis as a generous mentor who encouraged Schwarzenegger in his early Hollywood career when others told him his accent and foreign name were too much of a handicap. 'You are going to make it,' he recalled Tony telling him. 'Don't pay any attention to those guys. I heard the same thing when I came here.'

He said that Tony refused to feel old. 'I mean, who had the guts to take off their clothes at the age of eighty?' he said, recalling Tony's photoshoot for *Vanity Fair*.

Jill Curtis recalled how he so easily dismissed their forty-five-year age difference, and when friends asked if he was worried about keeping up with his wife, he replied deadpan, 'Well, if she dies, she dies!'

She said that among his simple loves were Krispy Kreme doughnuts, Splenda sweetener, his dog Bronx and white clothes. She urged family and friends not to dwell on his death but on his extraordinary life. 'He was, as one fan put it, a once-in-a-lifetime man,' she said.

As the service ended, a second montage was screened, finishing with the words, 'The End' over an image of Tony shaking his head as though he could hardly believe it himself.

Among the seven honorary pallbearers were Kirk Douglas, singer Phyllis McGuire and Kirk Kerkorian. The funeral was followed by a reception for more than a hundred invited guests at the Luxor hotel-casino on the Las Vegas Strip.

Tony was buried in his favourite white shorts and white sweater, his Armani scarf around his neck, and with his Stetson tucked under his arm. His travelling bag was placed with him, packed with his most favourite possessions – photos and letters of special meaning, a model of his car the twenty-fifth Anniversary Edition Trans Am, his driving gloves, some 'dough', a copy of the poem *Richard Cory*, the book *Anthony Adverse*, his navy medals from World War Two, grandson Nicholas' baby shoes, some of his gold coin collection, his two favourite watches, a yarmulke from the Dohany Synagogues in Budapest which the charity he founded had helped to restore, a collection of coloured stones that he gathered on his travels, including some from the grave of his friend Dodi Fayed, a DVD of his film clips, his iPhone, some items from his father's tailor's shop he had kept all those years, a pair of sunglasses and a pair of reading glasses, several packets of the sweetener Splenda because he had such a sweet tooth, a Percocet (painkiller), a pair of eye blinders (he always wore them to sleep or take a nap), a picture of his dog Bronx, the ashes of his dog Jack, his favourite paint brushes, some paint, sketch pad, pen, and a favoured fencing sabre.

Once asked what he wanted his epitaph to be, he replied, 'Nobody's perfect.' He knew he wasn't perfect, but he went through life trying to find happiness, and give happiness to others. When he led me on to the set of *The Persuaders* in 1971, with his arm linked through mine as if we were long-time friends rather than strangers who had met for the first time, he said, 'This is what I do. I do all this for you. And one day you're gonna say, "Gee, Tony Curtis gave me an hour each week of happiness." That's what it's all about.'

THE MOVIES

Criss Cross, 1949, Universal-International. Burt Lancaster, Yvonne De Carlo, Dan Duryea, Stephen McNally, Richard Long, (Bernie Schwartz uncredited). *Producer* Michael Kraike. *Director* Robert Siodmak.

The Lady Gambles, 1949, Universal-International. Barbara Stanwyck, Robert Preston, Stephen McNally, Edith Barrett, John Hoyt, Leif Erickson, (Anthony Curtis uncredited). *Producer* Michael Kraike. *Director* Michael Gordon.

City Across the River, 1949, Universal-International. Stephen McNally, Luis Van Rooten, Thelma Ritter, Peter Fernandez, Al Ramsen, Richard Jaeckel, Anthony Curtis. *Producer/director* Maxwell Shane.

Johnny Stool Pigeon, 1949, Universal-International. Howard Duff, Dan Duryea, Shelley Winters, Anthony Curtis, John McIntire. *Producer* Aaron Rosenberg. *Director* William Castle.

Francis, 1950, Universal-International. Donald O'Connor, Patricia Medina, Zasu Pitts, Eduard Franz, Anthony Curtis. *Producer* Robert Arthur. *Director* Arthur Lubin.

I Was a Shoplifter, 1950, Universal-International. Scott Brady, Mona Freeman, Anthony Curtis, Charles Drake, Gregg Martell. *Producer* Leonard Goldstein. *Director* Charles Lamont.

Winchester '73, 1950, Universal-International. James Stewart, Stephen McNally, Shelley Winters, Dan Duryea, Will Geer, Jay C. Flippen, Rock Hudson, Anthony Curtis. *Producer* Aaron Rosenberg. *Director* Anthony Mann.

Sierra, 1950, Universal-International. Wanda Hendrix, Audie Murphy, Dean Jagger, Burl Ives, Richard Rober, Anthony Curtis. *Producer* Michael Kraike. *Director* Alfred E. Green.

Kansas Raiders, 1950, Universal-International. Audie Murphy, Brian Donlevy, Richard Arlen, Scott Brady, Marguerite Chapman, Tony Curtis. *Producer* Ted Richmond. *Director* Ray Enright.

Meet Danny Wilson, 1951, Universal-International. Frank Sinatra, Shelley Winters, Raymond Burr, Alex Nicol. Guest appearances by Jeff Chandler and Tony Curtis. *Producer* Leonard Goldstein. *Director* Joseph Pevney.

The Prince Who Was a Thief, 1951, Universal-International. Tony Curtis, Piper Laurie, Everett Sloane, Peggie Castle, Donald Randolph, Jeff Corey. *Producer* Leonard Goldstein. *Director* Rudolph Maté.

Son of Ali Baba, 1952, Universal-International. Tony Curtis, Piper Laurie, Victor Jory, Morris Ankrum, Susan Cabot, William Reynolds, Hugh O'Brian. *Producer* Leonard Goldstein. *Director* Kurt Neumann.

Flesh and Fury, 1952, Universal-International. Tony Curtis, Mona Freeman, Jan Sterling, Wallace Ford, Connie Gilchrist, Harry Guardino. *Producer* Leonard Goldstein. *Director* Joseph Pevney.

No Room for the Groom, 1952, Universal-International. Tony Curtis, Piper Laurie, Spring Byington, Don DeFore, Lillian Bronson. *Producer* Ted Richmond. *Director* Douglas Sirk.

Houdini, 1953, Paramount. Tony Curtis, Janet Leigh, Torin Thatcher, Angela Clarke, Sig Ruman, Connie Gilchrist, Michael Pate. *Producer* George Pal. *Director* George Marshall.

The All-American, (aka *The Winning Way*) 1953, Universal-International. Tony Curtis, Mamie Van Doren, Lori Nelson, Richard

Long, Gregg Palmer, Paul Cavanagh, Stuart Whitman. *Producer* Aaron Rosenberg. *Director* Jesse Hibbs.

Forbidden, 1953, Universal-International. Tony Curtis, Joanne Dru, Lyle Bettger, Marvin Miller, Victor Sen Yung. *Producer* Ted Richmond. *Director* Rudolph Maté.

Beachhead, 1954, Universal-International. Tony Curtis, Frank Lovejoy, Mary Murphy, Eduard Franz, Skip Homeier, John Doucette. *Producer* Howard Koch. *Director* Stuart Heisler.

Johnny Dark, 1954, Universal-International. Tony Curtis, Piper Laurie, Paul Kelly, Ilka Chase, Don Taylor, Ruth Hampton. *Producer* Wlliam Alland. *Director* George Sherman.

The Black Shield of Falworth, 1954, Universal-International. Tony Curtis, Janet Leigh, Herbert Marshall, Ian Keith, Torin Thatcher, Barbara Rush, Dan O'Herlihy. *Producers* Robert Arthur, Melville Tucker. *Director* Rudolph Maté.

So This Is Paris, 1955, Universal-International. Tony Curtis, Gloria DeHaven, Gene Nelson, Corinne Calvet, Paul Gilbert. *Producer* Albert J. Cohen. *Director* Richard Quine.

Six Bridges to Cross, 1955, Universal-International. Tony Curtis, George Nader, Julie Adams, Sal Mineo, Jay C. Flippen, Jan Merlin. *Producer* Aaron Rosenberg. *Director* Joseph Pevney.

The Purple Mask, 1955, Universal-International. Tony Curtis, Colleen Miller, Gene Barry, Dan O'Herlihy, Angela Lansbury, George Dolenz. *Producer* Howard Christie. *Director* H. Bruce Humberstone.

The Square Jungle, 1955, Universal-International. Tony Curtis, Ernest Borgnine, Jim Backus, Pat Crowley, Leigh Snowden. *Producer* Albert Zugsmith. *Director* Jerry Hopper.

The Rawhide Years, 1955, Universal-International. Tony Curtis, Colleen Miller, Arthur Kennedy, William Demarest, William Gargan, Peter Van Eyck. *Producer* Stanley Rubin. *Director* Rudolph Maté.

Trapeze, 1956, United Artists, Hecht-Hill-Lancaster, Joanna Productions, Susan Productions. Burt Lancaster, Tony Curtis, Gina Lollobrigida, Katy Jurado, Thomas Gomez, Johnny Puleo. *Producer* James Hill. *Director* Carol Reed.

Mister Cory, 1957, Universal-International. Tony Curtis, Martha Hyer, Charles Bickford, Kathryn Grant, William Reynolds, Russ Morgan. *Producer* Robert Arthur. *Director* Blake Edwards.

The Midnight Story, (aka *Appointment with A Shadow*) 1957, Universal-International. Tony Curtis, Gilbert Roland, Marisa Pavan, Jay C. Flippen, Argentina Brunetti, Ted De Corsia. *Producer* Robert Arthur. *Director* Joseph Pevney.

Sweet Smell of Success, 1957, United Artists, Hecht-Hill-Lancaster, Norma Productions, Curtleigh Productions. Burt Lancaster, Tony Curtis, Susan Harrison, Martin Milner, Sam Levene, Barbara Nichols. *Producer* James Hill. *Director* Alexander Mackendrick.

The Vikings, 1958, United Artists, Bryna, Curtleigh. Kirk Douglas, Tony Curtis, Janet Leigh, Ernest Borgnine, Alexander Knox, Frank Thring. *Producer* Jerry Bresler. *Director* Richard Fleischer.

Kings Go Forth, 1958, United Artists, Frank Ross-Eton Productions. Frank Sinatra, Tony Curtis, Natalie Wood, Leora Dana, Karl Swenson. *Producer* Frank Ross. *Director* Delmer Daves.

The Defiant Ones, 1958, United Artists, Curtleigh, Stanley Kramer Productions. Tony Curtis, Sidney Poitier, Theodore Bikel, Charles McGraw, Lon Chaney Jr, Whit Bissell, Carl Switzer. *Producer/director* Stanley Kramer.

The Perfect Furlough, (aka *Strictly for Pleasure*) 1958, Universal-International. Tony Curtis, Janet Leigh, Linda Cristal, Keenan Wynn, Elaine Stritch. *Producer* Robert Arthur. *Director* Blake Edwards.

Some Like It Hot, 1959, United Artists, Mirisch Corp, Ashton Productions. Marilyn Monroe, Tony Curtis, Jack Lemmon, George Raft, Joe E. Brown, Pat O'Brien, Joan Shawlee, Nehemiah Persoff. *Producer/director* Billy Wilder.

Operation Petticoat, 1959, Universal-International, Granart Productions. Cary Grant, Tony Curtis, Joan O'Brien, Dina Merrill, Gene Evans, Arthur O'Connell, Dick Sargent. *Producer* Robert Arthur. *Director* Blake Edwards.

Who Was That Lady? 1960, Columbia Pictures, Ansask. Tony Curtis, Janet Leigh, Dean Martin, James Whitmore, John McIntire, Barbara Nichols, Larry Storch. *Producer* Norman Krasna. *Director* George Sidney.

The Rat Race, 1960, Paramount. Tony Curtis, Debbie Reynolds, Jack Oakie, Kay Medford, Don Rickles, Sam Butera, Gerry Mulligan. *Producers* William Perlberg & George Seaton. *Director* Robert Mulligan.

Spartacus, 1960, Universal-International, Bryna. Kirk Douglas, Laurence Olivier, Jean Simmons, Charles Laughton, Peter Ustinov, John Gavin, Tony Curtis. *Producer* Edward Lewis. *Director* Stanley Kubrick.

Pepe, 1960, Columbia Pictures, G.S. Posa Films. Cantinflas, Dan Dailey, Shirley Jones, Carlos Montalban, with guests stars including Tony Curtis, Janet Leigh and Jack Lemmon. *Producer/director* George Sidney.

The Great Impostor, 1961, Universal-International. Tony Curtis, Edmond O'Brien, Karl Malden, Raymond Massey, Gary Merrill, Arthur O'Connell. *Producer* Robert Arthur. *Director* Robert Mulligan.

The Outsider, 1961, Universal-International. Tony Curtis, James Franciscus, Gregory Walcott, Bruce Bennett, Vivian Nathan. *Producer* Sy Bartlett. *Director* Delbert Mann.

Taras Bulba, 1962, United Artists, Harold Hecht-Avala Film. Tony Curtis, Yul Brynner, Christine Kaufmann, Sam Wanamaker, George Macready, Perry Lopez, Brad Dexter. *Producer* Harold Hecht. *Director* J. Lee Thompson.

40 Pounds of Trouble, 1962, Universal-International, Curtis Enterprises. Tony Curtis, Suzanne Pleshette, Claire Wilcox, Phil Silvers, Stubby

Kaye, Larry Storch. *Producer* Stan Margulies. *Director* Norman Jewison.

Captain Newman, M.D. 1963, Universal-International, Brentwood/ Renard. Gregory Peck, Tony Curtis, Angie Dickinson, Eddie Albert, Jane Withers, Bobby Darin, Bethel Leslie, Robert Duvall. *Producer* Robert Arthur. *Director* David Miller.

The List of Adrian Messenger, 1963, Universal-International, Joel Productions. Kirk Douglas, George C. Scott, Dana Wynter, Clive Brook, Gladys Cooper, guest stars Tony Curtis, Burt Lancaster, Robert Mitchum and Frank Sinatra. *Producer* Eddie Lewis. *Director* John Huston.

Wild and Wonderful, 1964, Universal-International. Tony Curtis, Christine Kaufmann, Jules Munshin, Larry Storch. *Producer* Harold Hecht. *Director* Michael Anderson.

Goodbye Charlie, 1964, Twentieth Century-Fox/Venice Productions. Tony Curtis, Debbie Reynolds, Pat Boone, Walter Matthau, Martin Gabel, Ellen McRae. *Producer* David Weisbart. *Director* Vincente Minnelli.

Sex and the Single Girl, 1964, Warner Brothers Richard Quine Reynard Productions. Tony Curtis, Natalie Wood, Henry Fonda, Lauren Bacall, Mel Ferrer, Fran Jeffries. *Producer* William T. Orr. *Director* Richard Quine.

Paris When it Sizzles, 1964, Paramount. William Holden, Audrey Hepburn, Noel Coward, Marlene Dietrich, Tony Curtis. *Producer* George Axelrod. *Director* Richard Quine.

The Great Race, 1965, Warner Brothers, Patricia-Jalem-Reynard. Jack Lemmon, Tony Curtis, Natalie Wood, Peter Falk, Keenan Wynn, Arthur O'Connell, Dorothy Provine, Larry Storch. *Producer* Martin Jurow. *Director* Blake Edwards.

Boeing Boeing, 1965, Paramount. Tony Curtis, Jerry Lewis, Dany Saval, Suzanna Leigh, Christine Schmidtmer, Thelma Ritter. *Producer* Hal Wallis. *Director* John Rich.

Not with My Wife, You Don't! 1966, Warner Brothers/Fernwood-Reynard. Tony Curtis, Virna Lisi, George C. Scott, Carroll O'Connor, Richard Eastham, Eddie Ryder. *Producer/director* Norman Panama.

Arrivederci, Baby! (a.k.a. *Drop Dead Darling*) 1966, Paramount/Seven Arts. Tony Curtis, Rosanna Schiaffino, Lionel Jeffries, Nancy Kwan, Zsa Zsa Gabor, Fenella Fielding, Anna Quayle, Mischa Auer. *Producer/Director* Ken Hughes.

Chamber of Horrors, 1966, Warner Brothers. Patrick O'Neal, Cesare Danova, Wilfred Hyde-White, Patrice Wymore, Suzy Parker, Marie Windsor, Tony Curtis (uncredited). *Producer/Director* Hy Averback.

Don't Make Waves, 1967, MGM/Filmways-Reynard. Tony Curtis, Claudia Cardinale, Sharon Tate, Robert Webber, Joanna Barnes. *Producers* John Calley & Martin Ransohoff. *Director* Alexander Mackendrick.

The Chastity Belt (a.k.a. *On My Way to the Crusades I Met a Girl Who . . .*), 1967, Warner Brothers/Julia Film. Tony Curtis, Monica Vitti, Hugh Griffith, John Richardson, Ivo Garrani, Nino Castelnuovo. *Producer* Francesco Mazzei. *Director* Pasquale Festa Campanile.

The Boston Strangler, 1968, Twentieth Century-Fox. Tony Curtis, Henry Fonda, George Kennedy, Mike Kellin, Hurd Hatfield, Murray Hamilton, Jeff Corey, Sally Kellerman. *Producer* Robert Fryer. *Director* Richard Fleischer.

Rosemary's Baby, 1968, Paramount. Mia Farrow, John Cassavetes, Ruth Gordon, Sidney Blackmer, Maurice Evans, Ralph Bellamy. Voice cameo by Tony Curtis (uncredited). *Producer* William Castle. *Director* Roman Polanski.

Those Daring Young Men in Their Jaunty Jalopies (a.k.a. *Monte Carlo or Bust*), 1969, Paramount/Marianne/Mars/De Laurentiis. Tony Curtis, Susan Hampshire, Terry-Thomas, Eric Sykes, Gert Frobe, Peter Cook, Dudley Moore, Jack Hawkins. *Producer/director* Ken Annakin.

Suppose They Gave a War and Nobody Came? 1970, ABC Pictures-Cinerama Releasing. Tony Curtis, Suzanne Pleshette, Brian Keith, Ernest Borgnine, Tom Ewell, Bradford Dillman, Don Ameche. *Producer* Fred Engel. *Director* Hy Averback.

You Can't Win 'Em All, 1970, Columbia Pictures/RSO. Tony Curtis, Charles Bronson, Michele Mercier, Patrick Magee, Gregoire Aslan. *Producer* Gene Corman. *Director* Peter Collinson.

Lepke, 1975, Warner Brothers/Amerieuro. Tony Curtis, Anjanette Comer, Michael Callan, Warren Berlinger, Milton Berle, Vic Tayback. *Producer* Yoram Globus. *Director* Menahem Golan.

The Last Tycoon, 1976, Paramount/Academy/A.G. Prods. Robert De Niro, Tony Curtis, Robert Mitchum, Jeanne Mareau, Jack Nicholson, Donald Pleasence, Ingrid Boulting, Ray Milland, Dana Andrews. *Producer* Sam Spiegel. *Director* Elia Kazan.

Casanova & Co. (a.k.a. *The Rise and Rise of Casanova*), C.O.F.C.I. 1977. Tony Curtis, Marisa Berenson, Sylva Koscina, Hugh Griffith, Britt Ekland, Marisa Mell. *Producers* Franz Antel & Carl Szokoll. *Director* Franz Antel.

The Manitou, 1978, Manitou Productions. Tony Curtis, Susan Strasberg, Michael Ansara, Ann Sothern, Burgess Meredith, Stella Stevens. *Producer/director* William Girdler.

Sextette, 1978, Briggs and Sullivan Productions. Mae West, Tony Curtis, Ringo Starr, Dom DeLuise, Timothy Dalton, George Hamilton, Alice Cooper, Keith Moon, Rona Barrett, Walter Pidgeon, George Raft. *Producers* Daniel Briggs & Robert Sullivan. *Director* Ken Hughes.

The Bad News Bears Go to Japan, 1978, Paramount. Tony Curtis, Jackie Earle Haley, Tomisaburo Wakayama, George Wyner, Lonny Chapman. *Producer* Michael Ritchie. *Director* John Berry.

It Rained All Night the Day I Left, 1980, Cofci-Canearum-Israfilms. Tony Curtis, Louis Gossett Jr, Sally Kellerman, John Vernon, Lisa Langlois,

Guy Hoffman. *Producers* Sholomo Mugrabi & Claude Giroux. *Director* Nicolas Gessner.

Title Shot, 1979, Regenthall Film. Tony Curtis, Richard Gabourie, Susan Hogan, Allan Royal. *Producer* Rob Iveson. *Director* Les Rose.

Little Miss Marker, 1980, Universal. Walter Matthau, Julie Andrews, Tony Curtis, Bob Newhart, Sara Stimson, Lee Grant. *Producer* Jennings Lang. *Director* Walter Bernstein.

The Mirror Crack'd, 1980, GW Films. Angela Lansbury, Elizabeth Taylor, Rock Hudson, Kim Novak, Tony Curtis, Edward Fox, Geraldine Chaplin. *Producers* John Brabourne & Richard Goodwin. *Director* Guy Hamilton.

Brainwaves, 1983, Cineamerica Productions. Keir Dullea, Suzanna Love, Tony Curtis, Vera Miles. *Producer/director* Ulli Lommel.

Othello – the Black Commado, 1982, AMB Diffusion Eurocine Production. Max H. Boulois, Tony Curtis, Ramiro Oliveros, Joanna Pettet. *Producer* Maria J. Gonzalez. *Director* Max H. Boulois.

Where is Parsifal? 1984, (released 1988), Slenderline Ltd/Terence Young Productions. Tony Curtis, Cassandra Domenica, Erik Astrada, Peter Lawford, Ron Moody, Donald Pleasence, Orson Welles. *Producer* Daniel Carrillo. *Director* Henri Helman.

Insignificance, 1985, Zenith Productions. Gary Busey, Tony Curtis, Theresa Russell, Michael Emil, Will Sampson. *Producer* Jerry Thomas. *Director* Nicolas Roeg.

King of the City, aka Club Life, 1986, MRP Productions/VTC. Tom Parsekian, Michael Parks, Jamie Barrett, Tony Curtis, Bleu McKenzie. *Producer/director* Norman Thaddeus Vane.

Balboa, 1986, Entertainment Artists/Production Associates. Tony Curtis, Carol Lynley, Jennifer Chase, Chuck Connors, Lupita Ferrer, Sonny Bono. *Producer/director* James Polakof.

Welcome to Germany, 1988, Channel Four/George Reinhart Productions/Road Movies. Tony Curtis, Katharina Thalbach, Karin Baal, Charles Regnier, Alexandra Stewart. *Producers* George Reinhart & Joachim von Vietinghoff. *Director* Thomas Brasch.

Midnight, 1989, SVS Films. Lynn Redgrave, Tony Curtis, Steve Parrish, Frank Gorshin, Rita Gam. *Producer/director* Norman Thaddeus Vane.

Walter & Carlo i Amerika, 1989. Ole Stephensen, Jarl Friis-Mikkelsen, Tony Curtis. *Producers/directors* Jarl Friis-Mikkelsen & Ole Stephensen.

Lobster Man from Mars, 1989, Electric Pictures/Filmrullen Prods. Deborah Foreman, S.D. Nemeth, Anthony Hickox, Tony Curtis. *Producers* Steven S. Greene & Eyal Rimmon. *Director* Stanley Sheff.

Prime Target, 1991, Hero films. David Heavener, Tony Curtis, Isaac Hayes, Robert Reed, Andrew Robinson, Don Stroud. *Producers* David Heavener, Merlin Miller. *Directors* David Heavener & Phillip J. Roth.

Centre of the Web, 1992, Pyramid Distribution/Winters Group Prod. Tony Curtis, Robert Davi, Charlene Tilton, Bo Hopkins. *Producer* Ruta K. Aras. *Director* David A. Prior.

The Mummy Lives, 1993, Klondike Films. Tony Curtis, Leslie Hardy, Greg Wrangler, Jack Cohen. *Producer* Yoram Globus. *Director* Gerry O'Hara.

Naked in New York, 1993, Fine Line. Whoopi Goldberg, Tony Curtis, Kathleen Turner, Timothy Dalton, Eric Stoltz, Ralph Macchio. *Producers* Fred Zollo & Martin Scorsese. *Director* Daniel Algrant.

The Immortals, 1995, End Productions. Eric Roberts, Joe Pantoliano, Tia Carrere, Tony Curtis. *Producers* Kevin Bernhardt & Elie Samaha. *Director* Brian Grant.

The Continuing Adventures of Reptile Man and His Faithful Sidekick Tadpole, aka, *Brittle Glory*, 1997, Shoreline Entertainment. Tony Curtis, Arye Gross, Ally Walker. *Producers* Kelly Kiernan, Pierre-Richard Muller, Morris Ruskin, Mary Skinner. *Director* Stewart Schill.

Hardball, 1997, Cinepix Film Properties. Michael Dudikoff, Lisa Howard, Tony Curtis, Steve Bacic, L. Harvey Gold. *Producers* Jeff Barmash & John Dunning. *Director* George Erschbamer.

Stargames, 1998, Greydon Clark Prod. Tony Curtis, Travis Clark. *Producer/director* Greydon Clark.

Play It to the Bone, 1999, Shanghai'd Films/Touchstone. Antonio Banderas, Woody Harrelson, Lolita Davidovich, Tom Sizemore, Lucy Liu, Robert Wagner (Tony Curtis was billed far down the cast list with other guest stars including James Woods and Kevin Costner). *Producer* Stephen Chin. *Director* Ron Shelton.

Reflections of Evil, 2002, Pookie Prods. Damon Packard, Nicole Vanderhoff, Beverly Miller, Dean Spunt, Chad Nelson, Tony Curtis. *Producer/director* Damon Packard.

The Blacksmith and the Carpenter, 2007, Scottsdale Community College. Robert Picardo, Tony Curtis, Liz Sheridan, Hunter Gomez, Clint James. *Producer* Aaron Kes. *Director* Chris Redish.

David & Fatima, 2008, Karim Movies. Cameron Van Hoy, Danielle Pollack, Martin Landau, Allan Kolman, Anthony Batarse, Yareli Arizmendi, Colette Kilroy, Tony Curtis. *Producers* Tavia Dautartas & Tammi Sutton. *Director* Alain Zaloum.

TELEVISION SERIES AND FILMS

General Electric Theater series, episode 'Cornada'. Tony Curtis, Salvador Baguez, Pamela Duncan. Directed by Herschel Daugherty, 1957.

Schlitz Playhouse of Stars series, episode 'Man on a Rack'. Tony Curtis, Everett Sloane, Andra Martin, 1958.

General Electric Theater series, episode 'The Stone'. Charles Aidman, John Baragrey, Tony Curtis, Rita Moreno, hosted by Ronald Reagan, 1959.

Startime series, episode 'The Young Juggler'. Tony Curtis, Heather Ames, Robert Carricart, directed by Ted Post, produced by Curtleigh, 1960.

The Flintstones series, episode 'The Return of Stony Curtis'. Voice cast – Alan Reed, Jean Vander Pyl, Mel Blanc, Gerry Johnson, Tony Curtis (guest star). Directed by Joseph Barbera and William Hanna, 1965.

Bracken's World series, episode 'Fade-In'. Elizabeth Allen, Don Brodie, Dennis Cole, Tony Curtis (cameo). Directed by Walter Doniger, 1969.

The Persuaders series. Tony Curtis and Roger Moore appeared in all 24 episodes. Directors included Basil Dearden, Leslie Norman, Roy Ward Baker, Val Guest, Roger Moore, 1971–2.

The Third Girl from the Left. Tony Curtis, Kim Novak, Michael Brandon. Directed by Peter Medak, 1973.

Shaft series, episode 'Hit-Run'. Eddie Barth, Nicky Blair, Philip Chapin, Tony Curtis. Directed by Harry Harris, 1973.

The Count of Monte Cristo (shown on TV in America, released theatrically elsewhere). Richard Chamberlain, Tony Curtis, Trevor Howard, Louis Jordan, Donald Pleasence, Taryn Power, Kate Nelligan. Directed by David Greene, 1975.

McCoy series of five feature-length episodes – 'The Big Ripoff', 1975; 'Bless the Big Fish', 1975; 'Double Take', 1975; 'In Again Out Again', 1976; 'New Dollar Day', 1976.

The Users. Tony Curtis, Jaclyn Smith, Joan Fontaine, Red Buttons, George Hamilton, John Forsythe, Michelle Phillips. Directed by Joseph Hardy, 1978.

Moviola – The Scarlett O'Hara War. Tony Curtis, Sharon Gless, Harold Gould, Bill Macy. Directed by John Erman, 1980.

Inmates: A Love Story. Kate Jackson, Perry King, Shirley Jones, Tony Curtis. Directed by Guy Green,1981.

Vega$ series. Robert Urich, Bart Braverman, Phyllis Davis. Tony Curtis appeared in 16 episodes from 1978 to 1981.

The Million Dollar Face. Tony Curtis, David Huffman, Herschel Bernardi, Gayle Hunnicutt, Lee Grant, Roddy McDowall. Directed by Michael O'Herlihy, 1981.

Portrait of a Showgirl. Lesley Ann Warren, Rita Moreno, Dianne Kay, Tony Curtis. Directed by Steven Hilliard Stern, 1982.

The Fall Guy series. Episode 'Eight Ball'. Lee Majors, Douglas Barr, Heather Thomas, Tony Curtis (guest star). Directed by Michael O'Herlihy, 1983.

Mafia Princess. Tony Curtis, Susan Lucci, Kathleen Widdoes. Directed by Robert Collins, 1986.

Murder in Three Acts. Peter Ustinov, Tony Curtis, Emma Samms. Directed by Gary Nelson, 1986.

Charlie. Shirley Jones, Ned Eisenberg, Melody Rogers, Tony Curtis. Directed by Jack Bender, 1989.

Tarzan in Manhattan. Joe Lara, Kim Crosby, Tony Curtis. Directed by Michael Schultz, 1989.

Thanksgiving Day. Tony Curtis, Jonathon Brandmeier, Joseph Bologna, Kelly Curtis, Sonny Bono. Directed by Gino Tanasescu, 1990.

Christmas in Connecticut. Dyan Cannon, Kris Kristofferson, Tony Curtis. Directed by Arnold Schwarzenegger, 1992.

A Perry Mason Mystery: The Case of the Grimacing Governor. Hal Holbrook, Barbara Hale, Tony Curtis. Directed by Max Tash, 1994.

The New Adventures of Superman series – episode 'I Now Pronounce You', Dean Cain, Teri Hatcher, Tony Curtis (guest star). Directed by Jim Pohl, 1996.

Roseanne series – episode 'Ballroom Blitz', Roseanne, John Goodman, Tony Curtis (guest star). Directed by Gail Mancuso, 1996.

Suddenly Susan series – episode 'Matchmaker, Matchmaker'. Brooke Shields, Nestor Carbonell, Kathy Griffin, Tony Curtis (guest star). Directed by Alan Rafkin, 1998.

Hope & Faith series – episode 'Jack's Back'. Faith Ford, Kelly Ripa, Ted McGinley, Tony Curtis (guest star). Directed by Joanna Johnson, 2004.

CSI: Crime Scene Investigation series, episode 'Grave Danger Volume 1'. William Petersen, Marg Helgenberger, Gary Dourdan, George Eads, Jorja Fox, Eric Szmanda, Tony Curtis, Frank Gorshin. Directed by Quentin Tarantino, 2005.

BOOKS

Balatke, Joe, *The Films of Jack Lemmon*, Citadel Press (USA) 1977

Curtis, Tony, with Peter Goldenbock, *American Prince: My Autobiography*, Virgin Books (UK) 2008

Curtis, Tony, & Barry Paris, *Tony Curtis: The Autobiography*, William Heinemann Ltd (UK) 1994

Curtis, Tony, with Mark A. Vieira, *Some Like It Hot: Me, Marilyn and the Movie*, Virgin Books (UK) 2009

Fitzgerald, Michael G., *Universal Pictures*, Arlington House (USA) 1977

Haygood, Wil, *In Black and White: The Life of Sammy Davis Jr*, Aurum Press Ltd (UK) 2004

Hirschhorn, Clive, *The Universal Story*, Octopus Books (UK) 1983

Hunter, Allan, *Tony Curtis: The Man and His Movies*, Paul Harris Publishing (UK), 1985

Leigh, Janet, *There Really Was a Hollywood*, Doubleday & Co Inc (USA) 1984

Moore, Roger, *My Word is My Bond*, Michael O'Mara Books Ltd (UK) 2008

Poitier, Sidney, *This Life*, Hodder & Stoughton (UK) 1980

Shipman, David, *The Great Movie Stars*, Angus & Robertson (UK) 1972

Sinatra, Tina, *My Father's Daughter*, Simon & Schuster (UK) 2000

ARTICLES WITH BY-LINES

Cashin, Fergus, 'The Sweet One', *Daily Sketch*, 4 July 1963

Crane, Lionel, 'I'm Honest At Last', *Sunday Mirror*, 7 June 1970

Crawley, Tony, 'Tony Curtis', *Game*, August 1975

Curtis, Tony, talking to Michael Hellicar, 'My Regret', *Woman's Own*, 13 November 1982

Dangaard, Colin, 'Tony Lives On Love', *Daily Express*, 17 January 1979

Davis, Victor, 'Self-portrait by Tony Curtis Lands "Breakaway" Role', *Daily Express*, 26 January 1968

Edwards, Sydney, 'Why Does Tony Run and Run?', *Evening Standard*, 16 January 1976

Garvan, Frank, 'Tragedies That Made Tony Curtis "A Shambling Wreck"', *Weekend*, 15–21 July 1981

Le Blanc, Jerry, 'We Had Little in Common But He Made Beautiful Babies', *News of the World*, 7 January 1973

Kennedy, Philippa, 'Love . . . the Secret of Tony's Sex Appeal', *Sun*, 20 May 1974

Lewin, David, 'Tearful Nights of Lonely Tony Curtis', *Sunday Mirror*, 20 July 1980

Lewis, Richard Warren, 'The Story of Tony Curtis', *Photoplay* (UK), November 1969

Mann, Roderick, 'You've Got to Work at Romance, Says Christine', *Sunday Express*, 28 November 1965

Mann, Roderick, 'If Tony Curtis Had Been Ricardo Cortez', *Sunday Express*, 20 May 1973

Mann, Roderick, 'That Girl in the See-through Blouse', *Sunday Express*, 27 May 1979

Ottoway, Robert, 'How the Strangler Changed My Life', *Daily Sketch*, 27 June 1969

Owen, Michael, 'Angry Tony Curtis – "I Have Quit Films"', *Evening Standard*, 25 June 1973

Owen, Michael, 'The Bronx's Gift to Belgravia', *Evening Standard*, 18 October 1974

Rainbird, Walter, 'We Are Not the Happiest Couple', *Weekend*, 23–29 October 1963

Salisbury, Leslie, 'Why Curtis Feels Bitter', *TV Times*, 26 June – 2 July 1982

Short, Don, 'A New Stage in the Career of Mr Curtis', *Daily Mirror*, 1 August 1973

Taylor, Noreen, 'Starstruck – Not My Little Debbie', *Daily Mirror*, 16 January 1985

Wolf, William, 'I Spent £800,000 Learning About Women', *Weekend*, 17–23 May 1972

ARTICLES WITH NO BY-LINES
'Andria is Mrs Curtis No. 4', *Daily Mirror*, 3 May 1984
'Curtis Con Man McCoy', *Photoplay* (UK), December 1975
'Curtis Turning Over a New Leaf as Author', *Photoplay* (UK), October 1977
'Debee's Biggest Boo-boo', *Daily Mirror*, 17 February 1986
'Deb's Dollar Bill and Coo', *Daily Mirror*, 18 January, 1985
'My Slide to Drugs Hell', *Daily Mirror*, 13 August 1985
'Tony . . . Without Janet', *Photoplay* (UK), November 1962
'Tony's Girl', *Photoplay* (UK), October 1962
'What Do Newly Weds Do All Day?', *Photoplay* (UK), June 1963

DOCUMENTARIES
Tony of the Movies, Peter Jones Productions Inc for A&E Network, 2001
Hollywood Greats, BBC Scotland, 2002
Shrink Wrap, Finestripe Productions for Channel 4, 2008
Nobody's Perfect: The Making of Some Like It Hot, October Films Productions for BBC, 2001

Index